# Journalism in Practice

# Journalism In Practice

Hari Mohan Agarwal
(M.A., Ph.D.)

Reference Press

4831/24, Ansari Road
Darya Ganj
New Delhi-110 002
Phone: 51563444
Fax: 51563334
*E-mail: info@essessreference.com*
*url: http://www.essessreference.com*

**First Published 2005**

**ISBN: 81-88583-93-6**

**Rs.675/-**



Published by:
**Reference Press**
4831/24, Ansari Road, Darya Ganj,
New Delhi-110 002.
Phone: 51563444
Fax: 51563334
*E-mail: info@essessreference.com*
*url: http://www.essessreference.com*

Printed in India at:
Mehra Offset Press, New Delhi

# CONTENTS

# PREFACE

No doubt, the present world is the world of media and journalism. It is gaining its ground day by day and spreading its wings dominantly. The present book, 'Journalism in Practice' is a deliberate attempt on my part to endow the people, in the sphere of journalism, with such specific qualities, one generally lack is in his life. It has been endeavoured to understand such a concept, which might throw the light, how to improve yourself and emerge out successfully.

It substantially touches the diverse specific aspects, comprising way of expression, expression of facts, justice with facts, writing features, how to write for newspapers, how to write editorial, what should be the role of an editor or writer, how to substantiate copy-editing, how to provide excellent performance, what is column writing and how it is created, photo features, feature writing and many more such sorts of phenomenal subjects. All the above mentioned facts require intensive study to shine on the horizon of journalism and this book should prove to be a boon for its readers.

Other appended fields like role of law, legal protection, the techniques of advertising etc., have also been discussed comprehensively.

If this book satisfies even to a little bit, its readers, the undersigned would be pleased to feel that the motive to write this book has been fulfilled.

All valuable suggestions from critics and readers are highly solicited.

**Author**

# 1

# The Fundamentals

To the outsider, journalism and ethics are about as incongruous a mixture as you can get. Even to put the two words in the same sentence is to risk reducing the listener to helpless laughter.

To the insider on a mass-market tabloid, ethics are largely an irrelevance. Editors, pressured by intense competition for readers, demand that staff cut ethical corners; and competition among staff encourages some to respond. Lecturing these journalists about ethics is as pointless as advocating celibacy to sailors arriving in port after six months at sea.

To the insider working on a quality paper, where there is virtually unanimous agreement about basic professional morality, ethics are a code of principles to which all journalists should adhere, or at least feel guilty about if they do not. They are rarely, if ever, required to step outside this code.

Ethics, more than any other aspect of the job, are where personal circumstance produces experiences so that the different ethics employed are barely recognisable as the same thing. The reason is that ethics, as actually practised, are conditioned less by morals than by what is rewarded or punished in any given newspaper. On a British mass market tabloid (or agency serving one) journalists may be regarded, paid and promoted according to how many dramatic, possibly invasive, stories they produce. Not too many questions are asked about how they obtained them or what degree of exaggeration is involved. Indeed the news desk, or higher executives, often tell reporters what line they want, regardless of any reservations reporters have. Not much scope for Mr. or Ms. Proper here. At the other extreme - on a US paper enjoying a monopoly and sharing the same city as its sources and readers-reporters are judged and rewarded differently, with ethics playing a far greater part in their lives.

Ultimately the main factor in deciding what ethics are actually practised is competition. In monopoly situations, papers know that there is no rival paper to scoop them, and readers have no alternative to turn to-save for giving up papers altogether. This lack of competition gives the journalists the moral luxury of generally being able to apply far more idealised standards of professional ethics. In a mass market, highly competitive and with a macho culture, almost the only sanction on what papers will do to get a story, or publish once they have got it, is the prospect of upsetting readers, especially to the point where they will not buy the paper. Only then will word go out to the staff, and the little news agencies that feed them, that it is time to call a halt (perhaps only temporarily) to stealing pictures from the bereaved, invading hospitals where sick celebrities are being treated, publishing pictures of royal children in private moments, condemning a community for violence without sufficient evidence, or whatever. On tabloids especially, the periodic little eruptions of ethics that are sometimes seen nearly always come from proprietors acutely aware that readers can always, and maybe are about to, buy another paper. Or that the government is about to legislate.

But journalists have a sanction, too. We do not have to be mere creatures of the papers we work for; we have a choice. Just as readers can stop buying, so journalists can change jobs. We can decide that there are some things we will not do and leave the paper - either discreetly after having found another post, or publicly, in a blaze of righteous indignation. If more of us did that, and made clear our reasons for doing so, journalism would be better for it.

This element of moral choice, the distinction between how papers acting under commercial pressures expect us to behave and how we can choose to behave, explains why ethics have a daily purpose - or rather, two purposes. The first is to provide some kind of moral compass, telling us how far we are diverging from a desired route. So far as I know, the magnetic north in our trade is found in the clauses of an unwritten contract which should exist between all newspapers and their readers:

- Every story in the paper is a result of decisions made free of political, commercial or non-commercial pressure.
- None are there because of any favours or money exchanged.
- All stories are written and edited in a spirit of free enquiry, and chosen for publication entirely on their own merits, be they real or imagined.

Second, ethics provides a practical guide to the production of safe and credible journalism. Honestly, with plain dealing and with the removal of conflicts of interest are the best ways to do this job because they are the safest ways to do it. At the most base level, they keep you out of the courts and help you to sleep at nights. And, at the risk of shocking some of the more raunchy reporters, ethics are the most decent way to do the job, too, giving us attitudes to readers (and sources) that are based on some sensitivity, rather than mere sly commercial calculation.

## Theories and Guidelines

Viewed like this, ethics are not some optional extra but are integral to every aspect of the job. This book therefore deals with them as they occur - in handling sources, asking questions, writing, etc. - and not in some moral parking lot tucked away from the main action. There are, however, some general principles and these have been gathered here.

If you want to be a propagandist, then go and work in public relations, or politics. Journalists should owe no loyalty to anyone or anything else; not a political party, source, commercial interest, non-commercial interest or particular cause, however worthy. Balanced journalism is difficult enough to achieve without such conflicts of interest. The Washington Post newspaper has a rule that its journalists cannot take part in any political activity. That includes marching on demonstrations. So when several Post reporters were spotted on an abortion rights demonstration, they were told they would not be allowed to cover anything touching on the abortion issue.

The dangers of allowing a missionary zeal for some cause to infect reporting are even more obvious. One of the more notorious examples is Walter Duranty, the New York Times correspondent in Moscow in the 1920s and 1930s. So taken was he by the ideology of the new Soviet Union that his reporting was often little more than propaganda. At the height of the famine in the Ukraine, for instance, largely engineered by Stalin to break local resistance to Soviet control, Duranty wrote of 'village markets overflowing with eggs, fruit, poultry, vegetables, milk and butter' at prices far lower than in Moscow. 'Anyone can see this is not famine, but abundance', he added; and a Pulitzer committee, knowing no better, gave him a prize. In fact, millions died, and Duranty knew this full well, telling colleagues in private that he thought the death toll was around ten million. Malcolm Muggeridge, the Manchester Guardian's reporter in Moscow at the time, called him 'the biggest liar of any journalist I have ever met.'

Each story should be an open-minded attempt to find out what really happened, accompanied by a willingness to print that truth, however uncomfortable it may be to our own, or the paper's, cherished beliefs. Thus, journalists should not accept work which seeks to bolster a point of view in the face of evidence, or undertake reporting which aims to support a preconceived theory.

You would think this so self-evident that it would not need stating. But every day you can read reporting which stretches and strains the facts to fit a particular thesis. One of the worst examples in recent memory was committed by the Sun, Britain's biggest-selling daily. For reasons best known to himself, the then editor became convinced that Aids was a disease limited to drug addicts and homosexuals. On several occasions government statistics were wilfully manhandled to support this view. The most flagrant occasion was a story headlined 'Straight Sex Cannot Give You Aids —Official', which reported, among other absurdities, that the chances of getting Aids from heterosexual sex were 'statistically invisible. Anything else is homosexual propaganda.' Eventually, the volume of protests at this coverage produced an apology - which the paper ran at the bottom of page 28.

Here, and this is no isolated case, was reporting that deceived readers and possibly endangered them. Preconceived theories have no place in journalism. Newspapers should be at war with closed minds, not employing them.

This means not only money and free gifts, but also the promise of advantage or preferment. It specifically means two things. The first is hidden advertising, where journalists or their papers take money for writing public relations pieces about firms or people which then appear in the editorial columns parading as normal stories. In recent years this has become a widespread practice in countries like Russia, and the temptation to write hidden advertising in places where pay is very poor is understandable. But that does not make it journalism. It is advertising, PR, puffs, whatever you call it, dressed up to look like journalism. It is a deception, and a damaging one. First, it breaks the basic contract with readers, with stories, purporting to be a normal editorial in print only because money has changed hands. Second, such deceptions destroy any trust that should exist between readers and papers. Third, the practice makes editors suspect their staff have taken bribes to write about a company when their story may be perfectly honest. Fourth, editors and publishers will, like hotel owners paying waiters low salaries because of tips, use hidden advertising as an excuse not to pay journalists properly. Fifth, it establishes that the journalists who do it have their pens and minds available for hire. What will they accept money for next? Writing favourable stories about criminal groups% Keeping stories about wrongdoing out of the paper: That is but a short step away from collecting information with a view to selling its destruction or suppression. In other words, blackmail.

(Lest anyone think this a good original money-making scheme, an American publisher called Robert Harrison got there first in the 1950s with a magazine called Confidential. It specialised in Hollywood scandal and, by paying large sums for tips and information, he and his investigators obtained decidedly intimate details of the stars' private lives. Each story was well-researched and Harrison's staff were not fussy about their methods, hiring prostitutes to trap victims, secretly taping and filming encounters and confessions. Sales of Confidential soared and eventually hit four million. But soon the temptation to sell the negatives, tapes and other evidence to wealthy stars proved too strong. The inevitable court case happened, a staff member killed herself, the editor shot his wife and himself in a New York taxicab, Harrison sold the magazine and both he and it went into a richly-deserved oblivion.)

Hidden advertising (which should be correctly labelled 'advertising' and typographically treated accordingly), is very rare in developed countries. Far more common is the acceptance by journalists of what they call 'freebies', that is, free trips with vacation companies, free meals from restaurants or free tickets from theatres, all given so that journalists can review them. The danger here is that the writer will feel obliged to write a favourable piece. This need not be so, and the dangers can be minimised and faith kept with the reader if it is made plain somewhere in the piece or in a footnote that the ticket/trip/meal or whatever was given free to the newspaper.

It is not unusual, especially on smaller, less profitable or local papers, for advertisers to try to use their commercial weight to bully the paper. This pressure should be resisted at all times. It normally comes from the paper's advertising department who will say to the editor that it would be helpful if this important client could have some 'good coverage'. A few years ago the Riverside Press-Enterprize, a paper in California, published a total of eleven news pieces and 22 photographs of a new department store called Nordstrom's in the six days before, during and immediately after its opening in the town. These 400 column inches appeared in the same week as 20 full pages of ads for the store. A coincidence? Unlikely.

More rarely, groups of advertisers act in concert to try to force the paper to change its coverage. When I took over as editor of a British provincial paper, one of the things I did was to stop the automatic reporting of all shop-lifting court cases because they were so common as to be boring. Within a week, all the department stores in the city approached the publisher and told him that unless reporting of all shop lifting cases was resumed they would withdraw their advertising, which was considerable. They said the coverage acted as a deterrent to would be thieves. Luckily the publisher supported me. The advertisers' threat was not carried out.

The danger of giving in to advertisers' pressure, whether individual or collective, is that your content ceases to be freely chosen. You would also find that what is granted to one advertiser would soon be demanded by many. Give in once, and you would never be free of the pressure.

A journalist has power. It should never be abused, either in the course of a story or in one's daily life. Prosecuting personal disputes with stores, neighbours, etc. by threatening exposure or reference to high-placed connections is bullying, and unsafe bullying at that. How could you ever write a future story about any person or organisation you have threatened in this way? How could you write about the connections you have used in your threat? You will be in their pocket for the favour you owe them. Neither should you use your newspaper's headed notepaper to write a letter demanding preferential treatment, compensation for some alleged negligence or faulty service. It implies to the recipient that your paper exists as a sort of private protection racket for its staff.

It sometimes happens that you are asked by someone to 'forget' a story, or part of it, in return for some favour, or even cash. It is clearly wrong to accept such an offer, for the same reasons as it is wrong to put in a story for favours. When friends are involved, refusal might be more delicately phrased, but just as swift and sure. So should it be with colleagues, as these two stories illustrate.

The first case comes from Oregon in the United States where a few years ago a local television station reported that the long-time chief of staff of the state's Republican senator had served for 25 years as director of a bank that collapsed and was bailed out at a cost to taxpayers of $100 million. It was suggested that the man's involvement with the bank may have influenced the senator's position on bank deregulation and the subsequent bailout. The story was picked up by the Associated Press and was the talk of the state, but the main newspaper in the state, the Oregonian, chose to ignore it. It also ignored allegations a week later that the chief of staff's official travel, at taxpayer's expense, had included

52 trips to New York, where he published an annual guidebook to the city that had earned him more than $1 million.

The paper's reluctance to write this story may have had something to do with the fact that the chief of staff wrote a weekly column for the paper. It eventually published parts of the story only after the Washington Post gave the revelations national exposure.

Contrast this with a paper called the Daily Item in Sudbury, Pennsylvania. Among the daily stories from the police in one issue was an uncensored account of charges filed against a town resident for driving at an unsafe speed under the influence of alcohol. The item included the man's name, age, address and occupation - editor of the Daily Item. Which paper would you trust most, the Item or the Oregonian?

Inventing information is obviously wrong and dangerous. So, too, is even a light doctoring of the facts, embellishment of the truth or temporary amnesia about certain details that inconvenience the main thrust of the story. Your report will be a cheat. This applies with equal force to photographers and the dishonest 'set-up' picture, where an event or situation is staged to imitate some alleged reality.

Some news photographers in Western Europe also have been known to carry around in their cars certain 'props' to insert into pictures. A well-known ploy used to be to have a child's shoe, or teddy bear available, so that photographers covering disasters like train or air crashes, could set this prop among the wreckage for a 'poignant' picture. Such pictures have now become a cliche. Besides, there was always the danger that the passenger list, when finally issued, would reveal that there were no children aboard. Deliberate fakes, or at least the detected ones, are very rare. Perhaps the most famous recent example was Janet Cooke's Pulitzer-winning story in the Washington Post. It was called 'Jimmy's World' and told the story of an eight-year-old heroin addict. Jimmy, however, did not exist. The story was an invention from beginning to end. When the fiction was revealed the Post saw that, with hindsight, there were many warning signs. Some staff, for instance, had harboured doubts about the story at the time, but had either thought it best to keep quiet, or thought the story 'too good to check'. This journalistically-lethal attitude was encouraged by

Cooke's warnings that her (and Jimmy's) life would be endangered if checks were made. Nor did anyone think to check Cooke's own credentials. She said she was a graduate of Vassar, had a master's degree from Toledo, studied at the Sorbonne, was an accomplished pianist and spoke four languages. No editor thought this a tall order for someone aged just 25. Among these executives, ironically, was Watergate hero Bob Woodward.

Using information you have acquired in order to make a commercial gain before the story is published is a temptation most likely to be faced by business reporters. A few years ago a reporter for the Wall Street journal called R. Foster Whinans co-wrote a column based on information from sources that traded stocks. He decided to sell information to a stock-broker friend.

He was paid $31,000 to leak the contents of the column to several stock-brokers, enabling them to buy and sell shares in companies before this information became public and thus would affect the price of the stock. The brokers made about $690,000 from the leaked information. Whinans and the brokers were eventually caught and found guilty in court of violations of the Securities Exchange Act by misappropriating confidential information. Whinans was sentenced to 18 months in prison, five years' probation, 400 hours of community service and a $ 500 fine. Many Western papers now make their financial staff declare their investments and financial dealings.

## Facing Problems

The above issues are clear-cut. But a lot of issues in reporting are more complicated. Hard and fast rules are difficult to design and apply. Take phoney by-lines, for example. Plainly wrong if used routinely to give the impression a paper's staff is several times what it is, the practice is a good deal less harmful when sports editors use it to disguise the identity of, say, staff reporters from a daily moonlighting to cover events for a Sunday. Since the story purports to be written by someone who does not in fact exist, I would still contend phoney by-lines are a deceit. It is particularly unsafe where the story may be challenged, or even end in a law suit. Who do you produce in court', An actor taking the name of the fictitious reporter?

There have been many attempts to be dogmatic about privacy, but none can be sustained beyond the most simplistic instances. We all agree that if a President fools around with a junior employee in his office, there is a legitimate story. If someone is asking for our votes (and our taxes to pay their wages), we have a right to know about them, their lives and how they impact on their duties. On the other hand, few would suggest writing a story about a second junior employee fooling around, in their own time, with a third. The sex lives of private citizens, however fascinating, are not regarded as a legitimate target for a story, unless the law is broken. But between these two extremes, in all the less clear-cut cases, is the gaping space where we argue about privacy.

The conventional, and largely sensible, guideline is that the person should be a public figure and the invasion of their privacy must have a legitimate justification based on the public interest, not merely tickling the public's curiosity. If a man standing for public office makes a great deal of public fuss about morality and the virtues of family life, but you can prove he has a string of mistresses, then it is right to publish a story. His double standards are clearly relevant to public life.

There are two problems with this conventional wisdom. First, if a paper thinks the story is sufficiently entertaining or salacious, almost any 'public interest' pretext can be dredged up. Second, justifications tend to be applied in a partisan way: papers defend the privacy of those they admire and invade the privacy of those they seek to destroy.

Part of the answer lies in that traditionally most unjournalistic of qualities: sensitivity. Journalists must have very good reasons for invading someone's privacy and should also be aware of the consequences of such reporting. A few years ago in Britain a policeman began an affair. His wife learnt about it and persuaded him to give up his mistress. The jealous lover then told a national paper and her account was printed under the headline, 'The Love Life of a Detective'. As a result, the couple's child was teased at school, the husband had to give up his job and the family had to move. Some may think that a fitting punishment for his original sin. I do not think so, and neither would I like to justify that reporting.

An issue which comes up less frequently is where journalists get involved in wrong-doing in order to investigate it. This is not a good idea. Breaking the law in pursuit of a story is both wrong and unsafe. It removes whatever moral legitimacy their reporting may otherwise have had.

Sometimes reporters investigating drug-dealing, crime or prostitution learn information that should be passed straight to the police. I think you should do that. Otherwise you are compromising your legitimacy, and may also be putting the lives of innocent citizens at risk. Only the police - not you - can judge that. (This condition about the safety of citizens also applies to the situation where journalists are accused of merely spectating in disaster or war situations and not doing anything to help those who are in danger. Our rule should be that if you can have any influence on the outcome of a situation you should follow your normal instincts and act to help.) : Never accept a free ticket from a theatre manager, a free ride from the chamber of commerce, or a favour from a politician.

## Reorganisation Process

Regretfully, All India Radio (AIR) performance in informing, educating and entertaining its listeners has not been impressive and it has failed to come up to its promise as an instrument of mass communication. Its failure has been twofold: it has failed to provide a broadcasting service satisfactory to the community and it has failed to fulfil the purpose of the state to inform and educate the masses, to enthuse them with plans of social and economic progress and to enlist their cooperation in fulfilling them. This failure is attributable to many factors; basically they arise from organisational deficiencies and inadequate financial resources.

According to the Indian Telegraphs Act of 1885, as amended, the Government of India has the exclusive privilege of establishing, maintaining and working a broadcasting service. The Act provides that a licence may be granted to others also. This permissive provision was used when in 1926 the Indian Broadcasting Company Ltd., was granted a licence for the two stations at Calcutta and Bombay. Since 1930, when the broadcasting service was taken over by government as 'The Indian State Broadcasting Service' no licences have been issued except for small agricultural stations at Allahabad and Dehra Dun, both since defunct, and to the Madras Corporation for a restricted city service until the Madras station came on the air in 1938. AIR thus enjoys a monopoly in the field.

***Departments of Government :*** Since its inception AIR has been a department of the government. At present, its status is that of an attached office of the Ministry of Information and Broadcasting. The minister is responsible to the Cabinet and accountable to Parliament for all broadcasting activity. Except for short spells during the period 1947-65, the minister has not been a member of the Cabinet. Since January 1966, the ministry once again is put under a minister of state. It is unfortunate that it has been so. Effective mass communication in a developing country is essential for its economic and social regeneration. The minister at the helm should have suitable authority and status for the purpose. It is equally unfortunate that the Cabinet Committee on Information and Broadcasting has been recently discontinued. This again makes the link between the minister and the Cabinet tenuous.

The Director General is responsible to the ministry for the working of AIR as its executive head. He is appointed by the government in consultation with the Union Public Service Commission. It is usual to appoint an officer of the programme cadre of AIR to be the Director General, though the post is not specifically reserved for the cadre. There have been occasions when officers of the Indian Civil Service were drafted to be Director General.

Though the pay of the Director General is the same as that allowed to a Joint Secretary, he has not been equated in status to a Joint Secretary nor does he exercise any powers of government. The heads of two other similar organisations, namely, the Director General, Posts and Telegraphs, and the Director General Tourism, both have ex-officio Secretariat status and the former is remunerated by a higher salary.

The Director General is supported by a Chief Engineer ranking next only to him and three Deputy Directors General, one each for Programmes, Inspection and Administration.

The Deputy Director General (Programmes) is in charge of the preparation of programme schedules and recruitment and utilisation of staff artists, their emoluments etc. He is assisted by eight Directors, in the rank of Station Directors, nine Chief Producers, two Deputy Chief Producers and other staff.

The Station Directors of AIR administer the various stations on behalf of the Director General. Similarly, there are Directors in charge of Units such as the Staff Training School, the TV Service, the Transcription and Programme Exchange Service, the External Services, and the News Services. They are assisted by Station Engineers/Assistant Station Engineers, Assistant Station Directors and Producers or Assistant Producers.

Like all other departments of government, the entire expenditure of AIR is met by appropriations made by Parliament. In theory, the licence fee on receivers is levied to sustain the broadcasting service. But in practice, revenue derived from licence fees, after deducting collection charges, is credited to the Consolidated Fund and both the capital and revenue budgets of AIR are debated and voted upon annually by Parliament. There is thus no direct link between licence fees collected and amounts appropriated. In many countries the entire collection of fees reduced by the cost of collection is placed at the disposal of the broadcasting organisation either directly or through a vote of Parliament without a detailed control over its activities.

## The Procedure

We should now consider whether organised as it is today as an attached office of a ministry with concomitant financing arrangements, AIR can develop as a national organisation and provide a countrywide service of quality and excellence.

In the first place, a theme of centralisation runs through the fabric of India's administration. It is more marked in the field of financial administration. This by itself is a deterrent to the growth of departmental initiative and expeditious transaction of business. Even the ministries of government do not enjoy full financial powers over the appropriations made to them for purposes embodied in the estimates as approved by Parliament. They derive financial authority by delegations made from time to time by the Finance

Ministry. The principle that all executive levels should have administrative authority and financial power commensurate with their responsibilities and functions has yet to find acceptance. There is also a general disinclination to part with power and the Director General in his turn has been chary in delegating powers to the Station Directors.

A government department is subject to the discipline of rules and regulations both in regard to its employment policy and utilisation of resources allocated. These rules and regulations framed for administrative purposes are not wholly suitable for the commercial activities of government or for a creative medium like AIR. It is on this consideration that industrial and commercial activities of government have been entrusted to statutory corporations on companies. In the case of AIR no such dispensation has yet been made. The purpose of adopting the corporate form was to free the commercial activities of the state from inappropriate rules and regulations and to place them on a comparable footing with private enterprise.

We do not wish to overload this report with details but would refer to a few major limitations which impinge on the efficiency of AIR's administration. In the administrative field the Director General's powers for creation of posts only extend to minor posts of clerks and peons. Similarly, he can order transfers of only junior officials, not of Directors and not even of Assistant Station Directors if they hold independent charge of a station. His disciplinary powers are also extremely limited and hemmed in by archaic regulations. In this situation, it is difficult for him to administer the department efficiently nor can he command the respect of his subordinates.

His financial powers are even more limited. He cannot send out any officer on tour for more than ten days at a time and he cannot authorise air journeys where necessary. Even his powers in regard to programme planning do not allow him to make worthwhile adjustments. One might well say that he has responsibility without the authority necessary to fulfil it.

We now consider whether basic requirements of AIR would be met by enlarging the powers of the Director General.

First, he has to work within the limits of funds appropriated by

Parliament In the framing of estimates AIR's proposals are first scrutinised and usually pruned down by the Ministry and the process is repeated in the Finance Ministry. Thus, it is seldom that the reductions are made in a constructive way keeping in view the main purpose for which funds were demanded. Secondly, the Director General cannot spend the amounts voted according to his requirements without adhering to detailed allocations to different activities. He has hardly any powers of reappropriation.

Thirdly, the capital grant is determined by the Planning Commission's decision regarding the rate of development and the priorities in this development. As we have mentioned earlier, broadcasting does not figure in the list of priorities drawn up by the Planning Commission. We were informed that AIR's plan has just undergone a fifth revision to accord with the Commission's proposed total allocation of resources in the Fourth Plan. This has at one stroke nullified AIR's earlier intention to provide a medium-wave network to serve 95 per cent of the people by the end of the Fourth Plan.

Fourthly, the Director General is not competent to engage the type of people he needs and offer them salaries they are worth, as all recruitment has to be made through prescribed government channels and remunerations paid according to scales laid down by government. There is thus little flexibility in the selection of staff and in determining the terms and conditions of service'. And the Director General has no authority to dispense with the services of unsuitable staff.

We say all this to pinpoint the present disabilities of AIR, but we do not for a moment suggest that the Director General should be allowed to function without control and guidance or that he should be given all the resources he demands. He should, however, be brought into closer collaboration in the shaping of policy and programmes and given greater flexibility in their fulfilment.

Before we discuss what would be the most suitable organisation for AIR, we should make one point of substance and that is that the stations and other units of AIR must be given greater autonomy than they enjoy at present. It is the stations which are actually concerned with broadcasts and the test of a broadcasting organisation is the quality of its programmes. The need for speedy decisions and initiative at the stations is indisputable but cannot be met if their Directors have to obtain the Director General's approval for every little thing that they need or propose to do. Their status in the organisation has been progressively whittled down over the years.

For reasons we have developed earlier, it is not possible in the Indian context for a creative medium like broadcasting to flourish under a regiment of departmental rules and regulations. It is only by an *institutional chance* that AIR can be liberated from the present rigid financial and administrative procedures of government.

We first explored the possibility of adopting the form of one or other governmental agency which has greater freedom in movement than departments of government. The Railway Board, the Atomic Energy Commission, the Council of Scientific and Industrial Research, were suggested by some as a possible model for AIR.

Anxious as we were to limit structural changes to the minimum, we studied these organisations but came to the conclusion that none of the patterns would meet the needs of AIR. The reasons for our conclusions are as follows: There is a clear division of functions in Railway operations and it is not so in broadcasting. Secondly, the Railway Board is not engaged in creative activity. And thirdly, as a ministry of government, the Board has to work within the limitation of rules and regulations framed for recruitment, promotion, etc. On all these counts, the Railway Board pattern would not meet the needs of AIR.

Similarly, both the Atomic Energy Commission and the Council of Scientific and Industrial Research are engaged in specialised activities which do not make it necessary for them to be in constant touch with political, cultural and social developments with which Radio is intimately involved.

We, therefore, proceed to consider whether it would not be best to give AIR the corporate form which has been successfully adopted by broadcasting organisations in countries with a democratic constitution. In this consideration it would be relevant to examine the policy resolution which led to the acceptance of the corporate form for state industrial enterprises.

It was acknowledged that subject to the observance of certain general principles, the organisation of management suitable for each undertaking must necessarily be determined with reference to its particular requirements. The method of recruitment, the regulation of scales of pay, conditions of service and discipline of employees, the procedure for financial control, the system of accounting applicable to the normal activities of government could not obviously be adopted for the efficient administration of industrial enterprises. We feel that the same considerations apply with equal force in the case of AIR.

Experience has shown that the corporate form by itself has not brought about a psychological transformation nor given flexibility in operation because the Boards as constituted do not ensure independence implicit in the form. It is necessary to safeguard this position by making AIR a *national authority* in which major national interests would be represented to give it balance, quality, poise and purpose. Secondly, even with such a constitution the autonomy of the corporation would not be real unless it is financially independent and viable.

We have carefully studied in detail the major types of broadcasting organisations in different parts of the world. Major broadcasting systems are either in private hands largely exploited for profit, or they are owned by the state but entrusted to autonomous corporations subject to specified control over policies and programmes.

It is necessary at the outset to make the point that all radio and television organisations are subject to control and regulations by the state. First there is the international obligation in the use of wave lengths and frequencies. This requires the issue of a licence to operate as prescribed by the International Telecommunication Union. The grant of licence is subject to certain legal formalities and regulations framed by each government. Apart from legal requirements, no state can allow unrestricted authority to a broadcasting organisation to embark on programmes which offend against social and moral values.

These media have a tremendous potential in moulding public opinion; they can equally enslave or liberate the human mind. The state has to safeguard the public interest through its regulatory power. It is largely on this consideration that the Supreme Court of the United States of America had declared: 'Unlike other modes of expression, radio inherently is not available to all. That is its unique characteristic. That is why unlike other modes of expression it is subject to government regulations.'

The outstanding example of private ownership and management is provided by the United States of America where licences to operate Radio and Television Stations are issued by the Federal Communication Commission subject to certain laws and regulations. This system also operates in many other countries, notably, Japan, Canada and Australia. All the three countries have each a public corporation owned wholly by the state, but they have also licensed private stations which operate in competition.

There is a variation of this form which provides for joint state and private collaboration. The best examples of blending of public and private ownership are provided by the Italian and Swedish organisation. RAI, the Italian organisation, is a private limited company which has been granted a monopoly of Radio and Television and wire distribution. The majority of its shares are held by the Institute of Industrial Reconstruction which is a government agency. Although RAI enjoys a considerable measure of independence, it is subject to obligations and inspections by the state. The Board of Management and the Board of Auditors have government members.

In Sweden, programming rights are vested since 1925 solely in a company known as Sveriges Radio. The state owns the transmitting network and is responsible for its maintenance and operation. The programme company is privately owned; the state has no financial interest in it. Two-fifths of the shares are held by the Press, another two-fifths by large national organisations and popular movements and one-fifth by business and industrial interests. The government, however, reserves the right to appoint the Chairman and one half of the members of the Board of Governors; the other half being elected by the shareholders.

In the other category are public corporations constituted by Royal Charter of Statute. They are run independently by a body specifically set up for the purpose and are largely independent of government financially. All governments, however, retain overriding control by prescribing regulations under which the corporations must operate and also have discretion to alter the regulations from time to time. Theoretically the supervisory powers vested in the governments are extensive but in practice they are invoked only if the corporations tend to behave in an irresponsible manner or offend against the public interest.

Unlike privately owned corporations, they are not actuated by the profit motive. They are under an obligation to utilise their income to promote denned objectives. The best known examples of this type of broadcasting organisation are the corporations and commissions in the United Kingdom, Canada, Japan, Australia, France and West Germany.

We reproduce below an extract from the Beveridge Report on Broadcasting in the United Kingdom as an example to show how autonomy has been reconciled with control:

The formal power of the government over the British Broadcasting Corporation is absolute. The Governors who constitute the Corporation can be removed at any time by order in Council and can be replaced by others. The licence can be revoked by the Postmaster General, if at any time the Corporation in his opinion is failing in its duties. The Postmaster General can veto any proposed broadcast or class of broadcast, and in doing so can require the Corporation to refrain from announcing that a veto has been imposed. Any government department can require the Corporation to broadcast any announcement or other matter desired by it.

In practice it has become the agreed policy of successive governments, accepted by Parliament, that the Corporation should be independent of the government in the day-to-day conduct of its business, including both the making of programmes for broadcasting and general administration.

We now discuss the suitability or otherwise of the two forms we have outlined. On many consideration we are not attracted to the idea of entrusting radio and television to commercial interests.

First, there is the consideration that no commercial interest would be able to undertake the enormous capital outlay involved in setting up a radio and television organisation, unless it were given unfettered discretion to earn revenue from advertisements. They might not also provide requisite time and resources for programmes of educative value, and indulge in sensationalism, sacrificing objectivity and integrity in presenting news. We must, therefore, turn our face against this form of organisation.

The most important consideration on which we have rejected this form, however, is that radio and television have a purposeful role to fulfil in our developing economy. They have to mobilise public opinion to support the plans of development, they have to educate and inform the people and strive to better their social and economic life. That should be the major role and purpose of radio and television in India.

Several witnesses including some Union and state ministers and officials were in favour of allowing private stations to operate side by side with the national network. They felt that the national network should be supplemented by private endeavour to meet the requirements of the local communities. They also felt that independent private stations would be able to provide programmes which would give greater satisfaction to the listening public. This in our view is a danger. It may lead to a lowering of standards. We, therefore, are unable to subscribe to this view and would retain for the national network a monopoly in the field of broadcasting.

We are also averse to the system in which these two media are used primarily for purposes of propagating a particular ideology and regimentation of its citizens. We are thus left with the only alternative of entrusting the broadcasting services to an autonomous corporation set up by statute which would clearly define the authority and control which government would exercise over its activities. We found overwhelming support for this idea from the officials of AIR, distinguished witnesses whose advice we sought and from others who either sent in written memoranda or gave evidence in addition. The Press also largely supported the transformation of AIR into a Corporation.

There are other valid considerations which influence us in

making this recommendation. AIR must not be considered by the people as an instrument of the government of the day as it is widely regarded today. If its organisation were to be made autonomous and its programmes based on the concept of social responsibility, its value and effectiveness would be considerably enhanced. It would create public confidence and lead to the acceptance of its programmes as objective and unbiased and consequently their impact would be far greater.

## Political Aspects

There is also a political consideration which cannot be lightly dismissed, more so in a federal state. If some of the states come to be controlled by parties other than the one in power at the Centre, AIR would be exposed to stresses and strains which are best avoided.

We now turn to the nature of the Corporation we recommend. The Corporation should be set up by an Act of Parliament in which its objectives should also be clearly defined and be free of ambiguity. The right to require the Corporation to broadcast certain programmes as also the right to veto broadcasts in certain subjects may be reserved to government. It must be understood that such powers must be sparingly used and only when the national interest so demands. These reservations would automatically define the accountability of the minister to Parliament. We also consider that the Act itself should lay down the authority and powers of the Governors to prevent possible encroachment.

The constitution and composition of the governing body are all-important. The Chairman of the Corporation should be a *public figure* with a national reputation for his integrity, ability and independence. The members, the number of whom we consider should not exceed seven, should similarly be drawn from diverse fields of national life, each enjoying a reputation in his particular field.

One of the complaints in the functioning of autonomous corporations, here as elsewhere, had been that the ministers are able to influence their policies without issuing directives, thus escaping parliamentary accountability. This position can be safeguarded only when the composition of the Board is such that it will not be amenable to undue and unreasonable pressure.

The people who constitute the Board must understand fully the purposes of broadcasting and see that they are fulfilled. They must also take note of public opinion and ensure that the programmes respond to it.

Various suggestions for ensuring independence have been made. One is that appointments should be made by the President, the other that they should be made by him on the recommendation of the Chief Justice, a third is that public organisations and associations with related activities should each submit a panel and selections should be confined to the names included.

We do not favour any of these suggestions. A responsible government is expected to function in a responsible way and we would much rather leave selections to government indicating only the broad principles to be observed. Secondly, experience has shown that once selected to such autonomous bodies people act independently and do not sacrifice the interest of the organisation to outside pressure.

It now remains to consider whether members of Parliament and service personnel should be categories specifically excluded as suggested by some. We are against such a blanket ban and would not demur if, by reason of eminence and specialisation, one or two were drawn from these sources.

The term of office of the Chairman and Governors should, we feel, be six years and it should be provided mat for the sake of continuity two members should retire every other year in rotation.

The Director-General: The selection of the Director General requires equally careful consideration. As Chief Executive, on him will devolve the responsibility for maintaining objectivity, ensuring efficiency and economy and building up an attractive image of the organisation. He has undoubtedly to be a person with a dynamic personality endowed with drive, imagination and initiative, capable of creating a well knit team of devoted workers and giving it resolute leadership. It is difficult anywhere to find one with all these attributes.

It will be more so in India, particularly if according to present practice the selection is confined to government servants. The net will have to be cast much wider. It may even become necessary to persuade an outstanding personality in the fields of journalism, advertising, the film industry and the academic world to accept this assignment in a spirit of dedication and service. If a civil servant is selected by the Board of Governors, there should be a stipulation, as in the case of the Reserve Bank, that he should resign from service.

The question of the status of the Director General was also mooted by some, it being suggested that in a protocol-ridden society it is important that the Director General should be accorded a high rank commensurate with his responsibilities. We, however, do not attach importance to his suggestion. The status of the Board and its Chief Executive would automatically come to be determined by the place the organisation comes to occupy in our national life and the public esteem it is able to command by its independence, integrity and excellence.

Though the details of the organisation and the rules or business should be drawn up by the Board, we should suggest certain broad principles so mat in inheriting the organisation it does not inherit the deficiencies.

Even at the risk of being repetitive, we should stress once again the need for decentralisation of authority and functions. This is necessary in the interests of efficiency in any organisation, it is more so in a broadcasting organisation. For example, in a country so vast as ours with a multiplicity of languages and cultural patterns and with, regions in different stages of development, central control of programme planning and the imposition of uniformity in their contents and presentation would not only be inappropriate but would defeat the basic purposes of the broadcasting system. We would, therefore, give the Station Directors complete freedom in the matter and subject them only to policy directions as to the types of broadcasts which should be discouraged.

We do not suggest that this decentralisation should be absolute. It should be obligatory to relay the national news bulletins and other national programmes of interest. It is necessary though that determination of themes of broadcasts as national should be made with circumspection and discretion.

Another way to achieve decentralisation is to have several channels of broadcasting, one of which would provide the national programme, the other regional programmes and the third a local service on local transmitters which we have recommended earlier. The only practical way as we have stressed, is through such local stations.

The establishment of competitive channel of broadcasting was advocated by several witnesses. They argued that a monopolist enterprise tends to become complacent, stale and ineffective. It needs the stimulus of competition to make its staff more alert and enterprising and the programmes more lively. It was said that the establishment of the Independent Television Authority in Britain had a tonic effect on the BBC's TV Services.

We have considered this question carefully. We have come to the conclusion that having regard to the availability of resources both in manpower and in funds, and the role we envisage for broadcasting, we should not at this stage bring in considerations which might well come in the way of the development of radio.

We should, however, encourage universities to instal closed circuit radio and television services, or the state governments and major municipal corporations to set up local transmitters for agricultural, social and educational purposes to meet the needs of local communities which cannot be effectively served by the national network.

It is necessary to consider how the Corporation we have proposed should be financed. The question falls into two parts: capital expenditure to add to the network by installing additional transmitters, studios and other equipment; revenue expenditure for sustaining and improving the service.

We now turn to the question how future capital expenditure should be financed and how best the revenue of AIR should be augmented. In the case of state enterprises, government have provided both equity capital and loans to maintain a proper ratio between the two. While interest is chargeable on the loan (there has been a period of moratorium in many cases), the return on equity investment depends on the profits, if any earned. This is the policy adopted in the case of commercial activities. Similarly, government meet the capital expenditure on welfare measures, on education, health and activities necessary to increase agricultural production.

Broadcasting is not a commercial activity, though a monopoly, it cannot, unlike other monopolies, adjust prices, rates and fees to meet interest liability on capital expended. On all considerations and having regard to its primary role as a medium of education and information, we consider that capital expenditure is a legitimate charge on public revenues.

We propose, therefore, that the assets of AIR should be transferred to the Corporation without any interest or any other financial liability. Similarly, the allocation in the Fourth Plan should be made available to the Corporation free of charge. We consider that thereafter the proposals we make on revenue account, would make the Corporation fully viable, able to expand with its own resources taking resource to borrowing, if necessary, on its own financial standing.

We have one important observation to make in regard to capital expenditure. We find that organisationally AIR is geared to an expenditure of about Rs 2 crores a year. To enlarge its spending capacity efficiently, it would be necessary to bring about a reorganisation and the sooner it is undertaken the better it would be. The allocation in the Fourth Plan is bound to be larger and we have recommended certain priorities for providing local transmitters and the reorientation of the external services.

To fulfil this plan, AIR needs organisation and effort which should be preplanned.

There has been a suggestion that licence fees should be discontinued. We do not accept this suggestion. It would be unfair to burden the community at large to support a service when the beneficiaries are small in number. The fee should continue to be recovered from users of the service. (Licence fee has since been abolished).

We consider that considerable improvement in the recovery of licence fees is possible. It is common knowledge that a number of sets in the country are unlicensed; some suggest that it is as high as sixty per cent.

The steps we have recommended would give elbow room to AIR but would not make it fully viable nor enable it to finance.

By far the most fruitful source of additional revenue would be the acceptance of advertisement in programmes. In dealing with Television we have marshalled the arguments in favour of its acceptance with certain safeguards and restrictions. We do not feel that there are any special considerations which would justify making a distinction on this question between television and sound broadcasting. Consistent with our thinking on this subject, we would limit advertisements to the Vividh Bharati channel alone. By timing the spot advertisements suitably there need be no interference with a programme or its continuity. Vividh Bharati is a light programme predominantly of film music and the inclusion of advertisements is not likely to infringe on its quality or appeal.

Television is a comparatively new medium far more sophisticated than radio. There are basic differences between radio and television in important matters of technique and financing of operators and planning and execution of programmes. Television also presents other problems infinitely more complicated.

Even so, many countries with well-established broadcasting systems found it convenient to entrust the development of television to their existing organisations. This arrangement soon proved to be little more than a marriage of convenience. The rapid growth of television, the remarkable advances in its technology and programme planning, and its versatility in use, brought new responsibilities which could be hardly fulfilled within the resources of existing organisations. This difficulty has been sought to be met by investing the television wing with virtual autonomy. In the United Kingdom, the Union of Soviet Socialist Republics and in Italy, the television centre has now become a distinct, separate and powerful entity with tenuous links with the parent organisation.

In the light of these developments, it has to be considered whether it will be possible or wise to place television under the aegis of AIR. This possibility has to be ruled out as AIR is not organisationally and financially equipped to shoulder this responsibility. It would also be unfair to tag on television to AIR and expose it at its birth to prejudices which exist against AIR. On all these considerations, we would strongly advise against the development and management of this new medium, requiring a dynamic and imaginative approach and ample resources, being linked as an ancillary to an organisation which itself needs a major overhaul and refurbishing.

The question still remains whether the new organisation should follow the pattern of AIR and become an attached office of a ministry or whether it should be made an autonomous corporation, created by a special statute of Parliament. Having carefully considered the question in all its aspects, we have come to the conclusion that to develop on correct lines television must not be hampered by the limitations of a department; it should have a broader outlook, greater flexibility and freedom of action which the corporate form alone can give.

While discussing the future organisation of AIR we have already stated in detail the reasons for our recommendation that an autonomous statutory corporation would be the best form of organisation for providing a broadcasting service. These conside-ration apply with equal, if not greater force, in case of television.

We consider that to give shape to our recommendations immediate steps should be taken to invite a competent agency to prepare the project report. An officer of the status of a Chief Engineer, should be associated with their team in its preparatory work, who could later be selected to head the technical wing.

To ensure that the two processes of project study and operation planning go hand in hand, it would be necessary to form the Television Corporation with the nucleus of staff necessary to access the ultimate requirements of staff, organise training, draw up the programme policy and prepare an estimate of the finances required. It should also initiate negotiations with potential collaborators but keep government closely informed of developments. The agreements reached should naturally be subject to government approval.

We have already given our views on the staffing of AIR and suggested reorganisation. The staffing pattern and employment policy of the Television Corporation we propose will have to be differently conceived and designed.

As mentioned earlier, television is basically a different medium from radio and cannot be given the same treatment. Being, however, a part of AIR, the Delhi Television Centre has unfortunately the same organisation as a radio unit and has developed unsuitable trends and nuances. For one thing, it has tended to become a top-heavy organisation in which the more expensive technical staff was until recently being incorrectly employed; for another, its programmes being produced on the basis of radio techniques and experience, are indifferent and even colourless. It is essential that the two activities should be separated at the large scale inception of television, to give it a fair wind.

We are in agreement with our Consultant mat 'television needs a lively, decisive, imaginative, adventurous yet responsible staff. This implies that its control and operations should be in the hands of those who have these attributes.

Taking a look at the Delhi Centre, the first point that struck us was the strength of the staff deployed for its limited output. It appeared that there had not been a proper assessment of the staff required in different categories and that as problems arose they were sought to be met by hurriedly transferring whoever was conveniently available in the radio wing. As a consequence of this haphazard and irrational staffing, the sanctioned strength has been raised to 271 to allow for the recent extension of the service.

The Centre provides a one-hour evening programme of news and entertainment of which only about a third is produced at the Centre itself, the rest being films or recorded material obtained locally or from abroad. It also provides three twenty-minute school lessons a day for six days a week for each of the two shifts in the schools, giving a total broadcast time of about 120 minutes a day. But of these lessons one or two a week are repetitions of old lessons already recorded and telecast, thus reducing the output of the studio to about eight hours a week.

In the opinion of our Consultant, the Centre is grossly overstaffed. Our Sub-Committee concurs in this assessment on the basis of its study abroad. 'Telescuola' in Italy, running school and adult literacy programmes, is on the air for 41½ hours a week but it employs a total of 128 people only including 27 technicians and 16 teachers, e.g. Admittedly, its telecasts do not require certain categories of staff which an inclusive service of information, education and entertainment would need, but even so the contrast is striking.

Our Consultant also informed us that a firm International Television Consultants had recommended a total staff of approximately 50 for certain African countries embarking on television with a daily programme output of four hours. Similarly, a UNESCO Mission, which advised Israel on the introduction of television, recommended a total staff of 226 distributed between the three organisations of the Central Administration (the equivalent of the directorate general of AIR), the Jerusalem and the Tel Aviv Studio Centres. This requirement was based on a suggested output of 23 hours of programmes a week of which over 12 hours were to originate in the two Studio Centres.

The second point that struck us was that at its inception the Television Centre was manned largely if not entirely by people drawn from sound broadcasting without a mature consideration whether this arrangement was suitable either for the installation or the development of this medium.

Training is essential for the success of all human endeavour. The more difficult the objective, the greater is the need for training for its attainment. Yet the necessity of advance training of the required number of people in the difficult and varied techniques of television had been ignored before the Delhi pilot project was launched in 1959.

It was only after six years, in 1965, that a producer was obtained on loan from the BBC to give a course of training to a small number of selected production staff. We consider that this is totally inadequate even to sustain the extended programmes of the Centre and to improve their quality, leave alone to handle the expansion we recommend.

We have earlier mentioned that the installation of a television network needs massive financial outlay, a large part of it in foreign exchange. On both these counts, some acceptable form of foreign collaboration will have to be considered. Financing of the television service is another matter; it needs a different treatment.

Because of the low priority given to broadcasting, the allocation of Plan resources has so far been minuscule. We have already adduced many considerations why television should receive equal priority with industrial and agricultural schemes of development. Even so, the competing demands of other nation-building activities might make it difficult to allocate to television all the money it needs for developing a countrywide network by the end of the Fifth Plan. We have perforce to consider alternatives which would ensure adequate financial support.

We have made as detailed a study as is possible, in the absence of complete documentation, of developments elsewhere and the manner in which countries similarly situated have set about to bring the benefits of television to their people.

Foreign collaboration in two different forms has been adopted to cover fully the foreign exchange component of the project for the supply of capital goods such as transmitters, studio equipment, installation of links and other ancillary facilities. It has either taken the shape of participation in the equity issue of the corporation or it has been a straight loan with a period of moratorium before repayment commences. Some countries have adopted the former method in which a consortium of industrialists has a minority financial interest, the controlling interest being retained by government. Some others have preferred the latter method but have not encountered any lack of response because of this choice. We also consider that we must not have any foreign equity participation in the proposed Television Corporation. It is needles to add that the provision of a loan must not give any voice to the donors in deciding the policy of the Corporation.

In addition, it has been arranged either separately or as a part of the same scheme that the foreign exchange requirements of manufacturing television sets and the essential equipment would be provided by the foreign associates, the inducement being that they would themselves supply the television sets until, manufacture has been established but without an appreciable outflow of foreign exchange.

It is found impractical for a single county to provide the required financial support, the formation of a consortium might become necessary. The idea of forming a consortium has caught on even in the matter of international aid to developing countries. It should not, therefore, be difficult to bring about the formation of a consortium to assist our project should this become necessary. We contemplate a package deal in which the collaborator would also accept responsibility for the manufacture of television sets and other equipment. It may be necessary to set up a separate manufacturing unit.

The willingness to collaborate with technical assistance and a loan will naturally depend on the viability of the project and its ability to generate enough resources to be able to repay the loan in agreed installments. Under the plan we later discuss, we have no doubts that the revenues of the Corporation will be ample to meet all its commitments. We are confident that foreign collaborator would feel equally reassured.

The question will still remain how the rupee finance of the project can best be found. The allocation of a high priority for television together with the realisation that the acceptance of the plan we later unfold would make television a viable and even a productive venture should make it possible for the Planning Commission to release necessary resources. The expectation that television would become self-financing within a short time, if not at its inception, and that it would not, therefore, make annual demands for its running expenses should be a weighty consideration in the allocation of resources. It would imply that the initial investment needed would be little more than a capitalisation of a few years recurring expenses, provision for which would have to be made otherwise, being inherent in the acceptance of a television scheme, however, unambitious it may be.

There is another aspect developed earlier, that is the extensive use of television for educational, agriculture, health and other socioeconomic purposes. On a long term view, it may be found more economical, yet more effective to invest in television than, for example, to build schools for which teacher cannot be found, or equipment provided, or build health centres which can only be manned by indifferent and unimaginative people. Similarly, recurring expenditure on publicity to give an impetus to programmes for self-sufficiency in the production of foodgrains and other expenditure now incurred for popularising the introduction of improved strains of seeds, the use of fertilisers and pesticides, the rotation of crops, etc., could be considerably minimised by visual presentation which television alone can provide.

These savings would be a recurring annual feature and should give welcome relief to the budgets of these departments. Once his important aspect of television is realised, there should be no difficulty in either increasing the allocation for television by corresponding reduction in the capital budgets of the ministries concerned; alternatively, they should invest a part, albeit a small part, of their capital grants in building up a countrywide television network. A small advisory body of the participants in programme planning should ensure the allocation of adequate time to each.

The cost of operating the network depends on its output, the standard of the producers and artists it employs, the level of remuneration it pays, and the type and quality of programmes it provides. It must obviously be the aim to give the optimum output within the capability of the network and to plan and produce programmes of the highest quality employing first class artists. This implies that there must be resources available for establishing and sustaining a high professional standard comparable to other television services.

The method evolved by the British Broadcasting Corporation, and followed by some other broadcasting systems, is to levy a licence fee from the owners of receiving sets and to allocate the proceeds, after deducting the cost of collection, to broadcasting. The yield is thus directly related to the number of receiving sets held and licensed. The limitation of this arrangement is that the rate of levy cannot be easily adjusted to accord with the needs of the service. There are many factors including public resistance which have to be taken into account in a revision of the fee.

When the British Broadcasting Corporation entered the field of television, a separate and higher scale of levy was designed to finance its programmes and other operating costs. This levy has been adjusted upwards from time to time to sustain an expansion of programmes, to improve their quality and to neutralise rising costs. The public had gone along with these increases. More recently an Independent Television Authority was created by statute and was given freedom to run its services with advertising revenues without sharing with the British Broadcasting Corroboration the licence fees collected. This brought a new concept of financing television in tradition-bound and conventional Britain.

The programmes controlled by the Independent Television Authority not only proved attractive but were made available without any payment by the viewing audiences. We shall refer to the ITA later in the narration but mention it at this stage because of its indirect impact on the recent demand of the British Broadcasting Corporation for a substantial increase in licence fees both for existing services and for opening up a fourth channel which has become available. Government considered the increase demanded unreasonable and also unfair to licence-holders and conceded a smaller increase. This has left the British Broadcasting Corporation in a quandary.

It has to be appreciated that in a country like India the licence fees have to be kept reasonably low to accord with the people's capacity to pay. On the one hand, the number of sets in private hands in the initial stages will be small and the yield of licence fees negligible, on the other, there will be the need for a wide network to bring the social programmes within the reach of the community which needs them most. It will thus become necessary to accept commercial advertisements to supplement the revenue derived from licence fees.

We are aware of the opinion which still persists against the acceptance of commercial broadcasts. There is the apprehension that were commercial advertisements to be accepted television would become largely dependent on revenues derived from commercial interests and this might well lead to the political, economic and social policies of the organisation being influenced and even indirectly controlled by these interests. There is also the apprehension that the advertisements to have a popular appeal, might tend to become somewhat vulgar and demoralising.

Experience elsewhere has shown that the acceptance of advertisements to accord with the programme policy of a television organisation does not bring it even remotely under the control of commercial interests nor does it lead to the presentation of material which is in questionable taste.

It is necessary to review in a brief compass, the policy adopted by different organisations, discussing later their merits and demerits. In the United States of America and Latin American countries as also in Iran, Lebanon, Thailand and the Philippines, television is in the hands of private interests who finance their operations, including the setting up and expansion of their existing networks, from revenues derived entirely from the sale of time to advertisers. In the United States of America and most of these countries, the advertisers not only buy time but also provide programmes of their choice which go with the advertisements.

In Australia, Japan and Canada this system has been adopted by a number of comparatively small television stations which operate in competition with the national organisations which are maintained out of licence revenues. The acceptance of commercial programmes, known as 'sponsored programme' has resulted in the largest and most prosperous television network in the world being built up in the United States of America and it has also given impetus to the growth of television in the countries mentioned and in Latin America and some countries of Asia. The major undesirable feature of this system is that the television organisation has very little control over the programmes put on the air with the result that they are often in questionable taste and have a demoralising effect on impressionable and immature minds. It has been suggested that the increase in the rate of child delinquency in the United States of America is attributable to these programmes.

Benefiting by the experience of the United States of America, countries which entered the television field later, more particularly the European countries, evolved a new system. While accepting commercial advertisements as inescapable for supporting the growth of a sound television system and also the U.S. practice of selling time, they safeguarded the quality and standard to the programmes by refusing to allow the advertisers to produce them or even to have a say in the programmes which would include their advertisement material. By this method commonly known as 'spot advertising' or 'spot announcements', the organisations retained full control over their programme policy. An additional safeguard was also introduced, by stature where necessary, but mainly by a code of conduct voluntarily agreed upon by the organisations and the advertisers, to control the make-up of the advertisements. Italy went a step further and set up a corporation to handle and produce all advertisement shots.

Television stations in West Germany, Ireland, Italy, Spain, the United Arab Republic, Iraq, Pakistan, to mention a few countries, have adopted this system of spot advertising to raise resources to supplement revenues from licence fees. Some countries such as Italy and West Germany have introduced the practice of presenting in a single special programme all advertisements within an allocated period of time, usually 20 to 30 minutes, at an excellent viewing hour, between eight and nine o'clock in the evening. Other countries intersperse the spots, not exceeding five or six minutes in an hour, in their daily programmes.

It is necessary to discuss the two practices, their merits and demerits and their revenue potential. The practice of concentrating all advertisements in one programme has two attractive features: First, it enables the viewers who are not interested in commercials to switch off at the hour when they are on the air; secondly, by not breaking into a programme, it preserves the continuity and entertainment value of the programme and also the atmosphere it creates. The advertisers, however, do not consider this method as attractive as spots in regular programmes. They also consider that a spot should be repeated in a number of programmes in any one day to have worthwhile advertisement value.

The latter practice has undoubtedly greater advertisement value, as it provides a captive audience and a repeated presentation of the same spots in different programmes at different viewing hours. The irritation caused by the spots breaking into a programme has been sought to be removed by putting the advertisements at the beginning, the intermission and the end of the programmes.

This is an improvement from the viewers point and meets the advertisers' demands to a certain extent. The revenue potential of this practice is undoubtedly greater.

We have very carefully considered which of the two systems, the U.S. one of sponsored programmes or the European one of spot advertisement to recommend, or whether a combination of the two would be more suitable. We do not feel that one need be squeamish about sponsored programmes as such so long as they have an educative and cultural value and do not include any advertisement material except to mention at their commencement or conclusion that they were presented by the courtesy of so and so (naming the sponsors). Such programmes do not have the connotation or implications of sponsored programmes in the United States of America and should even be welcome as being useful and valuable additions to the repertoire of the television organisation. Such programmes are not uncommon elsewhere and have been viewed and appreciated by some of us abroad. These 'prestige' programmes are presented by sponsors who are inspired to contribute to the growth of the television system and incidentally bring their names and contributions to the notice of the viewing public. However, the revenues from this type of sponsored programmes will not be substantial but that should be no reason for excluding them.

The acceptance of advertisements should be considered only if it brings significant financial support to the growth of television. There is nothing non-ethical in accepting advertisements prepared in good taste provided that they do not affect the quality of the telecasts or make excessive demands. If the educational, social and children's programmes do not carry spots and they are confined to the entertainment programmes, there should not be any objection in adopting a practice which has now become more or less universal.

A 12-Member Working Group headed by B.G. Verghese was set up on August 17, 1977, to go into the working of AIR and Doordarshan and suggest changes. The following were the other members of his Group: V.G. Rajadhyaksha, Dr. Malcolm S. Adiseshiah, Chanchal Sarkar, P.L. Deshpande, Umashankar Joshi, A.G. Noorani, G.R. Subramanian, Mrs. Nayantara Sehgal and Dr. Ishwar Das (Member Secretary).

The group made wide-ranging recommendations to transform All-India Radio and Television into a more responsive organisation from a mere government department.

The two-volume report running into 405 pages was presented to Parliament on March 9, 1978. In its unanimous report, the working group suggested that the national broadcasting services should be vested exclusively in an independent impartial and autonomous organization established by law to act as a trustee for the national interest.

The legal framework of the autonomous national trust, as envisaged by the working group, was that the establishment of the corporation should not await a constitutional amendment. The law establishing the corporation could be enacted and the organisation brought into being to be followed subsequently by an amendment of the Constitution.

The autonomy of the corporation and its independence from government control should be entrenched in the Constitution itself and the idea of a trust woven into it.

In making recommendations, the working group was guided by a factor that mass media, radio and television must fit into a wider perspective of national communication policy or philosophy.

It rejected a proposal to create two separate corporations for All-India Radio and Television. However, it conceded the need to recognize the distinctive identity of radio and television within the ambit of a new integrated structure.

The group also did not favour the creation of autonomous regional corporations or even a federation of State Government corporations.

While rejecting the proposal to create two separate corporations or set up autonomous regional corporations, the working group argued that there would be a large measure of power delegated to the regional and local level.

This was kept to the fore so that the organisation enjoyed the advantages of quick decision making, sensitivity to local problems and tasks, and close linkages with various governments and institutions.

In recommending the new set-up, the working group did not apparently follow any model operating in any other country.

At the apex of NBT, the working group suggested a board of trustees consisting of 12 persons, and not exceeding 21 persons. The trustees would be guardians of the charter given to the NBT by statute.

The Controller-General of Broadcasting (CGB), heading the central executive board, was conceived by the working group as a link between the trustees and the entire broadcasting organisation. He would be ex-officio secretary to the board of trustees so as to provide an organic link between these two tiers.

Apart from the Chairman, the board of trustees would have three other full-time members to devote themselves to the fields of current affairs, extension and culture. They will operate through the CGB.

In addition to the Chairman and the three full-time trustees, the board would have two part-time trustees—one highly experienced in the field of finance and management and the other an eminent scientist or engineer familiar with the technology of broadcasting.

For the first time in the history of over half-a-century of broadcasting in India, there would be a complaints board comprising persons selected by the Chief Justice of India.

The recommendation of the working group for constituting a complaint board assumed significance in the light of the experience gained during the Emergency when the broadcasting system was blatantly used by the previous regime to further partisan ends.

According to the report, the board of trustees would be responsible to Parliament through its budget and an annual report. Together with accounts and auditor's comments, reports of the complaints board, among other things, would also figure in the annual report.

The complaints board would deal with complaints from the public relating to charges of unjust or unfair treatment including unwarranted invasion of privacy and misrepresentation, provided the right of resources to court was waived. The findings should be published by NBT in the programme 'Journal' and broadcast in special programmes.

In order to ensure the independence of the proposed NBT, the report recommended that the trustees, with six-year terms of office, would be appointed by the President on the recommendation of the Prime Minister from a list of names forwarded to him by a nominating panel.

The nominating panel for trustees would consist of the Chief Justice of India, the Lokpal and the Chairman of the UPSC. It would be a healthy convention if the Prime Minister consulted the leader of the Opposition before submitting the list of names to the President.

The trustees would enjoy the status of Supreme Court judges.

In regard to financial autonomy, the report recommended several measures. Initially, the government should make up the revenue deficit for a period of five years, after transferring the existing assets of All-India Radio and TV.

Later, NBT should be expected to stand on its own feet or raise additional resources by charging for broadcast time, made available by it to various users, including the Central and state governments.

It also felt that the Trust should undertake a comprehensive review of commercial broadcasting rates and procedures. The group also recommended an increase in broadcast receiver licences for certain categories of radio and TV sets.

The report comprehensively surveyed the entire scene of broadcasting and television network since the Chanda Committee submitted its report on radio more than 12 years ago. The Chanda Committee had also recommended an autonomous set-up for AIR.

According to the report, there were now some 20 million radio receivers and 600,000 TV sets. 'With population rising to say, 950 million by 2000 A.D. and 'an end to destitution' and fuller employment, at least 80 to 90 per cent of all households should possess radios,' the report added.

In a perspective study for 2000 A.D. there would be 160 to 180 million radio sets and between 12 to 15 million TV sets by the turn of the century.

In the opinion of the working group, AIR and TV combined in themselves the characteristics of the marketplace, newspaper, university, national extension agency and cultural academy. As such a unique institution must enjoy a unique autonomy.

The report called upon the National Broadcast Trust to bridge the urban-rural divide and combine modernity with relevant tradition.

It recommended the establishment of a strong audience research division. It noted that the audience research unit had a very limited staff and budget. It was, therefore, impossible to conduct any regular audience surveys or to operate on more than very small samples.

The audience research reports should be made available simultaneously and directly to the board of trustees, since these reports would constitute one of the most important antenna of the broadcasting organisation.

***Bill of Prasar Bharati :*** The Prasar Bharati Bill was introduced in the Lok Sabha on December 30, 1989, by the National Front Government led by V.P. Singh. The purpose of this Bill was to grant autonomy to the electronic media, that is AIR and Doordarshan.

The Lok Sabha passed the Bill on August 30, 1990 and the Rajya Sabha approved it on September 6, 1990. The President accorded assent to the Bill soon after.

The changes in the original Bill ran as follows:

> The autonomous Prasar Bharati or Broadcasting Corporation of India will be directly answerable to three authorities—a Parliamentary Committee, the Central Government and the proposed Broadcasting Council.

The original draft of the Prasar Bharati Bill introduced in the Lok Sabha did not contain any provision for the Parliamentary Committee. The government inserted this provision on August 29,1990, as one of the 65 amendments proposed by an all-party consensus. Members of the committee will be elected by proportional representation and will ensure that the Corporation functions in the manner set out in the Bill.

There was no opposition in Parliament to this particular provision as it was only intended to make the autonomous body accountable. Besides being answerable to the Committee, the corporation has to submit annual reports of its activities to Parliament.

The powers envisaged for the Central government, however, have given rise to immense misgivings. The initial draft said the Central government could give directions to make or not to make a certain broadcast only when 'the security of the state or preservation of public order' was at stake. But the August 29 changes widened the ambit by saying that the Central government can also issue directions 'in the interest of sovereignty, unity and integrity of India'. These concepts are very subjective and have been left undefined, tremendously increasing the scope for abuse of power.

Further, the Central government has been empowered to demand any information from the corporation. This means, for instance, that it can order Doordarshan to divulge the source of a news report. If the corporation 'persistently' refuses to comply with any direction, the Central government has been empowered to recommend to Parliament any action, including supersession of the Prasar Bharati Board. The government's recommendation has been given such weight that a ratification by a simple majority will be enough to supersede the board.

The only constraint is that the President, before issuing the notification of supersession, will have to give 'a reasonable opportunity to the board to show cause as to why it should not be superseded'.

The maximum permissible period of supersession is six months. The powers and functions of the board during that period will be discharged by 'such person or persons as the President may direct.'

The third authority which will be vested with some power over the corporation is the Broadcasting Council, which corresponds to the Press Council. The original draft of the Bill, envisaged as a watchdog to protect the interests of the citizens, empowered the Broadcasting Council to decide complaints against the corporation and recommend appropriate remedial action to it. What happens when the corporation rejects the Broadcasting Council's recommendation? An amendment provides for such a contingency: The Broadcasting Council will have the authority to force the corporation to broadcast the recommendation. This, in fact, is the only form of vindication the Bill offers to a citizen aggrieved by the corporation. If Doordarshan or Akashvani, after they are unfettered, broadcast a programme or news report defamatory to somebody, he cannot sue or initiate criminal proceedings against the corporation or anybody in it. This is due to a clause granting immunity against all legal action to the corporation and its employees.

Thus, on the one hand, the proposed corporation is sought to be given the freedom enjoyed by newspapers, on the other, the producers and reporters in the broadcasting field will not be liable for their mistakes as their counterparts in the print media.

The relevant section (24) in the initial draft grants the legal immunity 'for anything which is in good faith done or intended to be done in pursuance of this act or of any rules or regulations made thereunder.' The language is general enough to enable anybody in the corporation to take refuge under this clause for any error committed by him. Yet this section has surprisingly managed to survive the radical amendments made in the Lok Sabha to the original draft.

The Prasar Bharati Board which forms the core of the legislation has also undergone many changes. In the first place, its name was 'Board of Governors'. But the high sounding 'governor' has been replaced by the simple 'member'. The strength of the board has been increased by the inclusion of two ex-officio members—the Director-General of Akashvani and Doordarshan and two elected members from among the employees of the Corporation. The whole-time chairman has been made a part-time one.

All the whole-time members of the board have been made employees of the Corporation.

Among other amendments are: the inclusion of four MPs (two from each House) in the Broadcasting Council, the stipulation on the Broadcasting Council present an annual report to Parliament, deletion of the power to dismiss an employee without being given an opportunity to defend himself and the bar on the Corporation from ceiling its assets.

The Verghese Committee which also advocated autonomy to the electronic media wanted the Ministry of Information and Broadcasting to shed its control over Broadcasting. But the Prasar Bharati Bill puts a representative of the Ministry on the Board of the Corporation.

The most controversial clause as stated earlier is Parliament's power to supersede the Prasar Bharati Board.

In the original version of the bill, this power was sought to be vested in the government.

The present dispensation is an improvement but the effect is the same to ensure that the Prasar Bharati behaves. BJP leader, L.K. Advani sought to soften the blow by suggesting during the discussion of the Bill, an amendment that would have required any resolution on supersession to be passed by two-thirds majority instead of a simple majority. But surprisingly except for one member, nobody supported his suggestion. Strangely, the CPI(M) appeared particularly averse to Mr. Advani's plea.

Voting in Parliament is on strictly party lines and it is unimaginable that if an official resolution is moved for supersession of board of governors, the ruling party members would vote against the resolution.

The official justification for such sweeping Parliamentary control is that if the Prasar Bharati were to be left completely to its devices there was a danger of its being taken over by big business. According to P. Upendra, all autonomous corporations are accountable to Parliament and their functioning is supervised by the Committee on Public Undertakings. This according to him, has not led to interference in their day-to-day affairs, so why should there be fears about such interference in the case of Prasar Bharati.

The fact is that no political party, especially the Left and the Congress wanted an absolutely free Prasar Bharati. They wanted to avoid a situation when the corporation could go 'amuck' in the name of autonomy.

The Congress party also opposed the decision to transfer the assets of AIR and Doordarshan to Prasar Bharati. It is on the insistence of the Congress party that the Bill was amended to say that the new corporation would use the assets in accordance with the terms and conditions prescribed by the government.

Commenting on the question of how autonomous would be the electronic media under the new set up, B.G. Verghese said that the concept is to de-governmentalise broadcasting, both radio as well as television, by placing it under an autonomous corporation—as against where it is now as a subordinate department of the government. Its autonomy would be safeguarded by two or three things.

One is that, according to the Bill, the corporation's accountability is not to the Information & Broadcasting Ministry, but to Parliament. Secondly, the appointment of its top board will be done by a selection committee consisting of the Chairman of Rajya Sabha, the Chairman of the Press Council and a third member to be selected by the President and their decision will be final. This prevents the body from being packed by government favourites.

The third safeguard is that if these people are to be removed it will have to be by a special procedure which is applicable to the members and chairman of the UPSC. They cannot be sacked. And now, they have also added the clause that if the board collectively misbehaves by persistently defying the government directives, then the ministry can make a report to Parliament in which it could recommend supersession, and following a decision of Parliament, supersession can take place. According to Mr. Verghese, Parliamentary control is unnecessary and he feels that the contingencies in which these powers would be used are extreme. They are theoretically possible but in practical terms, they are unlikely to be used.

According to Mr. Khushwant Singh, the well-known journalist, freeing the electronic media from government control deserves to be applauded as the National Front government's biggest achievement of its nine-month rule. All our past Prime Ministers and Ministers of Information and Broadcasting paid lip-services to the principle of freedom of expression for Press, Radio and Television, but everyone of them meddled with their free functioning when they found themselves at the receiving end of criticism.

Jawaharlal Nehru was no exception. He was riled by what

Durga Das (father of Inderjit, Member of the Lok Sabha) wrote about him and did his best to damage his career. His Minister of Information and Broadcasting, Keskar, had Nirad Chaudhuri dismissed from AIR and then blacklisted for eulogising the British in the dedication of his autobiography of an unknown Indian. Keskar had not bothered to read the book.

Mrs. Gandhi had scant respect for Press freedom and blatantly misused Radio and Television to propagate herself and denigrate rivals like Jayaprakash Narayan. She pressurised proprietors of newspapers to remove editors she did not like. Her sycophantic ministers like N.K.P. Salve and H.K.L. Bhagat (Vasant Sathe was one exception) went a step ahead to cancel programmes like 'The World of Nature' which had nothing whatsoever to do with politics for the sole reason that it was written by someone who Mrs. Gandhi regarded as her critic.

It was the same during the short regimes of Morarji Desai and Charan Singh: editors were fired, broadcasters, they did not approve, removed. Blacklists continued to be maintained by AIR and Doordarshan throughout Rajiv Gandhi's tenure as Prime Minister. Who is the Congress (I) to talk about freedom of speech and expression? For Messrs Salve, Bhagat and their likes to extol them is like harlots extolling the virtues of chastity.

It is still not clear how free from political meddling will be the board that will control Radio and Doordarshan. However, a very bold and significant step has been taken. Full credit for this must go to P. Upendra and V.P. Singh.

This is what Mr. Nikhil Chakarvarty, a columnist, said about the electronic media's autonomy. He said there was little consultation even with the media circles before the Bill was drafted, but the criticism was more than negated by two things. First, the speech made by Information and Broadcasting Minister, P. Upendra, while introducing the Bill had a ring of sincerity that reassured many that the present government was earnest about autonomy for the government owned media.

Second, the Minister, on his own, announced that there would be free and wide-ranging national debate on the proposed legislation and the criticisms, suggestions and comments to be made in such discussions would be taken into consideration in amending the bill before it was taken up by Parliament. Not only that, his ministry promoted such discussions all over the country. But after the much publicised computerisation of proposals and suggestions, the amendments which the government announced came as a big shock. These were largely retrogressive.

Meanwhile, the government has been remiss on another count. Upendra had promised that there would be a non-official committee to oversee the functioning of the Akashvani and Doordarshan in the interim period until the proposed Prasar Bharati Corporation took over. It was stated that within a couple of weeks this interim set-up would start functioning. Nothing of this kind happened.

Looking at the amendments so far tabled in the Lok Sabha, I for one cannot be optimistic about our setting up a genuinely autonomous corporation. For instance, there is an amendment seeking to establish a Parliamentary Committee to control the set-up. This sounds very impressive as evidence of democratic control but in practice it would have meant not the autonomy of the media but its domination by the party bosses in Parliament.

Vasant Sathe, one of the more competent among the long line of Information Ministers, has been harping on behalf of the Congress, on the need for functional autonomy instead of a new autonomous set-up as envisaged in the Bill. Functional autonomy would mean that the functionaries of the Radio and Television set-up would be ensured autonomy irrespective of ownership-government or a corporation.

In fact, such functional autonomy would be needed even if and when the Prasar Bharati is set up.

The Prasar Bharati Bill was supported by the Congress under Rajiv Gandhi and received the President's assent on September 12, 1990. The election manifesto of the Congress party issued in April, 1991, contained a pledge to implement the Act. But the Congress government has now developed cold feet towards its implementation.

In March 1992, the Information and Broadcasting Ministry, in a note to Prime Minister P.V. Narasimha Rao, observed that the 'circumstances have changed' since the time when the idea of autonomy to the electronic media was mooted.

The note cites some of the fruits of the government's recent liberalisation policy on media, including the advent of satellite broadcasting, video news cassettes and cable TV networks as evidence of the fact that the government no longer holds a monopoly over the electronic media.

The ministry wanted the Prime Minister to consider whether the notification on Prasar Bharati should be deferred.

The note also sought the Prime Minister's opinion on whether second Doordarshan channels in the four metropolitan cities should be simultaneously leased out to one or more entities who may share time among themselves.

With regard to cable television, the I&B Ministry note solicited the Prime Minister's opinion on whether permission should be given for the cables to operate with or without dish antennae. It has asked whether such permission, if given, should be through a system of licensing, or a mere registration with a local authority would suffice.

The government constituted an interdepartmental committee on September 3, 1991, under the Chairmanship of K.A. Varadan, Additional Secretary, Ministry of Information and Broadcasting, to suggest options available for implementation of the scheme for offering broadcasting rights to public corporations. The committee submitted its report in October 1991.

A major recommendation of the Varadan Committee relates to leasing out the second channel of Doordarshan in the four metropolitan cities to suitable licencees. At the same time, additional radio channels including FM stations wherever available, could also be leased out.

The government proposed to set up a Broadcasting Council of India. The Council could, among other things, serve as the agency for redressal of complaints emanating from individuals or institutions in regard to any programme broadcast by a new channel.

The Varadan Committee's Report on leasing out broadcasting rights of Doordarshan and Radio channels has offered a way out to the Congress government dilemma of liberalising the media without upsetting the existing power structure or losing its propaganda advantage.

It has achieved this by watering down and moderating many of the radical reforms that the government had earlier proposed.

The government has refused to give broadcasting rights to individuals and private firms. Instead, it has recommended that the government would lease out parts of Doordarshan's second channel and extra channel of AIR to potential licences.

In addition, the Varadan panel has recommended that the so-called 'public limited companies' to which such broadcasting rights are to be granted are to be decided by a single statutory or autonomous body known as the Broadcasting Council of India.

By adopting a more cautious approach towards privatisation, the Committee has done well to ensure that the autonomy does not mean replacement of state control with market ownership.

In a developing society like India, privatisation would only succeed in promoting elitism and consumerism which could be socially disastrous. It would help prevent perpetuation of monopoly by industrial houses running the newspapers.

Unfortunately, the Varadan Committee does not effectively tackle the two most important questions before it—the threat of foreign TV networks' invasion and the related issue of improving Doordarshans' fallen credibility.

While cognisant of and cautioning against the evil design of media Multinational Corporations (MNCs) which subject newly freed countries to cultural imperialism, the Committee pleads that nothing can be done to stop these transmissions or ban their receptions. The government must establish some kind of regulatory mechanism to monitor the programmes being beamed into the country from outside.,

At the same time the government must implement the Prasar Bharati Act at the earliest. It is only by injecting professionalism and credibility into Doordarshan that the government can hope to wean away Indian audiences who are getting hooked to alien broadcasting networks.

# 2

# NEWSPAPER SETUP

The rapid development of industrialisation gave rise to new technologies which were instrumental in bringing about a change in the process of communication. The process of communication was fast and receipts of communication and the feedback were ensured. Mass Media and Communication technologies have become integral parts of our life and our society.

***How a System Functions ?*** Media are used to add new information to human knowledge and keep on upgrading it. Ignorance can not be eradicated without adequate information supply. The overall development is directly related to education. Media enable the spread of education through conventional as well as unconventional methods. The desire to have access to media increases the level of education and knowledge among the population.

Increase in media use increases the level of education. Thus, people's demand for education has given rise to the need for greater access to informations which has further boosted the media hardware production causing an unprecedented growth in the economy. This, in turn, has stimulated the expansion of communications industry including media industries.

The mass media has monopolised the leisure industry. Transactional media giants have started invading the continents via the sky, using satellite slots. The competition for audience attention has become fierce.

Mass media have also played a leading role in shaping, guiding and reflecting the public opinion. These functions of media help to establish democracy. Use of media in a democratic polity creates critical awareness among the people. The media may not be able to perform these functions unless the access to them is ensured to a large section of our population.

Access to media means access to facts and documents which help one acquire information and knowledge. In comparison with individuals, media have more access to sources of information due to their reach and institutional character. Media power makes access easy.

Media access is important in the political sphere. Access to media is access to public opinion, so essential to protect and preserve democratic institutions. It is advantageous to both the leaders and masses. Leaders can address masses depending upon their convenience. They reach widely dispersed masses simultaneously through the electronic media in particular.

## Free Press

As technological innovations improved, as the spread and reach of the press expanded, attention was focused on diffusion of information upholding the right of the public to the freedom of information. Originally, the freedom of information meant the people's right to information. In simple words, it was the right to know whatever affected the individuals themselves. New information technology has posed new dangers to the freedom of media person as well as media consumers. In theory, everybody enjoys the right to freedom of expression, but the huge capital needed for investment in new media of mass communication, has negated the whole concept since only the very-well-to-do, the elite can afford to launch the media ventures.

India is a classic example of communication contradictions. Certain media are allowed in the private sector while others are controlled by the Government. Newspapers in India have traditionally uphold the freedom of press. In India, with a low literacy level, the influences of print media are limited to the urban centres. Further, most Indian newspapers being privately owned, are supposed to guarantee free and unbiased reporting. Several defects have been identified. Most of the largely circulated newspapers are owned by big business and industrial houses, and thus political interests take precedence over any other human interests. A study conducted by the IIPA, Delhi, revealed that out of 54 dailies selected, 27 newspapers were owned either partially or totally by business and industrial houses and controlled about 50 per cent of the total circulation. For the purpose of unbiased and objective performance, delinking the ownership of newspapers from large industrial houses was suggested.

However, inspite of all this, the Indian Press enjoys credibility with reading audiences. Public opinion is reflected either in the editorials or letters to the editor published in newspapers. But, with 85% of the population totally unexposed to the press and its accessibility limited to just the elite, it is questionable how accessibility to the media can be a criteria for its high credibility. Further, how can editorials or letters to the editor from the literate few, constitute feedback of the entire nation.

Government controlled electronic media are anathema to the very concept of an open society. Frequent political interference has eroded the credibility of both AIR and Doordarshan. Added to this, bureaucratisation has affected professional aspects of their functioning. These two powerful media can cross the barriers of illiteracy and their reach is the reason why political authorities keep a stranglehold on them.

A community is an assembly of people in an identified geographical area. A community's development hinges on effective communication. The increased use of local media makes communication a vital input of every community development programme. Community participation in media programmes accentuates free flow of information. Consequently, the democratic process acquires more meaning and relevance. Community participation in mass media can be both at the level of decision-making and management.

The mass media are very important component of society. Their use in a developing country like India is considered most crucial in the challenge to mobilize people for development activities. Therefore, there must be a communication policy. The policy should give direction to the programmes which are channeled through various mass media networks.

## Critical Issues

The mass media systems may fail to perform their functions when unplanned use of such technology creates problems. For instance communication resources can be concentrated in a few centres alone. The mass media may be misused by the owners to exercise their power, or the media content may be manipulated to give as a result of the communicators biases. All these problems forced the formulation of a viable communication policy. If the policy itself becomes outdated in the face of technological developments, it will have to be suitably changed.

Traditionally, communications research in India has shown a remarkable orientation towards social problems. Studies on propaganda techniques, attitude change, effects of mass media, personal influence, diffusion of innovations, flow of information, media uses and gratifications and the economics of communication have been motivated by practical problems faced in society. These studies focus on the need to understand the role of communication in those problems and the desire to apply the knowledge gained from research to solve them.

In spite of a great deal of empirical research, no systematic knowledge about the nature, frequency and origin of communication problems in India is available. However, the situation is changing now. Demands are being made for improving existing regulations, resource allocation principles, institutional arrangements, and defining the rights and responsibilities of professional communicators, commercial communication organisations and the bureaucracies. A communication policy must give importance to these issues. The policy, in effect, is built on the body of knowledge developed by research.

***Press View :*** A Policy is a set of principles, rules and guidelines to help in the tackling of problems which may be faced by a society in any particular field. A communication policy is formulated in response to the challenges of new communication technologies. We can define communication policy as action-oriented principles, outlining objectives and means of achieving objectives, focusing on what needs to be done and what is to be avoided in dealing with current and anticipated communication problems in society. The policies are formulated on authoritative guidelines.

Given the centrality of communication in modern society, one should rightly expect that communication policy would have a distinct and independent role to play. It would take into account the problems that crop up when using communication in varied activities. Communication policy should be based on an understanding of the totality of communication problems. Such a policy should aim at achieving society's goals and expectations regarding the applications of communication.

The priorities according to which the developed and the developing countries formulate their policies differ, sometimes even contradict each other. The technologically advanced countries like USA and Japan are concerned with mobilizing world markets for their communication goals and services. The developing countries like India, on the other hand, are concerned with building and expanding their communication systems with indigenous and appropriate technology. One major objective of their policy is to eliminate the vestings of colonial dependency. A major thrust area of communication policy of developing countries is the implementation of viable alternatives to the one-way flow of information into their societies. Most of the developing countries are busy waging a constant battle against poverty, malnutrition, illiteracy and indebtness. Thus, communication development receives scarce priority in their national objectives.

The mass media can be tools of cultural enrichment, national cohesion and advancement. The media policy makers in India first have to bridge the gap between ground realities and ideal situations. Certain paradoxes exist in the field of communication which need to be considered by policy makers. Some of these realities are elucidated here-

(a) Whereas there is an urgent demand to realise the right to equal access to information, there is a widening of the information gap between the richer and the poorer sections of society.

(b) There is misappropriation of the mass media for commercial and political purchases, when the need of the hour is to apply the media to the task of propagating culture, education, information and leisure time entertainment.

(c) There is predominant use of media to impose foreign values.

(d) In India, by and large, the communicators don't desire to find out the reactions of the audience to their programmes.

(e) The increase in the number of channels is not matched by any corresponding increase in the standard of programming.

(f) While communication satellites remove the barriers to information and education across the national boundaries all over the world, the same technology pave the way for cultural imperialism and new communication colonialism.

The Doordarshan has always suffered from the dichotomy between policy pronouncements and the continuous drift and departure from them in actual practice. In developing and democratic country like India, access to television and the social benefit accruing from it, is a crucial test of the social relevance of such an expensive medium. The importance of utilising TV is not just for the idle entertainment of the elite but for the uplift of the poor. But in effect and in actual practice, the purchase of a TV set is seen as wholesale investment in entertainment which obviates the bother and expense of going to an auditorium or a stadium.

From inception, broadcasting in India has been looked upon as a public service for the promotion of social objectives. The concept of advertisements for the promotion of consumer goods was also considered incompatible with the prevailing philosophy of the "socialistic pattern of society". In a developing country like India, radio and TV should be viewed as a national resource for the uplift of the masses. It is only through a strong media network that the eight kind of information and education can be imparted to the people. But the media in our country, like elsewhere in the world, have buckled under the pressure of commercial interests. Mindless entertainment with little or no educative value defeats the very purpose of building up a strong media network.

The press in a democratic country plays a vital role in creating, moulding and reflecting public opinion. It is a fundamental institution of our society. Though the press in India is free, it suffers from many ills. There are a few in-built handicaps such as vast geographical area, illiteracy, poverty, multiplicity of languages and absence of adequate communication facilities. Some other bottlenecks exist like –

(a) the linking of ownership of newspapers with other industrial or commercial enterprises.

(b) limited newspaper ownership with closely held share interest.

(c) Urban-oriented expansion of newspapers leaving the vast country side population untouched.

(d) inadequate and expensive newsprint.

(e) the lack of local advertisement support.

Man's greatest invention is language. The invention of the script has helped mankind to preserve human thoughts and learning. It has helped society to conquer both space and time. An important product of the script was the book. The books helped older civilisations like the Chinese and the Indian civilizations to preserve heritage. Books spread ideas which set people thinking, as a prelude to individual and group action. For this reason, they met opposition from guardians of political and religious doctrines.

Plato argued that wise men alone could rule and the state would control education. For Machiavelli, the security of the state was supreme. Hegel regarded state as embodiment of morality. John Milton (1608-1674) in Areopagitica gave a solid reason for the freedom of the Press. In his essay on liberty (1859) John Stuart Mill (1806-1873) proclaimed that liberty was the right of the individual.

Today freedom of expression and speech are internationally

reorganised rights. The league of nations made the first organised attempt at the international level to proclaim rights of speech and expression by launching a series of conferences. In just a few years of its birth, the United Nations approved the UN Declaration of Freedom of Information (1946) and the Universal Declaration of Human Rights (1948).

With the gaining of independence, freedom of speech and expression were recognised as fundamental rights and were included in the Indian Constitution. They are provided in the Article 19(1) of our constitution. Article 19(2) provides reasonable restrictions on freedom of expression.

In U.S.A., freedom of the press was very clearly recognised for the first time in the Virginia Bill of Rights in 1776. Unlike U.S.A., Britain has no written constitution. But it has been the fountain of all philosophy concerning freedom of speech, expression and the press, as John Milton did most of his work in Britain. The rights of free speech, expression and the press are in a constant process of evolution.

In general press freedom means freedom, unless specifically prohibited by law, together, print and publish information and to set up technologies in pursuit of such objectives, to claim and gain access to information. In practice, freedom of the press means freedom of the owner of a newspaper. Journalists enjoy only that much freedom as is given to them by the owner of their newspaper/ magazine.

From the beginning, freedom of the press was sought and obtained on the ground that it was a prerequisite to democracy. The press demand freedom because of the functions they discharge for the benefit of the society. In today's context, freedom of the press is only an extension of the citizen's right to freedom of speech and expression. It is the press alone which can thwart the attempts of any government to deny this right to the citizen. Today, the press, the electronic media, wherever they operate privately, have information-gathering networks spread all over the world. They are the eyes and ears of the people everywhere.

In connection with the limitation, the very first thing is that the right of the freedom of the press is only an extension of the citizen's right to freedom of speech and expression. Therefore, all those laws imposing restrictions on this right of the citizen apply to the press too. It has no special privilege that the citizens do not enjoy in this area. In all western societies and in India, the constitutions as well as the general laws of the countries, set the limits for the exercise of freedom of the press. It goes without saying that with regard to freedom, the press is not on any higher footing than the ordinary citizen. Since the press is also a business and an industry, all those laws which apply to business and industry, also apply to newspaper organizations.

The theory of responsibility is simple that everyone is responsible for the consequences of his actions. 'No Rights without responsibilities'. Therefore, freedom of the press is also linked with responsibilities.' At least, the freedom should not be abused.

When we say that somebody is responsible, we mean that he has a duty to do something, when we say someone is accountable, we mean that if he fails to do what his duty is, he is accountable to some person or institution. Thus, the right to freedom of speech and expression carries with it, a duty not to disturb public peace. If he so disturbs it he is accountable to the state for such breach of responsibility. Since media circulates information for the consumption of members of the society, it is natural that they should be responsible in the dissemination of the information. With every increase in the power of media, this responsibility towards the society also increases.

Editors and others often say that they have a right to inform the public. These are self-imposed responsibilities. These arise from an unwritten understanding between the media and society. On the basis of the responsibility of the media to inform the public, media have fought for and gained the right to free speech and expression.

But state has also imposed some obligations on media like not to publish anything that leads to, or has a tendency to lead to, a breakdown of public order. These are responsibilities imposed in addition to, and sometimes in contrast to, self-imposed responsibilities.

***Role of Government :*** The First Press Commission was appointed in 1952, because after independence the role of the press was changing. It was fast turning from a mission to' business. The commission founded that there was a great deal of scurrilous writing often directed against communities or groups, of indecency and vulgarity and personal attacks on individuals. It felt that the best way of maintaining professional standards of journalism would be to bring into existence a body of people principally connected with the industry whose responsibility it would be to arbitrate on doubtful points and to ensure the punishment of anyone guilty of infraction of good journalistic behaviour. Second Press Commission was appointed in 1978 and it wanted the press to be neither a mindless adversary nor an unquestioning ally. It wanted the press to play a responsible role in the development process. From the role that the two commissions recommended for the press, we can summarise the responsibilities of the Press thus-

— Help the country in its development process both by making constructive suggestions as well as criticism of delays and distortions in the development process.

— Give the widest possible access to people, reflecting the pluralistic composition of Indian society.

— Maintain internal stability and safeguard external security.

— Prevent and deflate social conflict.

Complaints are heard throughout the world that a section of the press functions without regard to its responsibilities to the society. There is a vast area not covered by any legal regime. Media ethics apply mostly to cases not specifically concerned by law.

The Second Press Commission observed that one of the functions entrusted to the Press council was the building up of a code of conduct for newspapers, news agencies and journalists in accordance with high standards of journalism. The second Press Commission lists a number of codes drafted in India, the USA and Britain have through the years. The All-India Newspaper Editors' Conference formulated a Code of Ethics and a Charter for Editors in 1953. The National Union of Journalists (1981), the All India Small and Medium Newspapers Association (1975) had all drafted similar codes. But the Editors Guild of India refused to draft any code arguing that responsible people do not need such a formal code. The second Press Commission said that it would not be desirable to draw up a Code of Ethics for newspapers. The Code of Ethics (1953) of All India Newspaper Editors' Conference asks journalists to serve and guard public interest, to be alive to fundamental human and social rights, to observe restraint in reports dealing with tensions leading to or likely to lead to public disorder, to assume responsibility for all information published, to respect confidence, not to exploit their status for non-journalistic purposes, not to allow personal interest to influence professional conduct, to correct inaccurate information, not to demand or accept bribe. The National Union of Journalists' Declaration of 1981 is also largely on similar lines.

The idea of an Ombudsman is of Swedish origin. In Sweden the Press Ombudsman at the national level is appointed by all the newspaper organizations together. Ombudsman generally means an intermediary, investigating complaints by private citizens against government officials or agencies. However, at present private or voluntary organizations are also having Ombudsmen to decide public complaints made against themselves or their members. In India, the Lok Ayuktas in some states are Ombudsmen.

Although this concept first originated in Sweden, but it was first adopted by the Press in USA.

The world's first Press Council took its birth in Sweden in 1916. In USA, a Press Council (National News Council) worked for 11 years and today there are nearly 50 Press Councils all over the world. The Press Council of India was set up on July 4, 1966 and Justice J.R. Mudholkar, was its chairman. It consisted of 25 members who were editors, working journalists, proprietors etc. In 1970, news agencies were also put under its jurisdiction. The council has powers to levy a graded fee on newspapers and news agencies to meet its expenditure and to reduce its dependence on government's financial support.

The countries of North and South are separated by an enormous gap in their respective communication capacities. The developed countries continue to exercise considerable political, economic and technological control on information flows. Nearly 80 per cent of the information disseminated in the world originates from five largest transnational news agencies as told before. About 15 great media corporations dominate the production of the radio sets, television sets and printing equipment, ten of these corporations belong to the U.S.A. Due to our dependence on the media delivery systems of the West, we also become dependent on the West.

Self-reliance in news and information distribution, both in disseminating news to the outside world or in getting news and information from various places in the world, for internal consumption, is essential for the following reasons-

(a) To provide the media a national identity and personality.

(b) To facilitate the analyses of the world events not from the perspective of the West but from the national perspective.

(c) To foster better understanding among the developing countries, which is far more essential now than ever before.

(d) To prevent the unwarranted entry of foreign and alien ideas, cultures and life-styles, that always tend to contribute to shaping public opinion in favour of foreign countries, particularly of the West.

(e) To provide an objective account of the news and developments that were considered newsworthy by the indigenous media.

As per the directives of the UNESCO to establish a news pool or consortium of news agencies, the 'pool' of news agencies of the non-aligned countries was formally launched in July, 1976 at the New Delhi Conference of Information Ministers and Representations of the news agencies of the non-aligned countries. The objective of the pool is to expand the mutual exchange of information among the non-aligned countries in a spirit of collective self-reliance.

The Non-Aligned News Pool is not a transnational news agency, but a system of exchange of agency information, based on co-operation and co-ordination among individual news agencies taking part in these activities. The Pool is not based on any formal membership. The Pool has no single directing centre, nor does it have its own budget.

Many of the developing countries do not have an extensive and elaborate telecommunication network. For some, high tariffs are major barriers. Optimum information exchange depend on the level of development of communication systems in the individual non-aligned countries.

A few year ago, about 85% of the news items received by PT1 from the Pool partners were spiked. The reasons for this were given as delay in news reception, poor quality, low news value, or propaganda material.

The lack of proper training among the non-aligned journalists and their inability to match the professional standards of the journalists of the transnational news-agencies, are the reasons for the poor quality of material put out by the Non-Aligned News Agencies Pool.

In many of the non-aligned countries, the news agencies are under the strict control of the governments. The first casualty of such a solution is the objectivity of the news and information put out by their agencies.

The editors of private-owned newspapers in the democratic countries like India, either are not convinced of the need for such an inter-regional co-operation or they do not respect the news coverage of several agencies, which are participants of the pool.

While there has been a continuous effort to establish alternative news and information distribution systems in the world, the recent global changes have had a deep impact on the information scene.

The West has been for a long time using the concept of 'Freedom of Information' as an ideological weapon, and successfully deploying it to deflect the 3rd World from its pursuit of a new world information and communication order.

In the matter of broadcasting, the Western powers insist upon the 'open skies' policy, which they claim to be consistent with the principle of freedom of information. On the face of things, this seems a plausible argument. Open skies, seems to connote a situation of an unfettered information exchange of knowledge flowing freely across the national boundaries. On the contrary, the same western countries, show a complete disinclination towards free trade by imposing heavy tariffs to protect their own products.

These developments call for a greater unity among the 3rd World countries to come out of the dependence and dominance in the field of information, and promote self-reliance. The existing world information order provides an opportunity to the richer nations to use the scarce global natural resources, and exclude the poor nations from using the same. An attempt is made through the on going GATT talks to impose stronger forms of monopoly control over the content of information flows.

***World Standard :*** The developing nations campaigned for a 'new order' in the field of international information and communication, which would facilitate a 'free and balanced flow' of information capable of breaking through the stereotypes created and nurtured for over 50 years by the western media empires. The new order, they maintained, would create a new international information climate that would foster a closer and better understanding among nations and individuals. The most important step in this direction was the launching of the Non-Aligned News Agencies Pool, in 1975. The 'free flow' concept was amended to 'free-and balanced flow', when a declaration on the role of the media in the promotion of international understanding and peace was approved by the UNESCO in 1978. 'The right to know' was transformed into 'the right to communicate'.

The non-aligned nations coined the phrase, New International Information Order (NIIO). The MacBride Commission broadened the sphere by substituting the term 'world' for 'international' and incorporating 'communication' along with 'information'. Since then the phrase the 'New World Information and Communication Order (NWICO) has been widely used.

A major factor that helped the growth of US agencies was the wireless transmission technology, which reversed the world communication imbalance to the overall advantage of the American interest. Another factor was a general realization in the US of the advantages that world communication control bestowed on foreign trade and commerce. Following such realizations, ideas on unrestricted How of communication between nations began to crystallize in the US.

The following overlapping and mutually complementing factors are at the base of the demand for a new order in the field of information-

(1) The emergence of new nations following the dissolution of the colonial empires after World War II.

(2) The asymmetrical economic relationship between the new nations and the western industrialized nations which, while strengthening the latters' wealth and power, perpetuated the new nations' dependency, not merely economic but political and cultural as well.

(3) The coming together of the new nations under the umbrella of non-alignment in the wake of aggressive bloc-building by the US and the USSR.

(4) The new nation's realization that their under-development was related to their dependence on rich nations followed by a firm resolve to assertive actions to correct imbalances in world trade and commerce, and cultural exchanges.

(5) Their gaining in strength in international organization, such as the UN and the UNESCO. Four stages can easily be identified in the history of the NWICO. The first stage (1973-76) marked the evolution of a new order. The second stage (1976-79) saw the accumulation of data and empirical evidence to give credence to the new order demand. The third stage followed the publication of the MacBride report in 1980. The fourth stage is the period following the adoption of the NWICO Resolution in the UNESCO.

Generally, the evolution of the new order concept is credited to the NAM. Much of the credit for the enlarging communication agenda of the UNESCO in the 1970s goes to the Non-Alignecd Movement, which saw communication, at least in the early 70s, as a means to an end, the end being economic development of the poor nations.

The Algiers Summit of the non-aligned countries, held in

1973, is a major landmark, in the history of NWICO, for it was here that communication concerns were addressed directly in more than one paper in the context of their economic development programmes.

The 19th UNESCO General Conference adopted a resolution inviting the Director General to undertake a review of the problems of communication in modern society. Director General constituted a 16 member commission for the study of communication problems.

The 20th UNESCO general conference, held in 1978 was marked by a spirit of compromise. The new Mass Media Declaration (MMD) text now retitled as 'Declaration on Fundamental Principles Governing the contribution of the Mass Media in strengthening Peace and International Understanding and in combating was Propaganda, Racialism and Apartheid' was approved.

The 21st general conference of the UNESCO, held in 1980, accepted the MacBride report and unanimously adopted Resolution outlining the basic character and content of the NWICO. The establishment of the NWICO depended upon five major factors— (1) the will of the developed and developing countries to bring about changes in all areas of communication within their respective regions; (2) Co-operation between the developed and developing nations for removing all obstacles to a two-way and balanced flow of news and information among nations; (3) sharing of communication resources, including technologies, for countering monopoly of the international news flow by a few; (4) cooperation among the developing countries to correct imbalances with their own regions by increasing horizontal flows and (5) Co-operation between the media-rich and media-poor for mobilization of resources to strengthen communication infrastructure in the latter's region.

The 21st General Conference of the UNESCO approved the establishment of a news agency, the International Programme for the Development of Communication (IPDC) within the framework of the UNESCO to reduce the gap between the developed and developing countries by strengthening infrastructure and services through international cooperation and assistance. The objectives of the IPDC cover all facts of communication development.

The withdrawal of the US on December 31, 1984, and Britain and Singapore a year later, from the UNESCO, was not a deterrent to the objectives of the NWICO. Today, the evolving goals of the NWICO rest with not just the UNESCO, but a large number of international organizations such as the Organization for Economic Co-operation and Development (OECD), the International Telecommunications Union (ITU), the IPDC and the Third World and its organizations for moving the aim of the NWICO to a higher plain. The IPDC has done its best to help develop communication capabilities of the media-poor regions. Between the second session in 1982 and the seventh session held in January 1986, it had allocated US$ 9.74 million for some communication projects in the developing countries. Those included 3 regional news agency projects Pan Africa News Agency (PANA), the Agencia Latino American De Servcios Especiales do Information (ALA SEI) and the Asia-Pacific News Network (ANN) and 14 national news agency projects in different 3rd World countries. These agencies and news exchange arrangements operating within the developing countries, no matter how inadequate they are, indicate that the NWICO has set itself on its evolutionary path. But there is more to be achieved.

Imbalances in the flow of news and information at international level have not ceased to exist. The one-way flow is still very much in evidence. Most of the news flowing through the transnational agencies into the developing regions concerns the developing world. The agencies continue to view the developing world's events and issues from their own perspectives. As a result, news everywhere is seen through the prisms of the West, the developed world. The Western media giants continue to set the world's news agenda.

The developed countries should be more open to redress the ever-increasing asymmetrical economic relations between them and the poor countries. This calls for hastening the pace for the establishment of the NIEO as it is linked with the NWICO. The developed world could make available resources for communication specific projects in the poor regions of the world. New technologies needed to be viewed as resources for the benefit of the mankind, and not as a new tool for exploitation of the disadvantaged.

Steps are needed to establish a balance in the information flow by devoting more space and lime to news and issues concerning the developing countries. The developed countries should join hands with the developing countries in making the telecommunications tariffs more suitable for a better use of existing systems.

The developing world, on the other hand, needs to formulate communication policies, without which the media development would get hampered. The press must make conscious efforts to free itself from the attitudes fostered by the Western news criteria.

The free flow of information is a Western concept, by which almost all western countries rationalise the operation of their media and information agencies. The term means that any person or persons and any organization or organisations can own and operate any media or information agency, gather any information, and disseminate the same, if they so desire, to any target audience, wherever and whenever they want. The concept is basic to the history, culture and life of the liberal capitalist western society. Any challenge to this concept is rejected on grounds that it is undemocratic, inhuman and even uncivilized.

The philosophy of free flow resulted in the consolidation of the centres of information gathering and dissemination in the western countries. The socialist and the 3rd World countries could see that they were not represented objectively in the western media. Significant happenings in their countries were paid scant attention and whatever done, those were only half truths coloured by the Western perceptions. Slowly, this situation got concretised, and the leaders of the 3rd World countries endured the situation as they were unable to take steps to change the situation. The 3rd World countries had no infrastructure or active network to make a difference. There is imbalance in the flow of information between the developed West and the developing 3rd World countries, which can not have any say on the mechanism of gathering information as they do not own and control the technology of the giant information agencies of the West. Moreover, the 3rd World countries, knowing fully well that the information disseminated from these agencies doesn't represent all the truths about them. The imbalance is in terms of volume of information, flowing into the 3rd World countries, when compared to the volume of information flowing out from them.

The root of the problem goes back to the late 1950s and 1960s, when the concept of 'Development Communication' was born. The communication specialists thought that what the West achieved in centuries, the 3rd World could achieve the same in a matter of decades if aided by the mass media. Two eminent western scholars-Daniel Lerner and Wilbur Schramm-were in the forefront to suggest this theory. Their theories were tried in many 3rd World countries.

It was assumed that mass media used for creating a stable and sustainable democratic nation and implementing programmes to uplift the living conditions of the common man in society would transform the developing societies into modern, vibrant and stable societies. However, a decade later, it was found that most of the social problems remained unsolved. Instead more problems were created. The western media organizations focused the negative developments of the developing society. In such a situation, an American author, Herbert Schiller articulated something very new. He said that the free flow of communication was essentially meant to safeguard the economical growth of the West. And any attempt to regulate the flow of information beyond borders is seen as a threat to the western economies. Thus, it is termed as interference with the basic human right. Hence, the concept of 'imbalance' is an economic issue, and the international flow of information is just another fact of this issue.

Although the flow is still imbalance, exchanges of TV programmes, specially educational programmes, are quite frequent. More western programmes are seen on the TV screens of the 3rd World countries. Despite the large scale changes brought about by technology, imbalance persists in the media and coverage of the development west vis-a-vis the developing countries of the 3rd World.

## Basic Setup

Although the government doesn't own a majority of the newspapers and magazines, yet it is the government that remains at the helm of affairs in matters such as newsprint allocation, Registration of newspapers and periodicals, conduct of research and collection and maintenance of exhaustive reference and archive material.

PIB is the central agency of the Government of India for the dissemination of information on government policies, decisions, programmes, initiatives and activities. It puts out this information to daily newspapers, periodicals, news agencies and All India Radio and Doordarshan. The PIB has its headquarters in Delhi. The Bureau in Delhi consists of information officers attached to different ministeries and departments of the Government of India. It also has the job of evaluating public reaction and accordingly renders advice to the Government of India on its information policy.

This is the largest publishing house in the public sector. It is the media unit of Ministry of Information and Broadcasting. Earlier it was known as Foreign Branch of the Bureau of Public Information and was renamed in December 1944. It has many wings to oversee the production of print material. These are Editorial Wing, Production and Art Wing, Business Wing, Administration Wing and Employment News Wing. Employment News Wing brings out the weekly Employment News and Rozgar Samachar. The Publication Division also publishes Kurukshetra, Aajkal, Bal Bharati, Yojana, Mass Media in India etc.

This is an agency that conducts research and provides reference information on a variety of subjects. Compilation work is carried out by the documentation and catalogue section of the library. There is a separate wing that specifically collects and maintains newspaper cuttings.

A Reference Annual is published every year by the division. The National Documentation centre on mass communication, set up as a part of the division in 1976, documents and indexes news items and information about the mass media.

The Photo Division comes under the administrative purview of the Ministry of Information and Broadcasting. It documents the socio-economic progress and cultural activities of the country through photographs. The photographic prints of major events in the news are distributed to the media through the Press Information Bureau. It has its head office in New Delhi, with regional offices at Mumbai, Kolkata, Chennai. It also has a photo unit at Guwahati.

The Press Council of India is a quasi-judicial body, constituted by an Act of Parliament. It has 28 members headed by a Chairman, who has traditionally been a sitting or retired judge of the Supreme Court. Twenty members are press personnel, five are members of parliament and one each nominated by the University Grants Commission, Sahitya Academy and Bar Council of India. It hears complaints by the Press and against the Press regarding freedom of the Press.

It was established in 1948 under the Imperial Library Act, 1948. It is situated in Kolkata and has more than 20 lakh volumes in its custody, excluding the maps, manuscripts, official documents and books received as gifts or in exchange schemes. It is a subordinate department under the Ministry of Human Resources Development, Department of Culture, Government of India. The special feature of this Library is that it organizes exhibitions, lectures and seminars at the national and international levels. It is headed by a Director in addition to a librarian.

We have already dealt with the growth and evolution of PCI. Here we will look into the principles, structure and function of the Press Council.

The guiding principle of the Press Council is that if any section of the Press violates the tenets of journalistic ethics, whether written or unwritten, the Press itself should take appropriate action against it rather than the authorities punishing newspapers. The PCI was first set up in 1966 under the Act of 1965, and was abolished after the proclamation of emergency in 1975. However it again came into being in 1979. The council comprises a chairman and 28 other members. Until now, only former Supreme Court judges have been selected for the chairmanship of the council. 13 members are nominated from among working journalists including six editors and seven other working journalists. Not less than three editors and four other working journalists should be from newspapers in Indian languages. Out of the six owners or managers of newspapers, two each should be from small, medium and big categories of newspapers. One person is nominated from among the managers of news agencies.

The term of the chairman and of the council is three years. While the members retire on the expiry of the term of the council, the chairman may continue in office until a new incumbent is nominated, but not for more than six months beyond the three year term. A retiring member can be re-nominated for not more than one term. That is a person can be a member of the Press Council for maximum period of six years. Three person having special knowledge in respect of education and Science, law and literature and culture are nominated, one each by UGC, the Bar Council of India, and the Sahitya Academy. The PCI has very wide functions in furtherance of its dual objectives of preserving Press freedom and maintaining and improving standards of print journals. But it does not deal with the electronic media.

It has also been vested with powers of a civil court. It can summon and examine witness, require the discovery and inspect documents, receive evidence on affidavits, issue commissions for examining witnesses or documents, or any other matter which may be brescribed. The council holds open inquiries on complaints received both against newspapers and news agencies, journalists as well as authorities, individuals, associations or groups of people and on the basis of its inquiries the council declares its adjudications.

The Working Journalists and other Newspaper Employees and Miscellaneous Provisions Act. 1955, is a welfare measure meant to regulate conditions of service of the people employed in the newspaper industry.

Its provisions relate mainly to (a) special provisions in respect of certain cases of retrenchment, (b) payment of gratuity, (c) hours of work, (d) leave, (c) fixation of revision of rates of wages, (f) enforcement of the recommendations of the wage fixation machinery i.e. wage boards and wage tribunals, (g) employees' Provident fund and (h) recovery of money due from the employer.

A work of literature, drama, music or art is an intellectual property. It must be protected from illegal copying or reproducing.

The Copyright Act 1957 accords this problem. Copyright has been held to be a right which a person acquires in a work which is the result of his intellectual labour. The primary function of the copyright law is to protect from annexation by other people the fruits of a man's work, labour or skill.

## News Agencies

It is an agency of the U.N. All UN Member states have a right to belong to it. UNESCO has been concerned both with the development of the media and also the problems such a development brings with it. It is always alert to find out how the media and development work in the 3rd World countries. For UNESCO, it is necessary to understand that the purpose of the organisation is to contribute to peace and security by promoting collaboration among nations through education, science and culture. It also realised that only a few of the developing countries had any newspapers and more so, news agencies, which could provide the media with news.

The role of UNESCO became more significant in the context of the demand by many developing countries for a better deal from the developed countries. The first step in this direction was a call for the establishment of a New International Economic Order (NIEO) and was realised that NIEO can not be independent from socio-cultural factors, apart from political and economic factors. The 5th conference of the Heads of State of the Non-Aligned Countries (1976) and the 19th General Conference of UNESCO crystallised the idea of a New International Information and Communication Order (NIICO).

ITU was founded in Paris in 1865, as the International Telegraphic Union to co-ordinate and monitor the development of the telegraph, which was a new invention. With the development of other systems, the name was changed to International Telecommunications Union.

In 1947 ITU entered into an agreement with the United Nations and thus became a specialised agency for telecommunications. The ITU secretariat is in Geneva and works at various levels. The main functions of ITU are to—

(a) allocate frequencies to avoid interference

(b) co-ordinate efforts to eliminate interference

(c) foster the creation of telecommunication in newly independent developing countries

(d) promote safety measures

(e) undertake studies in the area of telecommunications.

Although ITU performs a very technical function, it is an important agency that is central to communication development.

In addition to UNESCO and ITU, there are other UN organisations whose activities have a bearing on communications developments. Regional intergovernmental organisations, such as Council of Europe. European Economic Community, Organisation of American States, Organization for African Units, South Asian Association for

Regional Cooperation and Association of South East Asian Nations are active in the Communication field.

The essence of any interregional cooperation in the field of information is to bring about a new sense of common destiny, and unite news agencies operating under different levels of development.

The fundamental problem in the inter-regional news networks and co-operation is that the participating news agencies in the network being, essentially, domestic agencies are geared to serve purely national needs in their news coverage.

Another area is about the issue of relevance. Most of them are editorially ill-equipped to produce copy for the consumption of the other agencies in the region. They are mostly irrelevant to each others, needs.

In most of the networks, almost all agencies are in principle, committed to producing a regional file containing news reports and features, especially prepared for the consumption of the readers outside their national frontiers. However, the tendency that persists is to move copy originally written for domestic readership for the network transmission without necessary rewriting. A great deal of information may be missing in such reports for the readers abroad, or much more than necessary is included. But, criticism on several agencies, which are part of such networks are a large majority of reports transmitted in these networks are hard news, which rarely attract the attention of the editors in other countries.

Another criticism is that they do not make amendments and changes in the news reports, keeping in view the requirements of the readers abroad.

Information can be defined as facts about an event, a place, a person, or whatever is communicated, by a person or persons to another person or persons. Mere facts do not generate knowledge. The human minds in interaction with facts produce knowledge. This knowledge has helped and is helping the human race generation after generation. Knowledge is wealth and when this wealth is used properly, it brings power.

## World-wide Agencies

There are hundreds of agencies, which are in the business of supplying information to the mass media. These agencies are referred to as news agencies, feature services, and syndicates. The impact of these agencies on what we read and see is quite significant.

A news agency generally deals with news coverage. It combines spot coverage with interpretation of the important political and economic events. Although its emphasis is limited, the news agency plays a very important role in shaping public opinion on crucial national and international affairs. The news agency doesn't deal directly with the public. It works through the intermediary of the other means of mass communication, namely the press, radio and television. For a majority of the news media, the news agencies are a major source of news supply. The two leading news agencies in India are United News of India (UNI) and Press Trust of India (PTI), which have contractual agreements with these global news agencies. Certain studies reveal that there are about 1200 news agencies operating in the world. However, the five transnational agencies, Reuters, Agence France Presse (AFP), Associated Press (AP), and United Press International (UPQ and Telegrafnoi

Agentsvo Sovetskavo Soyusa (TASS) put out around 35 million words per day, and claim to provide nine-tenths of the total foreign news output of the World Media. Other major agencies are Deutsche Press Agenteur (DPA) of Germany, Kyodo of Japan and Xinhua of China.

## Agencies in Different Hue

This news agency takes its name after its founder, Paul Julius Reuter. Around 1850, he set up a carrier pigeon service. Initially his services were confined to commercial information. His first major breakthrough came in 1859, when he sent a dispatch for shadowing a war in Italy. Since then the agency has expanded. Reuters supplies news to its media clients such as other news agencies, newspapers, the radio & television stations. Under its present form of ownership Reuters claim that it can ensure that no particular group or faction can have control. Consequently, it hopes to preserve its integrity and freedom from bias.

The impetus to provide speedy transmission of news was given by the telegraph invented by Samuel F.B. Morse, in 1844. The telegraph enables many small town newspapers in the US to get their news. The meeting of the leading New York publishers was held in this context in 1848. Although a decision was made to start a news agency, the name, Associated Press, was not used till about 1860. Associated Press took a concrete form in 1900 as a modern news gather association. The struggle by AP to establish its base and the restrictions the rivals placed on it is often cited as a case that is reflective of many 3rd World countries wanting to break the monopoly of the 'big five', which ironically includes AP.

AP with its wide communications network using advanced technology has bureaus in more than 100 countries. Its 5000 plus correspondents and a host of stringers cater to about 1300 newspapers, 3400 broadcasters in the US and 1000 private subscribers.

The growth of AP spurred the rise of competitors. Edward Willis Scripps formed the United Press Association in 1907. Scripps started two regional news services to cater to his own newspapers.

At the same time, there was another association the Publisher's Press Association formed in 1898 by the Non-AP newspapers. In 1907. Scripps merged his United Press Association with the PPA to form United Press Association. A major set back occurred in 1918. It sent a report that the war had ended, and later it turned out to be false. Its credibility suffered. But slowly it recovered. The backgrounds and personal accounts enabled UPA to score over AP. Parallel to these developments emerged a third press association, the International News Service (INS). It faced severe competition from AP. Although, it was emerging as a major service, by 1956, it decided to merge with AP in 1958 to form United Press International. UPI claims to have an overseas electronic strength of about 200 journalists overseas distributed in Europe, Latin America, Asia and Australia. Its broadcast related services are considered to be a specialisation.

AFP, founded in 1835, has the maximum representation on its board of directors. Although AFP is described as an unsubsidiscd autonomous organisation, in effect, the French government and various agencies under its control subscribed to AFP, and provided good support. AFP is regarded as one of the major global news agencies. It has more than 10,000 newspapers and 70 agencies as its subscribers. Its operations are in more than 150 countries with a network of 110 foreign bureaus.

Often it was customary to exclude TASS from the 'globals' as the transnational news agencies are called. However, in terms of influence, impact and coverage, TASS was in no way different from the other agencies.

TASS began on the foundation of what was known as the Petrograd Telegraph Agency, in 1917. It supplied news through a network of correspondents in all regional and territorial centres. TASS has approximately 20,000 subscribers both domestic and foreign.

The work of TASS was complemented by another information agency, Novosti Press Agency (APN), established in 1961 by the Union of Soviet Journalists, the Union of Soviet writers. TASS and APN merged to form anew Russian information agency called ITAR-Information Telegraph Agency of Russia.

The International broadcasting by different countries are aimed at serving their people settled in other countries, and also to propogate the policies of the respective countries.

BBC occupies a central place in terms of its international reach and influence. Now through satellites, millions have the benefit of watching the BBC-TV. BBC is a central institution in the broadcasting system of the United Kingdom. In 1922, several radio manufacturers established the BBC. In 1926 it became a public corporation. BBC draws international news from its correspondents.

The operations are not commercial, and finance is provided in the form of a special grant approved by the British Parliament. Consequently, the Government is directly involved in the international broadcasting system. The External Services Department has responsibility for international broadcasting. The scape, nature and character of BBC External Services was affected during the Falkland crisis. It was also the target of criticism during the Iranian Revolution and the Gulf war. However, contemporary developments indicate that international broadcasting is here to stay.

Another country which has systematically used and realised the potential of the radio and television in international affairs is U.S.A. During the World War II, two government organisations, the Office of War Information and the Council of Inter-American Affairs were responsible for international broadcasts during the period. The programming titled Voice of America was done on a contractual basis by the private US broadcast corporations. And when US. Information Agency (USIA) was established in 1953, VOA became one of its divisions. Apart from VOA, there is a separate television service of the USIA. Through satellite networking, it also arranges for direct telecasts.

It is a London based international TV news film agency owned by a consortium of the BBC, Reuters, Canadian Broadcasting Corporation, Australian Broadcasting Corporation and New Zealand TV. It is related to the international broadcasting service in the supply of audio-visual material. The service has over 170 subscribers in 95 countries.

## Basic Foundations

The degree of formal organization given to the media information service depends to some extent on the size of your organization or, for a consultancy, on the size of the fee paid by the client. Some large organizations have specially designated press officers working within a press office which, though coming under the surveillance of the public relations department, is separate from it. Other organizations designate a press officer within the PR office and others simply expect all the PR staff to act as press officers as the need arises.

It probably does not matter what title is held by the people who will be dealing with media enquiries, but what does matter is that they should be reasonably au fait with the company and its products. The lack of even basic knowledge is probably a fault encountered more when dealing with a consultancy than with in-house PROs. If the query is of a complicated or technical nature it is quite acceptable to pass it on to the expert. And you really should have price lists and stockists handy.

As well as having a good working knowledge of the subject with which you are dealing, you, as an efficient PRO, should also have at your fingertips the names and telephone numbers of people within the organization who are competent to speak to the media on specialist subjects, and this list should include others apart from the brand managers and marketing department personnel. It is annoying to a journalist who is working on a story to be told that the PRO will ring back with the relevant numbers and then not to get them for another two or three days.

If the queries coming into the public relations or press office are short questions they can usually be answered on the spot, but quite often they will be in the form of a general request for information on a specific topic and it could be that your organization has in its files material which could be sent out. Do make sure that all this material is filed in such a way that it is easy to find and is related to any photographic or other reference. Some information services are organized in such detail that they have a grandiose title such as 'The Barbed Wire Information Bureau', information sheets and a direct telephone line. However, such a detailed service is usually organized primarily for the consumer rather than for the media, though answering press queries will be part of its function.

If you do have a fairly sophisticated information service it is easy to think that you have all the answers to hand, but this may not be the case. So when taking down details of media enquiries don't just record them: listen, be constructive and ask questions. If you know what the story or feature is to be about and the angle from which the producer or journalist is approaching it you will be able to be more helpful. There may be a booklet on the subject, a special expert in the technical department who has sat on the relevant government fact-finding commission or a market research survey giving the latest market trends, any of which would help the journalists far more than the standard handouts.

## Working Aspects

Most journalists agree that the telephone manners of some PR departments leave much to be desired. Some of them leave the impression that they are really too busy to deal with media enquiries and unless the journalist can use the name of a welt-known programme or a national daily the service is grudging to say the least.

However, there are other PROs who are extremely friendly and helpful on the phone. This immediately puts their organization in a good light and the journalist is disposed to feel that this outfit may be a useful source of information in the future. If this friendly attitude is followed up with prompt service the good impression is stamped even deeper. Too often the executive forgets to phone back until the next day. Or even worse, the material promised does not arrive until the end of the following week. It has even been known for a company to respond to a request for information six weeks after the initial query and then to complain that their product had been left out! There also sometimes seems to be a feeling that the media could have got themselves better organized and asked for the material earlier. There is occasionally some truth in this, but very often the journalist's deadline is looming close, and the PRO is supposed to be providing a service not a favour.

### *Checklist for an Efficient Enquiries Procedure*

1. Be friendly and helpful throughout; do not give the impression that it is all too much trouble.
2. Record the details of the request and ask for further details about the proposed story so that you can dig out the most useful in-depth material. Indicate that this is the reason for your questions.
3. Drop everything and treat the request as extremely urgent Even if you know that the answer can wait until the next day it is far better to deal with it at once. It may be forgotten later on.
4. If you need to phone back, do so as soon as possible. Phone back within hours to report progress even if you do not yet have the answer.
5. If you leave a message for someone else to phone the journalist back, check to see that they have not missed the message or forgotten to fulfil it.
6. If the request is for an expensive sample use tact in discovering whether it has a genuine background. You may not have heard of the journalist or author concerned but that does not mean that they are not engaged on a bona fide testing programme or working on a first-class magazine feature.
7. Where necessary send material by cab or messenger.
8. Check to see that both postal or hand-delivered material has arrived and whether the journalist needs any more material.

## Working Nature

Getting the enquiries procedure right is only the first stage in setting up a good media relations programme. The second stage is the much more active one of going out and securing a steady stream of coverage for the company and its products or services. Start by making a list of the areas in which you think you might be able to generate coverage over a three-month period. Such a list of objectives for the PR department of a food manufacturer might look something like this:

1. Feature material on cooking with a variety of the products in women's magazines and in regional media.
2. A series of radio interviews on local radio.
3. A feature on the use of some of the products in pubs for a catering trade magazine.
4. An in-depth feature on the new soup production line in a leading food production magazine.
5. An in-depth feature on the work of the new product development team in a food technology publication.
6. A visit to the Peterborough factory-where new jobs are coming on-line-by the industrial editor of one of the national newspapers.
7. A feature on the activities of the Skelmersdale factory social club in the local media and a possible visit by the local radio station disc jockey to a social evening.

***A Similar List for a Heavy Goods Vehicle Manufacturer might Look Something Like This***

1. A release on the year's export success for both the heavy goods vehicle publications and all the publications covering the industries to which the goods were sold.
2. Local radio sponsorship of a motoring and good driving show.
3. An in-depth feature on the conversion of a stand ard line for use in a mountainous area for a leading magazine in the field of civil engineering and for publication in the country concerned.
4. An on-site demonstration of the current range of earth-diggers for publications covering public works and civil engineering generally.
5. A feature on the new managing director for the heavy freight publications.
6. A feature on safety aspects of carrying chemicals and other dangerous substances for a lorry drivers' magazine.

To achieve the list of objectives set you will need to be in constant contact with the leading media in your field and in occasional contact with all the other publications which might be useful. This contact may be by post, by telephone or by personal meetings. Some enterprising PRs have also used humorous tapes and promotional videos to put their ideas over. The choice will depend on how important you are to a magazine or radio and the magazine or radio to you and thus how often you are likely to be working with this particular publication, how physically near you are to each other and indeed how well you get on at a social level.

However, if you have creative ideas and good material, face-to-face contact is by no means necessary. Unfortunately many editors feel that this kind of creativity is absent from the activities of a number of PROs. The only material they receive is the syndicated material which is sent out to everyone on the mailing list, and there is little attempt at placing original and exclusive material.

Syndication of material can work quite well at a regional level, though even here blanket coverage can be a real waste. If for example, you are running a recipe or a beauty information service you will be able, over time, to build up a list of regional dailies and weeklies who use the material regularly. Some sophisticated services send out portfolios of material to selected users and these are updated from time to time. If the subject is one which is likely to be covered fairly regularly the expense of such an operation will be recouped. But for most products and services this sort of exercise would be too expensive. Others run food and cookery programmes on their local radio stations or even sponsor national radio slots. The success rate for syndicated material can also be increased by sending out material with themes which are relevant to the local area or which are topical.

For national media the approach must be rather different. Monthly mailings are no use at all, and ideas are needed in the first instance rather than completed material. Once you have sold an idea to an editor you can then discuss how much material you will supply and how much the newspaper or magazine will want to write or photograph for itself. Some magazines are pleased if you can produce an illustrated feature to an agreed plan. Others have a large enough budget to be able to retain their independence, and these publications will probably ask for background material only or will send a journalist to cover the story on the spot.

However, if you are to write the feature remember to check on the editor's requirements as to length, the number of illustrations, the date of issue of the article and the copy deadline. Sometimes it is worth thinking about getting a well-known person in the field to write features for you or at least to suggest his or her name to the publication. This will be a more expensive way of producing feature material but it may also make it more acceptable.

If your work is mainly in the trade and industrial area it is even more important to keep in constant touch with the leading publications in the field. An editor will appreciate it if you supply him or her regularly with information about the company, giving advance warning of changes and additions to the product range, the factory or indeed any aspect of the company's activities. A good relationship in this area can mean extra coverage since the editor will be more inclined to ring your company for quotes or for filler items. Editors have also been known to remind PROs that their exhibition details have not yet been received. Nor should you forget the media local to your offices and factories. Community relations can be extremely important but they are often relegated to the bottom of the list of PR activities.

List areas which are likely to generate coverage during a set period. Look at this list in terms of the relevant media and make a list of objectives to achieve within the period.

Send out syndicated material to specially selected regionals and place specific features ideas with nationals and specialist magazines. Be as original and creative as possible by letter or phone.

Once features have been placed take care to fulfil the editor's requirements.

***Press Releases :*** Some PROs like to put together a newsletter to send to the media, outlining all the things that have happened to their company over the previous three or four months. These are often quite stylishly produced with a scanner and desk-top publishing packages. The idea is that journalists will pick up just those stories which are of particular interest to their publications.

The problem is that these newsletters are often so well produced that they look far too much like sales promotion material and they may indeed be of use in selling-in to the trade. Journalists are likely to bin this type of material before they even read it, assuming that it will be full of puffs and exaggerated claims.

Far better to forget the clever design and pretty colours and stick to the news. Write up the facts following the Who? What? Why? Where? When? If possible include some information on forthcoming events as well as past history and make sure that the latter is not too out of date.

It is quite permissible to include ideas for features, but it is a waste of time to write the whole piece. It is better to negotiate the placing of the complete material into those sections of the media that are likely to use it.

***Various Angles :*** Though entertaining is not an essential part of the media relations programme it can help to smooth the way. Discriminate in your entertaining. If you are taking a journalist to lunch you should know exactly why you are doing it and what you expect to achieve from it. Even more important, you should know what you have to offer. Journalists will not appreciate your wasting their time, however good the lunch. Indeed 'launching' in the old-fashioned sense is on the decline. So do not be surprised if a journalist simply cannot find the time to join you.

Reasons for individual entertaining might include any of the following:

- Briefing editors or journalists on changes and developments within your organization which could affect the industry as a whole.
- Briefing a newly-appointed editor or specialist writer on your company and its activities and the service you have to offer.
- A 'thank you' for successful cooperation throughout the year, usually coupled with a briefing on the coming year.

- An introduction for yourself to editors or specialist writers in an area of the media which is new to you.
- A general briefing for editors or journalists with whom you are not often in contact, usually coupled withideas for specific features.
- To introduce new senior members of your organization to key journalists.

The question of where to entertain is a function both of your budget and the inclination of your guest. It might be a pleasant gesture to ask your guest where he or she would like to go. On the other hand, if you have reasonable in-house facilities this might be a better venue as it will be free from distraction.

It is sometimes even more valuable to entertain a group of journalists together. This can serve both as a briefing meeting and as a discussion group. It is a good idea, for example, to gather together representatives of your immediate trade or industrial publications, together with specialist writers from the national media, at a briefing lunch on the forthcoming year. Such an event enables the senior personnel within your company to meet the leading journalists in the field and to tell them first hand of the company's plans for the coming year. The journalists can ask their questions direct and can also air any grievances or problems in an informal atmosphere.

It is important that the senior management is briefed to be as open as possible at such meetings, otherwise the value of them tends to be diminished. The representatives of the media should see the meeting as a constructive activity and not just a propaganda exercise.

Another example of extremely useful group entertaining is illustrated by a luncheon arranged by an organization which was moving into sports sponsorship for the first time. Leading journalists covering the particular sport were invited to attend the lunch and to give their views on how the sponsorship could best benefit the sport and on how they would like to be kept in the picture. The lunch also served the purpose of introducing the company's executives to this particular section of the media, and much was learnt about how to get the most out of the sponsorship.

Some companies operating in the consumer field have also seen the value of group luncheons in generating special features around products which are not very exciting and which do not really merit a series of individual lunches. Journalists must be told that this is a speculative lunch with only a small information content and that the genera! intent is to discuss the subject in broad terms with the injection of a few ideas from the PROs. The discussion around the table often generates even better feature ideas which can be taken up by one of the journalists present. The trick is to ensure that there are no magazines represented which compete directly with each other. A luncheon to talk about nail care and nail care products might take in one representative of each of the following types of publication: general women's interest magazines, teenage publications magazines, holiday magazines, regional newspaper, London office women's editors, retirement publications and secretarial magazines. There is very little clash of interests here and it will be quite obvious which magazine will be interested in which idea.

***Checklist for Informal Entertainment***

1. Entertain only if you have a good reason for doing so and only if you have something of value to impart to the guest.
2. Decide whether it will serve your purpose better to entertain individually or in a group.
3. Make sure that colleagues who are to be present from sections other than the PR department are fully briefed on their role and on what can and cannot be said.
4. Have a variety of ideas ready to throw into the conversation and listen carefully to the resulting discussion. Make a note of all requests made for further information and of any interest expressed in ideas for features.

Whatever the means of communication has been, it is important to follow up properly. If a specific idea has been discussed over the phone confirm the details in writing. If an outline idea has been discussed over the lunch table ring up to carry it further, and if you have floated an idea by post and heard nothing phone up to see if it has fallen on stony ground. And when an idea has been fully agreed make sure that you deliver on time. But whatever you do, do not send out a general mailing and then ring up and ask whether the recipient is going to use it or not. If they are, your phone call will merely be a slight irritant, but if there is no appropriate slot at that particular time your call could cause enough irritation to prevent the material ever seeing the light of day.

It is worth mentioning here that the PRO's job should be a two-way one. So far we have been talking about the flow of information from the company, but it can be equally important for management to receive information on how the world is thinking about the company and its activities, about rival companies and about the industry in which it operates. Thus a press monitoring service becomes even more important. If your organization is involved in foreign markets then reaction in these countries would also be important.

The Media Relations department may also be called upon to act as a general information service, in addition to media directories you may need to keep company and financial directories-*Who's Who* and the like. These may be physical or electronic.

The choice of electronic reference works includes CD-ROMs such as *Microsoft Encarta.* This is a kind of electronic encyclopaedia which you can use to find all kinds of facts and figures. Your electronic database might also include the *Oxford English Dictionary, Grolier's Academic Encyclopaedia* (US) or *Microsoft Bookshelf* (half a dozen standard US reference books).

Alternatively you can subscribe to a variety of services such as CompuServe which provides access to large commercial databases such as Reuters News, Associated Press On-Line and Dun and Bradstreet. Others include the Financial Times 'Profile', British Telecom's 'Gold', 'Prestel' (which will also get you into the French 'Mintel') or 'Gateway' the international airways guide, all of which offer a variety of services. 'Profile', for example, holds every word published since the early 1980s in every national newspaper save a couple of tabloids and a few of the more important regional newspapers. BBC Enterprises have also made their database available.

The Internet is another vast source of information and it is growing all the time. Whole newspapers and magazines, complete books, hotel and restaurant guides, tourist information, weather forecasts-the list is endless-can all be downloaded from the Internet. A useful book which will give you some idea of what is available on the Internet is *The New Rider's Official Internet Yellow Pages* published by New Riders Publishing.

The choice of which kind of electronic reference base to use will depend upon the time taken to access it and the cost. The Internet is often the cheaper option but it can take a long time to find the information you need.

***The Principalities :*** In essence, the mass media are the tools or technologies that facilitate dissemination of information and entertainment to a vast number of consumers. They are the tools of large-scale manufacture and distribution of information and related messages. These tools 'mediate' the messages; they are not the messages themselves. However, Marshall McLuhan, the media prophet, liked to proclaim that 'the medium is the message', though the title of one of his books suggests rather that 'the medium is the massage.' The media are technologies; they are also messages and massages. They can also be looked at as industries, as cultural or entertainment industries. While cinema, radio, television, cable, and the press can easily be recognised as 'mass media', it requires some stretching of the established meaning of the term to include recent technologies (sometimes termed the 'new media') such as pagers, cellular phones, satellites, computers, electronic mail and the internet as 'mass media'. More correctly, these new media may be termed 'interactive media' for they are not as much transmission technologies from one source to many receivers, as interactive technologies, which involve feedback, exchange and participation.

'A mass medium' says Wilbur Schramm, 'is essentially a working group organised round some device for circulating the same message, at about the same time, to large numbers of people.' Such a definition excludes the folk media, group media, and interpersonal communication such as rumour, education and preaching, where communication is not 'mediated' by a 'device'. Further, the pejorative term 'mass' (a way of looking down at people as 'masses') suggests that the modern media are 'experienced' not by individuals and groups in terms of their own cultures but as part of the 'mass' and as 'mass culture.' The term 'mass' also suggests that people's interaction with media is homogeneous, inactive and unquestioning. In communication studies today, however, the term 'mass media' has come to be a useful collective phrase, though it slurs over the distinctions among the various media.

As generally interpreted the 'mass' media are the press, cinema, radio and television. But books, magazines, pamphlets and direct mail literature and posters also need to be included in the label. They are so termed because their reach extends to vast heterogeneous masses of the population living in a wide and extensive area of a country. The means they employ to communicate messages to the masses are technological—printing machines, records, cameras, cable, modems, computers and satellites. Their communications are thus interposed and mediated; they are not as direct or face-to-face as in interpersonal exchanges.

The organs of the mass media are technological means of transmitting messages to large numbers of people. Indeed, they are much more than that. As they are very expensive media, (particularly the cinema, radio, television, video, cable, computers, and satellites) they have to be run by institutions like the Government or well financed private commercial bodies. They require a group of people to organise and administer, to produce, distribute and constantly maintain in working order the whole set up of, say, a studio, a transmitting centre, or a publishing house.

Yet another feature of the mass media is that they are founded on the idea of mass production and mass distribution-the marks of an industrial society. Copies of newspapers and magazines, for instance, are printed in thousands (some national and regional dailies in India have a circulation of over half a million) and are circulated over a vast area. But to enjoy a mass audience, the media have to cater to a taste that is not very 'cultured' or sophisticated. What the mass media therefore reflect and propagate is a popular culture. The culture made popular by Hindi films in our cities is a case in point. With the rapid expansion of television and video in cities and towns, popular culture is likely to take on new forms; the 'myths' of our culture will find expression in ever-new ways.

But the mass media in India are in fact a minority media as access to them is still restricted because of poverty, low literacy levels, and familiarity with Hindi and English, the major languages used in the various media; moreover, reach is limited to populations living in metros and large cities. The folk media, in contrast, have a wide audience; they are media close to the hearts and minds of the people, suited to a poor country, and help facilitate identification and participation.

Modern mass media serve functions very similar to those fulfilled by traditional media in some ancient societies, and in some developing countries today. Western media theorists generally identify three major functions; surveillance of the environment, interpretation of the information and prescription for conduct, and the transmission of heritage. The developmental and liberation or empowerment functions, or even the ritualistic or celebratory functions of the media rarely find mention in Euro-American media theory. South American media theorists have contributed to our understanding of media for 'liberation' while African and Asian scholars have explored the relevance of media to 'national development.'

***Moral Principles :*** Surveillance of the environment relates to information or 'news' about happenings in society. The mass media carry out this function by keeping us posted about the latest news in our own region and around the world. In rural societies, however, the word-of-mouth method is still the most credible means of spreading news.

But the mass media cannot or should not stop at watching the horizon for us, through news bulletins or through advertisements of documentaries. They need, and often do help us to correlate our response to the challenges and opportunities which appear on the horizon and to reach consensus on social actions.

In rural India, the panchayat meetings help the village elders to decide on the challenges and the opportunities.

The mass media help us to keep the culture and heritage of our society alive, and to transmit it to others. This is what the media should ideally do, but often don't. Folk media serve a similar purpose in developing countries.

A fourth function is the vital function of entertainment. Entertainment has been a legitimate function of the traditional folk media, but the mass media provide it with a vengeance. They help to pass the time, and to relax with family and friends.

Anthropologists of culture and communication discern a symbolic function of the media: the media provide a 'shared symbolic environment.' George Gerbner, for instance, sees television as the central symbol of American culture today. Horace Newcomb and other 'culturalists' (such as James Carey and Robert White) perceive the media as providing a ritualistic and 'liminal' experience.

An equally vital function is that of the mass media helping to sell goods and services through sponsorships and commercials. The commercial function has indeed been served well, perhaps too well, especially in the United States, where the networks would have to close down if the support from commercials were to dry up. At the same time, it would be suicidal to let this function dominate the mass media at the expense of the other four functions. India too promotes the commercial function, and though it has not allowed its representatives to take over the programming of radio and television, the influence is still strong. This is equally true of the press and its dependence on advertising.

In the developing countries of Asia, Africa and Latin America, the mass media, which include traditional media have a different function to perform. In a word, development communication i.e., communication that focuses on the information needs of the poor and the oppressed, and their socio-economic and cultural interests.

While these may be the five functions of the mass media, it does not necessarily follow that audiences go to them for the same reasons. In his book The Play Theory of Mass Communication, William Stephenson argues that fun is both the greatest impact and the greatest public service of the mass media.

Audiences use them as a form of play, or lila. Victor Turner, the anthropologist, believes that the media provide a 'liminal' ritualistic experience. James Carey, Horace Newcomb and others of the 'culturalist' school have developed this approach further by analysing the television experience in terms of 'ritual.'

So, for a good number of the audience, the mass media may be marvellous time-fillers, like listening to the radio while cooking or while driving, or reading during a long train journey. Further, some people use the media to fulfil psychological and social needs. They perhaps get vicarious enjoyment out of sex and violence in the media, and use the media to get topics for conversation at work, or to solve their own problems.

Still others might seek information, merely to be well informed, or perhaps to learn how higher-status people dress and live. Or, they might watch advertisements on TV not so much to know more about a product as to assure themselves that they have bought the best product. These are the 'uses and gratifications' of the media.

So whatever functions the media pundits say the mass media have, the people will continue to use them in the way they (the people, not the pundits) like. It is in this sense that audiences are 'active' rather than 'passive' receivers.

***Ethics of Journalism :*** Western theories of the mass media (particularly of the news media) were first propounded by Fred Siebert, Theodore Peterson and Wilbur Schramm in their book Four Theories of the Press.

These theories have now come to be termed 'normative' in the sense that they 'mainly express ideas of how the media ought to, or can be expected to, operate under a prevailing set of conditions and values.' So, strictly speaking they are hypotheses rather than theories. These 'theories' were first enunciated in the United States during the height of the 'cold-war' against communism and the Soviet Union. They were thus part of American propaganda and only loosely based on actual practices in the media. They idealise the American practices, which are touted as being democratic and socially responsible, and deride 'Soviet' and 'Communist', practices as being 'dictatorial' and 'authoritarian.'

They do not take into account the 'public service' models of print and electronic media widely accepted in Western Europe, and in many countries of Asia and Africa.

The 'original' four theories of the press/media are authoritarian theory, libertarian theory, social responsibility theory, and Soviet media theory. Each of them suits particular political and economic circumstances, and focuses not so much on the relationship between the press and readers as on the relationships between the press and Government. The major concern is with ownership and control rather than with different perspectives of Journalism or the people's right to information. Siebert, Peterson and Schramm limit their analysis to 'four' theories; three more need to be added to the original four to take account of circumstances in the developing countries of Asia, Africa and Latin America. The last three could be termed 'Developmental or Alternative Theories' of the media.

According to this theory, the mass media, though not under the direct control of the State and the ruling classes, must do their bidding. The press and other media are expected to respect authority, to be always subordinate to established power and authority, and therefore should avoid offending the majority or dominant moral, political and economic values. Journalists lack independence and freedom; their reports have to be submitted for advance censorship. This censorship is justified on the ground that the State must always take precedence over an individual's right to freedom of expression. Such censorship is more rigidly enforced in times of war and during 'internal' and 'external' emergencies. It needs to be noted that both dictatorial and democratic regimes resort to such authoritarian control of the media. The strictness with which the Official Secrets Act is enforced in Britain and in India is a case in point.

The basis of this 'free press' theory goes back to 17th century England when the printing press made it possible to print several copies of a book or pamphlet at a comparatively low price. In contrast with the authoritarian theory, libertarianism is founded on the fundamental right of an individual to freedom of expression. Western liberal democracies swear by this belief. The First

Amendment in the American constitution is an embodiment of this theory; it flows from the individual's right to life, liberty and the pursuit of happiness. The individual, not the State or society, is supreme, and popular will (vox populi) is granted precedence over the power of the State. The argument is that 'truth' can be arrived at only through the free expression of diverse points of view, no matter how erroneous. The great apologists of this theory were John Milton, the epic poet (in his Aeropagitica) and John Stuart Mill (in his essay, On Liberty). A free press is seen as essential to a free society and the dignity of the individual. Moreover, the freedom to publish is often linked to the right to property, and the free market system.

In practice, however, the theory provides the prerogative of free speech only to the rich and the powerful elites of a society. The marginalized groups do not have access to, and indeed, cannot afford the means or the tools of free expression. What happens on the ground is that media merchants and media monopolies (e.g. the big newspaper chains, the television companies) exploit that freedom to expand their empires. Market forces rather than public good mould the kind of information to be purveyed. The theory thus protects media owners rather than the rights of editors and journalists, or of the public. What the theory offers, in sum, is 'power without social responsibility'.

This theory can be said to have been derived from the Hutchins Report (entitled 'A Free and Responsible Press: A General Report on Mass Communication: Newspapers, Radio, Motion Magazines and Books'). The Hutchins Commission on Freedom of the Press (1947) was established and financed by Henry Luce of Time Magazine at a time in the history of American Journalism when press barons like Luce sensed that government regulations on 'yellow journalism' were round the corner. Moreover, the years following the Second World War witnessed the rise of the Democratic Party in the United States, the restraints on business under the New Deal, and the strengthening of the trade union movement. The American press (which was known to be largely pro-Republican) feared that the federal Government would issue legislation to regulate the 'freedom of the press', despite the First Amendment.

Robert Hutchins, the Chairman of the Commission, was the Chancellor of the Chicago University at the time, and he was assisted by twelve others who were experts in different fields. The Report appeared in two volumes: the first on newspapers, the second on the other media.

The Commission found that the free market approach to press freedom had not met the informational and social needs of the less well off classes; in fact, it had increased the power of a single class. There was little expression of diverse views; the emergence of radio, film and television also suggested that some public control and some means of accountability had become necessary.

Thus, the theory had its roots in the view that the media had certain obligations to society-to serve its needs, rather than that of the free market. Hence the need for high professional standards; of truth, accuracy, objectivity and balance. Self-regulation and also state regulations were imperative. Public interest was a greater value than unregulated freedom of expression. So news offensive to religious and ethnic minorities, or news likely to lead to social violence needed to be underplayed. The Hutchins Report led to the establishment of Press Councils, the drawing up of codes of ethics, anti-monopoly legislation, and to press subsidies to small newspapers. State and public intervention in the exercise of free expression was therefore considered legitimate under certain circumstances.

This theory is derived from Lenin's application of Marx and Engel's dictum in The German Ideology that, 'the ideas of the ruling class are in every epoch the ruling ideas.' The media are thus a means of 'mental production' of the ideology. Hence the need for their control by the working class, that is, through the Communist Party, so that the interests of the working class rather than those of the ruling or elite class are projected. In a Socialist society, therefore, the media should be used as tools to 'socialize' the people; the primary functions of the media are to educate, inform, motivate and mobilize citizens, and to support 'progressive' movements everywhere. What is expected is 'objective' (or 'scientific') presentation of society. Censorship and restriction on the media are legitimate for the media are accountable to the State, to the public and to the Party. The public is encouraged to provide feedback, as it is only in this way that the media will be able to serve the public interest.

The 'four theories of the press' are not fully applicable to the experience of the non-aligned countries of Asia, Africa, and South America. While in most Asian and African countries, the media (especially the broadcast media) are owned and run by the State, in Latin American countries, commercial ownership of all the mass media is the norm. A common factor in the experience of the majority of the non-aligned countries is the dependence on industrialized countries for both hardware and software. Another common factor is the commitment of these nations to social and economic development on their own terms; they would like to employ the mass media as tools for 'development', for 'nation-building.' The larger national interest and the public good are of paramount importance to them. So certain freedoms need to be curbed in the interest of say national integration, and economic and social development. Hence the stress on 'development communication' and 'development journalism'. According to development theorists, journalists have the responsibility to support national governments in their efforts at eradicating illiteracy, promoting family planning, promoting national integration, and increasing production and employment. The weakness in the theory is that 'development' is often equated with government propaganda.

Latin American critics (notably Paulo Freire, Reyes Matta, Luis Beltran, Diaz Bordenave and Valerio Fuenzalida) of commercialized ('commodotized') media have come out strongly against the top-down, one way and non-participative character of contemporary mass media. Like the development theorists, they lay stress on the positive uses of the media, on the need for 'access' and the 'right to communicate.' They insist on the need for local and community participation in media and news production. The people must speak for themselves, they argue, not through professional journalists and producers.

What is vehemently opposed also is commercial, political or

bureaucratic control of the media, which exist to serve audiences, not the interests of government or commercial enterprises. The 'demassification' of the media, according to this theory, is as vital as 'democratization.' The ultimate purpose is to put the media in the hands of communities (as in people's radio) for their own 'liberation' through a process of 'conscientization.' Thus is created, in Reyes Malta's words, a 'critical national audience.'

***Mutual Relationship :*** Successful media relations involves understanding the media, how they work and what their requirements are. It also involves relating this knowledge to the needs of your own organization and the objectives of its media relations programme. It is important to work out the best strategy and to plan accordingly.

This book is essentially practical. It is concerned with the tools, the organization and the planning of the media relations programme. But it also seeks to show how a thorough knowledge and understanding of the media can make your efforts more effective.

There is, after all, no point in spending a fortune on trying to communicate an important story if you are telling the wrong people, in the wrong way, at the wrong time. Putting yourself in the recipient's place and deciding exactly what will be of interest and what will not will be much more useful from everyone's point of view.

This kind of practical knowledge of the media will put you in a better position to build up a harmonious and helpful relationship with those sections of the media which cover your organization's particular activities. And this relationship will in turn help you to establish a smooth communications channel between media and management.

Unfortunately, the senior managements of some organizations tend to view the press or media relations department as a buffer between the media and themselves. This can only lead to trouble. Very often the Public Relations Officer (PRO) is not qualified to answer detailed and possibly highly technical questions. Nor does he or she have the authority to answer for the company on important issues. Such an attitude inevitably leads to an unnecessarily bad press and a lack of cooperation by the media on future occasions.

Rather, the PRO should be the means by which the two sides can talk to each other more easily and with more understanding. You must stick to your professional guns in telling senior management what the consequences of their actions in the media relations field are likely to be. You must, however, also follow up such a stand with sensible advice on dealing with the media and be on hand to see fair play.

Of course, there are occasions when certain sections of the media behave with some dishonesty and as PRO you must watch out for signs of such a situation arising and warn your management in time. But the vast majority of dealings with the media will not be like this, and management must be encouraged to be as open as possible.

Building up a favourable relationship with the media often involves building up a good personal relationship with key journalists in your field. You cannot hope to achieve this if you are not convinced yourself. If you do not think you can be committed to an organization's activities, do not work for it. Honesty is as important at this level as it is on individual issues.

This applies equally whether you are planning to work directly for the organization or for its PR consultants. Indeed everything in the book applies to both situations, for they differ only in their organization and lines of control. To all intents and purposes a PR consultant must act as though he or she works directly for the client organization. 'Public Relations Officer' has also been taken to be synonymous with Press or Media Relations Officer' for the purposes of this book.

Of course a harmonious relationship with the media does not mean that everything will always go smoothly. Sometimes your objectives and those of your media friends will be in conflict and this is where your powers of diplomacy will be tested to the full. Competent journalists will be probing critically. That is their job. Yours is to present the facts in the most favourable light for your organization and, if the problems are severe, to ensure that ultimately your organization's worst story receives the best hearing.

A good example of successful media relations concerns a multinational oil company, one of whose oil tankers was wrecked, causing extensive spillage along the Californian holiday beaches. Sales at petrol stations immediately started to fall. The company instituted an expensive and wide-ranging mopping up programme including very quick cleaning of the popular beaches and a bird sanctuary, a marine life survey and a restocking operation. Full details of the disaster and the company's prompt action were relayed to the media at once and this, coupled with the previously good relationship between the oil company and the media, ensured that most of the coverage was concentrated on the mopping up operation. This resulted in the company being seen as a responsible, socially conscious organization rectifying an inevitable disaster, rather than as an irresponsible multinational with no concern for the environment. Sales not only recovered but exceeded the previous norm.

There are times when the disaster is less obvious to the public view and this is when there is a strong temptation to deny everything. The short answer is, don't allow your management to do so either. If you or any of the representatives of your organization do lie, your reputation in the media will be shattered and its loss will precede you into whatever industry you go. It is very rare for the truth not to emerge, given time, and once a journalist has been castigated by his or her editor for believing your lies the journalist will, understandably, never trust you again. In future, the journalist will be suspicious of everything you and your organization have to say and will tell associates to be wary too.

Successful media relations, then, means understanding the people with whom you want to communicate-producers, editors and journalists-appreciating their problems, needs and audiences and treating them with honesty, efficiency and common sense. It is this principle that underlies all the detailed information and advice.

The term 'media relations' refers to the communication Pattern between an organization and those sections of the media which are interested in its activities. Such communication may be concerned with anything and everything which happens within and around that organization. It may also be concerned with local and national issues, with finance and legislation and with public opinion.

Communication between organization and media may be initiated by either side, but from the organization's point of view media relations is concerned with achieving the most favourable coverage possible. This can sometimes be achieved by reacting to individual happenings or to media enquiries, but at best this approach is haphazard and at worst it is inefficient and potentially dangerous.

It is far better to plan a media relations programme within the framework of your organization's objectives as a whole. This not only helps to channel your efforts into the most effective areas, but also ensures that everyone who comes into contact with the media knows what their organization is trying to achieve.

***Real Situations :*** The first step is to define and analyse the problems in order of priority and then to set objectives to be achieved. The problems will, of course, vary according to the field in which your company or organization is operating and what it is trying to achieve. However, for a manufacturing company the problems might include any of the following:

- The product range is seen as too expensive.
- The proper use of a new product is not really understood.
- The company has a reputation for bad service.
- The company is moving into a new high technology field and needs to upgrade its scientific image.
- The company is not thought of as a good employer.
- The more expensive end of the product range is not being retailed through the right kind of outlets.
- There is an important technical development behind the introduction of a new product which is not fully appreciated.
- The company is thought of as being old-fashioned.

All these and other problems will come in as feedback from

the marketing and other departments. Obviously they need to be countered and an objective must be set. Ideally objectives should be measurable and achievable. If you set unobtainable objectives you will be seen to have failed even if you do a wonderful job. To some extent this is also true if the objectives are not measurable.

Whatever you do, do not try to link your objectives to sales. There may be a great temptation to do this as part of a justification for the very existence of the media relations programme. But you are unlikely to be able to show a link which is directly attributable to your activities and you will be encouraging the view that media relations is simply a cheap form of advertising.

If an objective is to be measured effectively it needs to be defined clearly. There is no point in stating that the objective is 'to increase awareness' or 'to change an attitude'. This is not enough. You must include the answers to the questions 'of what?' and 'by whom?' which will lead you into defining your target audiences. The answer to 'who are you trying to influence?' will in turn lead you on to 'how are you going to reach them?', and once you have reached this stage the programme starts to become viable.

Here is a very simple example of the start of a media relations programme for a small company producing torches.

Market research has shown that the company's torches are seen as dependable but rather old-fashioned and there is little awareness of the newer products which have been introduced to fit the contemporary life-style.

***Objectives***

1. To increase awareness of the more recent products.
2. To show that these products are up to date and invalu able to the modern man or woman.
3. To give the company a more go-ahead image, while retaining the dependable aspect.

The torch-buying public includes the following markets:

- Women buying torches for domestic and car use.

- Men buying torches for similar uses.
- Industrial buyers, for security services.
- The police and the armed services.

The media reaching the ultimate target audience include the following groups:

- Women's interest programmes and publications.
- Men's and general interest programmes and publications.
- Motoring programmes and press, and the caravan and holiday press.
- Security and safety publications (both consumer and trade).
- Police and armed services press.

This sort of analysis makes the rest of the programme much easier to plan. Working against the background of known developments and plans for the torch company for the coming year a single idea for each area will start the programme off. There may, for example, be plans to launch a new pocket or handbag version of one of the company's torches; if it is sufficiently different from anything else on the market this could form the basis for an onslaught on the women's interest press.

The frustration of life without a torch, illustrated by either a feature or a demonstration, could interest the men's press, and special car fitments for fixing a torch inside the car would be of great interest to the motoring media. Similar ideas for features, visits and events could be thought up for the remaining areas.

A plan like this not only shows up the priority areas and assists a sensible organization to plan its workload; it also shows where effort should be concentrated and helps in the measurement of success.

Massive coverage may look good but it is less valuable if it appears in media which are not seen by your ultimate target audience. There could even be occasions when extended coverage in a large number of regional and provincial newspapers is much more useful than a short piece in *The Times.* The temptation is, of course, to impress management with national press coverage, but this may not always be the most effective approach. It may be good for your ego, but is it good for the company?

Once you have an outline of your media relations programme worked out, and preferably written down, you will be ready to start thinking about the detailed use of tools such as media lists, press releases, competitions, press receptions, workshops, visits and special events.

However, the media relations programme does not end here. It must be assessed. Is the right message reaching the right people in the right volume or are you wasting your efforts talking to the wrong audience or giving the wrong signals? There are various ways of evaluating a media relations programme.

# 3

# News Stuff

Newspapers are not literature. But then nor is most literature. Writing for papers is different from writing a novel or short story, but not as different as some would like to think. All good writing has some things in common. It is clear, easy to read, uses fresh language, stimulates and entertains. Those things are as true of the well-written newspaper story as they are of the well-written novel. And they are true whatever language you are writing in.

Now for the bad news. Learning how to write is hard, lonely work. We all know people who say they want to write. What they often want is merely to walk around saying they are writers. What they do not want to do is to put their butts on a chair and stay there until they have covered some paper or a computer screen in words. That is what you have got to do. Many, many times. And the way you progress and develop whatever talent you have is to write hundreds and hundreds of stories and make mistakes. You leave vital things out and put irrelevancies in, write half the piece, then realise it is going wrong and have to start again, write clumsily, pompously or stiffly, turn in work that is confusing or trite, and commit to paper or screen whole paragraphs so silly that if you had to speak them, your voice would trail off in embarrassment mid-sentence.

Now for the good news. After a while, by hanging around a

good newspaper and listening, by reading, studying the good and the bad and being your own sharpest critic, you begin to see away. There will still be times when you take along time to get a story to work, but by and large, the more you write, the more fluently you write. Writing is like a muscle, it will be a lot stronger if you exercise it every day; you will waste less time in false starts and chasing down the wrong route, less time in writing stories at the wrong pace for the length they should be and less energy trying to think of a fancy phrase when a simple one will be better.

And you find that essential thing without which no one can call themselves a writer- your voice. No more will you be experimenting with a style that is over-elaborate, too formal or too colloquial. Instead, you will have found a natural style that suits you, is consistent, has rhythms and expressions recognisably yours and- the crucial test - if read aloud would sound like an only slightly tidied up version of your speech. It will be your own. Not put on, not affected and not borrowed. Of course it will owe something to the writers you admire, your background, education, reading and so forth. But it will be yours - your words and idioms, your pattern of sentence lengths and your rhythm within sentences. It will be like a signature. Only more readable.

## Thinking Process

The most important part of writing is what happens inside your head between finishing your research and putting the first word down. You have got to think about your material and decide what it is about and what you want to do with it. Composition is not merely the business of arranging words, it is the business of organising thought. It does not matter how wonderful you are at conjuring up colourful phrases or witty remarks; if you do not have a clear idea of what you want to say it will show.

This is easy enough on some cataclysmic event or short, straight forward news stories, but most journalism is not like that. Stories can be complex, not as strong as you would like, or they can be long features covering many different aspects, or commissioned pieces where you are unsure if the subject is interesting to the reader. Then you have to think hard about what the story is actually about. And sometimes it is not immediately obvious. A feature, for example, about a man collecting and keeping exotic frogs in his apartment is superficially about amphibians, not a subject in which most people are automatically interested. But it is also a story about eccentricity and obsession, about how a hobby has taken over someone's life (and his home). That is a far more promising topic than frogs.

The other thing you have to work out is the treatment for the story. Is it hard news? A soft news story or light human interest? Should it be told chronologically or by covering each aspect in turn? All these different ways of handling the story (and there are many more) affect the construction, the main framework of which you need to know before you start. In the case of simple news stories, planning what you want to say and the order in which you want to say it can be done quickly in your head. But with longer, or more complex, articles you need a written plan. Never be afraid to make a plan on paper. It is not the sign of an untutored novice, but someone who wants to get it right. It does not have to be very detailed -just the main building blocks of the story in order, with maybe a few notes of how to link them.

Construction gets its own chapter, as does the intro, that all-important first paragraph. Those sections discuss how you can grab the reader's attention immediately and sustain it through the piece-both essential features of good writing. There are, I think, six others: clarity, fresh language, honesty, precision, suitability and efficiency - and they are the subjects of this chapter.

## Thought to be Clear

Each story must be clear in thought, organisation and language. If it isn't, it needs rethinking or rewriting. You don't just have to take my word for that. The French novelist Stendhal wrote, 'I see only one rule: to he clear. If I am not clear then my entire world crumbles into nothing.' The British writer H.G. Wells put it less dramatically, `I write as straight as I can, just as I walk as straight as I can, because that is the best way to get there.' Of no writing is this more true than that for newspapers. They are often read in distracting, noisy surroundings by people with other demands on their time and easier, albeit inferior, ways of getting news. There are specific points to watch for.

*Achieve clarity before you have even put a single word down.*

To explain something to others, you must first fully understand it yourself. Until you do, don't write it down. A good tip for the confused is to tell the story to a colleague or friend. The obvious nub of the story (and its innate pattern) will probably come out of your mouth almost unconsciously.

*Be careful to include each stage in a narrative, each event in a sequence and each step in an argument.*

Jumping from A to C leaves readers having to work out that B happened In between. That's annoying, confusing and sometimes misleading, especially in the cases when B actually happened out of place. And don't make leaps of logic. You may understand your thought processes but readers won't unless you explain them.

*Don't assume readers have special or prior knowledge.*

When you spend a lot of time delving into a specialist or technical area. It is easy to forget that readers know only as much as you did before you began your research. Don't. And on stories that run for many days weeks or months, don't assume that readers have a photographic memory of what has gone before or have dutifully made notes when they read your previous stories. They haven't. Instead, work on the assumption that until something has passed firmly into general knowledge, readers will need reminders and recaps.

## Group of Professionals

The normal instruction on this subject is to avoid using all jargon, whether it is scientific, technical, bureaucratic or whatever. I think this is a mistake. Some jargon is useful. It takes readers inside a formerly closed world, adds to their knowledge of the language specialists use and, especially with bureaucratic jargon, shows the often-ludicrous phrases that officials dream up and thus their mentality. For these reasons, and for lovers of irony, it should never be banned from stories. What, however, should be censured is the failure to explain in everyday language what the jargon means.

This is not to say that jargon should be used often, even if it is explained. Journalists, especially specialist reporters, can easily slip into using jargon because they want to display their knowledge and sound like an insider. Well, by all means do so at a party if you think it will impress people, but not in your paper. Trying to come across as an insider or writing for insiders is elitist and obscurantist, neither of which characteristic is wanted on newspapers.

Then there is commercial and political jargon, which these days is perhaps the most damaging kind of all. It is widespread, sometimes difficult to detect, and journalists are especially prone to repeat it unthinkingly. Spokesmen for large companies say that their 'operation' (firm) is 'undergoing temporary cash-flow difficulties' (running out of money) due to 'market positioning problems' (people are not buying what they make) and so there will be a 'rationalisation of the work force' (people will be sacked). Government officials tall, of 'correctional facilities' when they mean prisons and 'an imbalance between the supply and demand for domestic units' when they mean that there is a housing shortage.

These are euphemisms, a form of linguistic dishonesty which is particularly common where public relations people proliferate. They play on the natural tendency of politicians and business leaders to, if not lie, at least try to hide the truth when under pressure.

***Clear Sentences :*** Don't write confusing sentences that oblige readers to go back to the beginning and read them again. Instead, you go back and rewrite it. This is different, of course, from the deliberate device of writing sentences that lead readers to expect one thing and then deliver another. Surprise is important to keep the writing lively.

***Tricky Writing and Tricky Language :*** Any writing that is self-consciously clever is almost certainly self-evidently bad. The idea is to communicate your meaning to others, not to keep it to yourself. So if you find yourself writing a showy phrase that you are particularly proud of, strike it out; if you verbally have to explain a passage to someone, change it, and if you feel tempted to use words to display your erudition, resist.

*One final word on clarity - simplicity.*

This virtue is normally urged on journalists when they are writing, especially for mass-market newspapers. It is good advice, up to a point; and that point is where simplicity becomes simple-mindedness. Some papers, particularly in Britain and Australia, severely underestimate the literacy of their readers, with the result that they use a vocabulary and language which is restricted and stylised.

They defend this on the grounds that they know their readers - a questionable assertion. If they actually knew them, they would know that in speech and thought their customers' minds operate several levels above that of the paper. If anyone doubts that, they have only to compare it with the vastly more complicated language and vocabulary of television that their readers cope with every day. When simplicity means linguistic inbreeding, it is time to let in a little new blood.

***New Stuff :*** The whole point of articles in newspapers is to give readers something they have not had before-information, insights, observations, thoughts. It is therefore a terrible waste to relate this novelty in language that is tired and worn-out through over-use. Do that and readers will feel even the newest material has an old, familiar ring to it. Points to watch out for are:

***An Individual, New Thing :*** Don't fall into the trap of formula writing, where you say to yourself, 'Ah, here's "a he said -she said argument story" and then trot it out to a well-worn pattern. Of course there must be a limit to the types of stories around, but that does not mean you must make all which bear a similarity to each other conform to a set formula. Professor John Carey, in his introduction to *The Faber Book of Reportage,* writes: 'Massive accumulations of standardised language and hackneyed story-lines lie in wait, ready to leap from the fingers to the typing page.' As he says, reporters have to see their story and tell it, as if for the first time. In this sense, beware especially a story which appears to write itself. If that starts to happen, stop, think and you write it instead.

***Avoiding Cliches :*** And here, for once, is something that is as easy to do as it is to say. Cliches are words and phrases that are familiar, too familiar, so recognising them should not pose any problems. A good rule is that anything you suspect of being a cliche undoubtedly is one and should be removed. Some are in general use, others seem to be purely confined to newspapers and are dealt with later in this chapter. But whatever they are, they are expressions so old and worn-out that they have ceased to have any impact.

Those that are similes pose an especial danger because their automatic use means they are often applied in the wrong place. For instance, describing a crash scene as 'like a battlefield' is both unoriginal and wrong, as those who have seen both accident scenes and battlefields will know. But whether they are similes, metaphors, catch phrases or single words, the cliche (a feature of which is that it is out of your head and into the story almost before you have realised it) should be deleted and something fresher put in its place.

***Automatic Words Avoided :*** These are normally adjectives which some reporters instinctively link with certain nouns. All deals have to be 'huge', all reports 'shock', all murders 'brutal', all concern `widespread' and all wants 'long-felt'. The adjective has become like a parasite living on its host and has long since sucked the phrase of any impact it might have had. There are also phrases which seem to be used automatically in certain circumstances. Each country's newspapers have them. In English-language papers, for instance, disasters always have investigators 'grimly sifting through the wreckage' (as if they would be laughing) and civil disturbances overseas have 'baton-wielding police' and 'stone-throwing demonstrators'. These are not just automatic, but cliches and used so frequently that they cannot possibly be accurate in all cases.

***Carefulness :*** An outright ban would be a bit severe, because once in a while (say every three years) somewhere in the world a journalist comes up with a good fresh one. Meanwhile, many millions more that are anything but fresh get published. They normally take two forms: first where the writer on a certain subject thinks of every possible word associated with that subject and loses no opportunity to fill the story with them (as in 'Tennis Player Nets Fortune'): second where the story, normally a light one in a mass market paper, seems to consist of nothing but word play. To those in the know, such puns are an infallible giveaway that the story is being written by someone with no imagination and also that the story is not worth the space it has been given.

There are no absolute rules in writing, but one that comes close is: never write the obvious. If you go to Las Vegas, don't write about the slot machines; if London, try to get to the end of the piece without reference to rain or Big Ben; if Paris, leave observations on the way women dress to someone else. So, too, with puns. They cannot put you in prison for writing a light story about cats which avoids all play on words like paws, nine lives or tail.

And contrary to the myth peddled by newspaper journalists whose stock in trade are puns, they are not at all difficult to write. If they were, there would be fewer of them in newspapers. A good general rule would be to allow someone else the glory of being the once-every-three-years hero who comes up with a pun worth repeating, and remove yourself from that competition by never writing with them.

*Work hard at creating new similes, metaphors and phrases.*

Whenever you find yourself reaching in a semi-automatic fashion for a phrase, simile or metaphor, stop and think. Think hard about the real nature of what it is that you are trying to convey and try to find a phrase that fits the bill perfectly, not just the nearest off-the-shelf option. Experienced writers have all kinds of devices where they deliberately and cleverly invert or fool around with familiar phrases to give them new life. But they also put a lot of brain power into trying to describe something or communicate its nature exactly, and that means the hard work of inventing a phrase especially for it.

They also fight and argue with editors for the right to use colourful language. Sometimes this is necessary when you work on a paper which seeks to force a literary straitjacket on its staff. The editing staff at the *New York Times,* for instance, used to be notorious for the dead hand they would lay on the prose of its writers. Consider the experiences of Molly Ivens in the late 1970s. She once wrote that a man had 'a beer gut that belonged in the

Smithsonian'. The copy-editor changed it to, 'a man with a protuberant stomach' - accurate, but dull. Then, another time, she wrote that a guy 'squawked like a two-dollar fiddle', and it appeared in the paper as 'an inexpensive musical instrument'. Editors who do things like that to fresh language should be working in a museum.

***Fashionable Word or Phrase, not Required :*** Language has its vogues, just like hemlines and hair-styles. Each new fashionable word or phrase, however, rapidly becomes irritating to read. So do your writing a favour - be a trend-setter rather than a trend follower. Use your own words, phrases and voice and let others mimic the passing fancy. As the style book of the London *Daily Telegraph* says: 'If you are tempted to use a word because all the smart writers are using it, change the word, your reading matter or your job.' Or, as Bernard Kilgore once wrote to his staff, 'If I read upcoming in the Wall *Street journal* again, I shall be down coming and somebody will be outgoing.'

## Truth's Value

There are aspects of the process of journalism which often compromise truth. The lack of time to collate a totally comprehensive account the lack of access to all the sources and information and the need to write the story to a finite, often quite short length-all these factors can prevent us presenting an account that is as complete (or as accurate) as we would like. That is fine as long as we are aware of these limitations and don't claim that we are presenting the definitive account in each story. And it is even better if we are doing all we can to overcome these limitations and difficulties.

But often when writing and editing news stories, journalists do things which actually put even more distance between their story and the truth. Writers know what editors prize as a strong news story and in writing the story as strongly as they dare, they often make omissions and use language which exaggerates or 'hypes' the story beyond its true value. And, on popular papers especially, if they do not do that, the chances are that an editor will. Avoiding this sometimes inadvertent, sometimes deliberate process is not easy, but here are a few points.

This is obvious and should not really need saying, but it does. Quite a lot of reporters when challenged on a part of a story will say, 'Well, it must be true.' Suppositions like this might be good enough for a chat in the kitchen with a friend, but not for newspapers.

This is a tall order. It is not just a question of making sure you have included both sides (normally there are more than two) to the story and have quoted accurately. It is a question of making sure what you have put in the story accurately reflects what you know to be the whole picture. You may, for example, spend a great deal of time interviewing someone who is perfectly even-tempered, except for their response to one question. Of course you are entitled to report that touchiness, but even if you quote it with total accuracy, the whole piece would be dishonest unless you indicated that their general mood was benign. Anything else is slanted selection with a dishonest purpose.

***No Hypes :*** This is the process whereby journalists use words that convey a stronger meaning than the material justifies. A lot of it is done automatically to conform to what the writer thinks are the required journalistic conventions, and thus is also a cliche. But whether his or her intention is conscious or not, the effect is to over-cook the story. Words like ,sensational', 'shock', 'dramatic' and 'disturbing' are used to describe things which are normally a good deal less than sensational, shocking, dramatic and disturbing. As one commentator once said: 'When you hear something described by a journalist as disturbing, you know you cannot take it seriously.'

There are two other bad aspects of this habit. First, all these words involve a value judgement, which has no place in a straight news story. And hyping is the worst kind of comment - a sneaky comment posing as a legitimate description. It does not declare itself, but goes under an assumed identity. Second, let the facts speak for themselves. If the story is sensational, shocking, disturbing or whatever, tell the readers all about it and let them judge for themselves. Good journalism involves not only the readers trusting the paper, but the paper trusting the readers.

The final problem with this sort of breathless, exaggerated language is that it bears no relation to the language real people use. And in almost every country, many newspapers have evolved this 'journalese'. In Britain, for example, it is a world where two people disputing a point are 'confronting' each other, and where 'amid extraordinary scenes' (anything remotely out of the ordinary) 'soap-stars' (any actress who has had a walk-on part) have 'miracle' babies (used to describe infants born in anything but the most routine circumstances) which are 'dashed' or 'mercy dashed' to hospital to be operated on by 'heroic' doctors. Reporting in journalese is dishonest, at least several steps removed from reality and, because it is so over-used, ultimately has no impact on readers. It is a fossilised art form, performed to a set of rituals. It has no life. Replace it with fresh, honest language.

***Simplistic, Black and White Headline Language in Stories, not Welcome :*** There is a great deal of difference between writing that brings an issue or subject to life and writing that gives the material a phoney life. A prime example of this is using words that have no shades of meaning, but are either very black or very white. This is best explained by relating briefly the roots of this in European mass-market newspapers. Over the last 50 or so years on such papers, headlines have become progressively larger in size. The unavoidable result of this is that the words used in headlines have got much shorter. And there is one great problem with short words: in almost every case they are far less good at conveying shades of meaning than longer words. They tend to deal in extremes of meaning, black and white and not grades of grey.

Thus if you and I hold different opinions on a subject and discuss it, we could be said to have a disagreement. If we are sufficiently interesting for a popular paper to want to report our debate, how will they describe it in their headline: Well 'disagreement' cannot fit, neither can 'debate', because all they have room for in type 4.5 cm high is a word of four letters. So our disagreement becomes a 'row' or a 'feud', something very different. Or we have a 'bust up', or I 'lash' you, or 'rap' you or 'blast' you, none of which happened. Typography and design has made a dishonest account of our meeting.

In many British papers, annoyance (meaning you are not pleased) is invariably now 'fury' (suggesting anger beyond control), an arrangement (meaning an informal agreement) is a 'deal' (meaning a far more formal agreement, with definite overtones of a financial, possibly even shady, side), bad luck is a 'curse', to criticise is 'to slam', failure to attend is a 'snub', internal dispute is 'civil war', possibility is 'threat', a proposal is a 'plan', to replace is to 'oust', a traffic jam is 'road chaos', etc. All of these examples (and there are many more to choose from) are shorter, more extreme and more brutal than the reality they describe. It is as if the story is being translated into another language by an angry man with a limited vocabulary.

This inaccuracy might be confined to the headline were it not for one thing: the language of today's headlines is the language of tomorrow's news stories. Editors and their senior executives control the culture of a paper partly through the language of headlines, which they approve. Reporters read the words used for headlines on their stories and, wanting to be thought in tune with the culture of the paper (and their editor) or a 'bright, lively' writer, they adopt it. And provincial reporters see such language in national papers and they imitate it, often badly. And then even some flagging quality paper, wanting to make its image more youthful, or its appearance more lively, will adopt larger headlines and thus imbibe some, if not the worst, of these excesses. Thus, in varying degrees, does the whole journalistic stream become polluted. It' the language of your papers has not yet been invaded by the little black and white words, keep a wary eye out for them.

***Answers to All Questions :*** Journalism should be the enemy of imprecision. Stories should be written to answer questions in the readers' minds, not to raise them. And the questions a reporter should be trying to answer, and answer precisely, are:

- What? - What has happened?
- Who? - Who has it happened to? Who has done it? Age, appearance, position, credentials and any relevant background.
- Where? - Where did it happen?
- When? - When did it happen? What time, day, month?
- How? - How did it happen? Explanations.
- Why? - Why did it happen?

Other points to watch for are:

> Writing which is not specific is not wanted. Reporting that talks of 'official organisations' without naming them is no good. Use specific words, name names, make lists and pin things down. You have to be careful where in the story you itemise these details, but they should be there. And don't just call a building 'tall'. How tall is it? In metres, please, plus some graphic idea of what that means.

*Use known quantities rather than unknown ones*

Writers often use words like 'really', 'considerably' and 'very' to express values or scale. But how much is 'very'? Be precise, use known values.

A leading US copy-editor has rightly pointed out the infuriating habit of reporters of being mealymouthed with numbers, as in: 'An average case worker might handle up to 100 cases a month or more.' As he says, this could be 'up to' (i.e., anything from 0 to 100) or 'more' (i.e., from 101 to infinity) - and it only 'might' be at that. Sentences like this say literally nothing. You can fiddle with this sentence a bit ('It's not unusual for a case worker to handle 100 cases a month') but for all you know 100 cases a month might be extremely rare. The only real solution is that the reporter should go away and ask for specific data.

There are some phrases in common use which communicate only vague ideas. 'Expensive tastes', for example, tells you that these tastes are not cheap, but that is all. What does expensive mean here? What the reader wants to know are concrete examples of what the money is being spent on, preferably with brand names and prices. Similarly 'fast car' - is it a Porsche, a second-hand police car or a Ferrari? And 'luxury' - what is that?

The answer is, it is different things to different people. You should tell readers something that means the same to all of them. This applies also to descriptions of people. 'She is tall and attractive.' What does that mean? But if I write that she is blonde and stands six feet, then we both know what we mean. 'She is intelligent' is meaningless, except as a general indicator that she is not actually mentally handicapped. But if I write that she has a degree in politics, we begin to learn something.

This is the language of people hiding from reality. They speak, for instance, of someone 'passing on' when they mean dying, they refer to sex as 'being intimate with'. Victorian England was a rich source for the more absurd euphemisms: 'nether garments' for underwear, 'maleness' for penis, 'in a state of nature' for naked, 'smallest room in the house' for toilet, 'in an interesting condition' for pregnant. Even now, people invent words or phrases to describe the things they feel uncomfortable with, whether it is death, sex or their own emotions.

Journalists should not use euphemisms, unless with irony. But that does not mean that every last detail of sex cases, or killings, has to be spelt out. Most newspapers are produced for a general readership which embraces an enormous range of people with different sensitivities. You should neither write for the most shockable, prim and proper, nor for the most bloodthirsty.

When writing about violent deaths, be they the results of crime, war or accidents, use your judgement about how graphic you can be without making your readers feel sick. Precision does not have to mean gloating. It means describing things in sufficient *relevant* detail, without being insensitive. You should have a reason for giving the detail. In some situations, like plane crashes, readers will not be surprised to learn that the force of the crash or explosion has dismembered and mutilated the corpses. You need only spell out what is necessary.

In other situations, like war or terrorism, people need the horrors of what has been done brought home to them. You will do this all the more effectively if you use measured, cool language. Here is Robert Fisk, then of *The Times of* London, describing the scenes he found when he went to investigate reports of a massacre of Palestinians at a refugee camp at Chatila in September 1982:

> What we found inside the camps at ten o'clock next morning did not quite beggar description, although it would perhaps be easier to retell in a work of fiction or in the cold prose of a medical report.

> But the details should be told for - this being Lebanon- the facts will change over the coming weeks as militias and armies and governments blame each other for the horrors committed upon the Palestinian civilians.
>
> ... Down a laneway to our right, not more than fifty yards from the entrance, there lay a pile of corpses.
>
> There were more than a dozen of them, young men whose arms and legs had become entangled with each other in the agony of death. All had been shot at point-blank range through the right or left cheek, the bullet tearing away a line of flesh up to the ear and entering the brain. Some had vivid crimson scars down the left side of their throats. One had been castrated. Their eyes were open and the flies had only begun to gather. The youngest was perhaps only twelve or thirteen years old.
>
> On the other side of the main road, up a track through the rubble, we found the bodies of five women and several children. The women were middle-aged, and their corpses lay draped over a pile of rubble. One lay on her back, her dress torn open, and the head of a little girl emerging from behind her. The girl had short, dark curly hair and her eyes were staring at us and there was a frown on her face. She was dead.

Fisk's report continues for another eleven paragraphs. Neither in these or the preceding thirteen is there is single word of comment, or emotionalism. You can be sure that is not because he feels no emotion, but knows that as soon as the reporter lets that infect the writing, then the impact - and veracity - of the story is lost.

For many years newspapers all round the world used the language of the nunnery to describe anything remotely sexual. Readers had to guess, rather than know, what was being described. Phrases like 'intimacy took place' and 'improper suggestion' were not only imprecise but also often left the reader with the impression that far worse had happened than actually did. One of the most abused terms was 'interfered with', which once led to the headline in a British paper: 'Girl Stabbed 65 Times But Not Interfered With'.

Yet the replacement of such bashful language with a clearer one is not a licence to write soft pornography. Detail should be given to explain and not to arouse. You will also find that being forced to describe events in a way that is acceptable to the broad band of your readers will frequently produce original and evocative writing. Here is Ben Hecht, an American reporter from the 1920s, writing the final line of a story for Chicago's *Daily News* about a priest who regularly made love to a girl in the basement of his church - until, one day, he accidentally kicked the gas jet open and died while having sex: 'Preoccupied by love, he had smelled no fumes than those of Paradise and given up the ghost while still glued to his parishioner.'

## Style Matching

Suitability is matching the style, tone and pace of the story to the subject. By no means all subjects require special handling, but some need more sensitive treatment than others. Most are obvious. Matters of life and death, for example, should always get serious treatment (unless you are writing a column and specialise in bad taste). Here are a few guidelines for the more straightforward situations.

The language and construction should be taut, the verbs active and direct, sentences economical and adjectives should be used sparingly. There are few better illustrations of this than Sergei Kurnakov's description of the frenzy in St. Petersburg, August 1914 in the hours after Germany declared war on Russia. It is a model of how to write something that reads at the same fast pace as the events it reports:

> When I got to the St. Isaac Square it was swarming with people. It must have been about nine o'clock, for it was pretty light yet - the enervating, exciting twilight of the northern nights.
>
> The great greystone monstrosity of the German Embassy was facing the red granite of St. Isaac's Cathedral. The crowds were pressing around waiting for something to happen. I was watching a young naval officer being pawed by an over-patriotic group when the steady hammering of axes on metal made

me look up at the Embassy roof, which was decorated with colossal figures of overfed German warriors holding bloated cart horses. A flagstaff supported a bronze eagle with spread wings.

Several men were busily hammering at the feet of the Teutons. The very first strokes pitched the mob to a frenzy; the heroic figures were hollow!

'They are empty! A good omen! Another German bluff! Hack them all down! No, leave the horses standing!'

The axes were hammering faster and faster. At last one warrior swayed, pitched forward, and crashed onto the pavement one hundred feet below. A tremendous howl went up, scaring a flock of crows off the gilded dome of St. Isaac's. The turn of the eagle came; the bird came hurtling down, and the battered remains were immediately drowned in the nearby Moika river. But obviously the destruction of the symbols was not enough. A quickly organised gang smashed a side door of the Embassy.

I could see flash lights and torches moving inside, flitting to the upper storeys. A big window opened and spat a great portrait of the Kaiser at the crowd below. When it reached the cobble stones, there was just about enough left to start a good bonfire. A rosewood grand piano followed, exploded like a bomb; the moan of the broken strings vibrated in the air for a second and was drowned; too many people were trying to out shout their own terror of the future.

There is not a spare word in this description. Each detail is fixed precisely with the minimum of adjectives. Like all the best writing, it defies editing.

The lure to over-write is always greater when your material is extraordinary. Let the events themselves make the impact. And do not try to add drama by characterising the events in any way. Do not, for example, write that the story is 'sensational', 'disturbing', 'horrific'. Present the story without such comment and let the reader judge.

In the movies, theatre and books, humour should have no taboos. Death, sex, cancer and hunger should all be fair game. But joking about these general subjects is a very different matter from trying to have a laugh about some specific person's misfortune in the following day's paper. Giving a light-hearted treatment to a story which involves injury, distress or upset is never a good idea. It is insensitive, and actually pointless. If there is a genuinely comic element to the story (of however questionable taste), people will find it and laugh anyway, especially if the tale is told straight.

Most journalists would agree that humour is very difficult to write. The trouble is, it does not stop them attempting it. Indeed so much writing in newspapers is humorous in intent, if not effect, that the failure of journalism text-books to address this issue borders on the criminally negligent. Just the two words 'think twice' would be valuable. Of even greater worth would be for them to point out one of the basic truths of humour, because that at least might stop at the drafting stage a lot of the laborious, creaking efforts that get into print. And this truth is: being funny on paper is a God-given talent not granted to many of us.

Writing humour is like singing in tune. If you can do it, you don't need to be taught; if you can't do it, no amount of teaching will help. And comedy out of tune, like singing, is excruciating to experience and embarrassing to do. Or should be. However, if you have got the talent, it comes relatively easily. Your ear instinctively recognises the rhythm that humour writing must have, and the words that are almost funny in themselves. You won't need to be told that jokes are funnier when delivered with a straight face rather than the literary equivalent of a whirring bow-tie. Your eye will see comic possibilities where everyone else sees what is merely on the surface, and your brain will be full of all the little cultural, social and historical references that make a joke.

If you have a good comic idea for a piece that is suitable, then work on it. It has to be tightly written, surprise the reader (which is why puns are not funny) and it has to have the punch line at the end of the sentence. Right at the end. Not in the pen ultimate phrase. Finally, if you are giving an article a particular humorous treatment or framework, it has to be strong enough to carry the whole piece right to the end. The soundest policy is always to let the humour flow naturally from the events and innate absurdities of your subject, rather than being a 'joke' that you impose on it from outside. Here, for example, is an intro written by Wall Street journal reporter Tony Horwitz. Just after the end of the Gulf War, he filed a piece about Kuwait, the invasion of which by Iraq had started the conflict. Kuwait is an oil-rich, semi-feudal state presided over by a fabulously wealthy royal family. This is what Horwitz wrote: 'The emir of Kuwait, Jaber al Sabah, returned home yesterday, 15 days after the liberation of his land, and 10 days after his furniture.'

The moral of this section is that if you have any doubts about a joke or allegedly funny line, leave it out. If you have no doubts, then imagine standing on a stage delivering it to an audience of 500 readers. Only if you still think it will get a laugh should you go ahead with it. And remember that the addition of an exclamation mark at the end of a sentence does not render it funny! just amateur!

## Expertise in Job

In the last century and quite a way into this one, journalists in Britain and the United States were paid by the line. This system of payment gave birth to a generation of journalists who could write impressive amounts about nothing and almost endlessly about very little. And this in turn produced a bloated style of writing whose chief characteristic was its exponents' ability never to knowingly write one word where four or five could be deployed. As a result, their pompous and excessive language (a football, for instance, was known as 'the elusive leathern spheroid') made a lasting if inadvertent contribution to British humour. It was writing so spectacularly inefficient that, in its way, it was almost admirable.

Thankfully, journalistic style (and, in most cases, systems of payment) have moved on a little. Payment by the word has long since been recognised as a way of bribing people to write badly. Yet enough of the lineage men's spiritual descendants live on to make a few notes about writing efficiency worthwhile.

They must either convey fresh information or otherwise help move the piece forward. If any part of the story does not do this, cut it.

Every language has phrases that are used in speech to give the speaker time to form fully the thought that is coming. In English, examples would be: 'It is a well-known fact that...'; 'Indeed, there is no doubting the fact that...'; 'We can also observe that...'. Avoid these and avoid also the leisurely constructions that slow a piece down. Journalism, especially news reporting, has to have pace. It can't if sentences like the previous one are constructed thus: 'It is an essential requirement of most journalism-features, sport, profiles and features, but particularly news reporting - that they should move forwards with that quality known as pace.'

You will write more quickly and more efficiently if you do so without looking at your notebook every five seconds. You should not even start to write unless the story is clear in your mind, and if you write without notes only the essential material will go in. The details, spellings and figures you can check with your notebook afterwards. There will almost certainly be one or two points you will add as a result, but the main draft will be written far more efficiently from your head than by copying out large chunks of notes.

Even the most experienced writers find themselves writing the most pitifully obvious things sometimes. These are often links between paragraphs that you have struggled over, and, in your desperation to try to weld one part of the story to another, you find yourself writing the purest nonsense. Only the other week I cut from a story the phrase, 'Of course, a ballet dancer's life is not all applause...'. Well whoever thought it was? You often find that you do not need these links at all. Most readers can handle a small change of direction if it is accompanied with a change of paragraph.

People and things do and say things, so it is always best to write this directly. Thus: 'Heathrow Airport will open another runway in 2003' and not 'It has been established that another runway will open at Heathrow International Airport in 2003.' Certain verbs, like come, leave and give, are frequently used for the passive voice as in: 'The demand came when Yeltsin asked...' (better to say 'Yeltsin demands ...'), 'The earthquake left 3,000 people dead...' ('The earthquake killed...') and 'The move gave a boost to...' ('The move boosted...'). The active voice is not just more efficient, it is also, as the name suggests, more active.

This can be overdone in a paper, but is very useful when you have a long catalogue of points to make. Instead of taking several long paragraphs to describe the effects of, say, government spending cuts on transport, itemise them like you would on a shopping list. But beware of doing this and then finding that you have to mention most of the points again in order to add detail to them. Put the detail with the list.

Phrases like 'serious danger', 'unconfirmed rumours' and 'unduly alarmed' are, if you think for a second, complete nonsense. What, after all, is unserious danger? And if a rumour was confirmed it would no longer be a rumour, it would be a fact and an attributable one. Such automatic phrases can be cut down to the second word, along with other meaningless modifiers like 'rather unique'. It either is, or is not, the only one of its kind, and if it is not, then it is not unique, rather, slightly or otherwise.

This is the use of words that say the same thing twice. For instance, *'Some* of the remarks *included...'* and 'it is an *essential condition'.* In both cases (and many others that could be given) only one of the italicised words is needed.

This is a common and wasteful habit, as in: 'The ministry denied this. A spokesman said, "We do not accept this allegation."' Write one or the other, preferably the first.

'The subject to which I refer', for instance, amounts to the one little word: 'this'.

Finally, a useful exercise is to take a few of your recent published stories and, with a red pen, reduce the number of words used, without eliminating any essential fact. You will be surprised how wasteful you have been. That is why it is a very good experience for a writer to work for a period as a copy editor. There is nothing like the discipline of telling complex stories in 250 words to teach you efficient writing.

Writers have to be their own fiercest critics. It is essential that you read back what you have written, looking for any flaws, and revise it if you are not happy. Normally, by the time the story reaches another pair of eyes it will be too late - either for improvement or for your reputation. Some writers prefer to write a version of the whole story before subjecting it to, perhaps heavy, revision. Others, perhaps those who know more clearly what they want, revise as they go. The method does not matter, what is important is that the revision is comprehensive and not just a superficial search for spelling mistakes.

George Orwell, the author of *Animal Farm* and 1984 whose writing was noted for its clarity, thought there were four questions that any writer should ask of each sentence. This sounds laborious, and would be if this questioning did not become automatic and almost sub-conscious after a while. His questions were:

What am I trying to say?

What words express it?

What image or idiom will make it clearer?

Is the image fresh enough to have an effect?

Then, by way of important afterthoughts, he added two more:

Could I put it more simply?

Have I written anything avoidably ugly?

Those writing regularly will soon learn to ask those questions of their writing with no more conscious effort than they use to move their eyes from left to right as they read. I would, however, suggest that a couple of questions are knowingly asked of the drafted piece.

Are there any loose ends, is everything explained properly? Does it read flowingly?

If it does, then leave it alone, resist the temptation to throw in a few more colourful phrases, as if you were a cook tossing a few more currants into a cake. And if it does read awkwardly, it may need more than a bit of light tinkering to put right. Punctuation, for instance, is not a quick way to give the kiss of life to dying sentences. Rewrite and restructure until you are happy.

And then cut it. Are there any words, phrases or sentences that slow the piece down? I rarely come across an article that could not be improved by cutting. It is like tightening the nuts and bolts on a piece of furniture. If left undone, the thing would be loose and unstable. Beware especially of anything that sounded good when you wrote it. As Samuel Johnson once said, 'Read over your compositions and, when you meet a passage which you think is particularly fine, strike it out.' Such parts often don't work as well as you first think.

## Enjoying the Role

Inexperienced journalists can be almost overwhelmed at times by the problems of writing something clear and interesting that people will want to read. Older writers are not exactly immune from this sinking feeling, too, and to hear them speak of the pains of composition you would think that no sane person would write, unless at the point of a gun. The great American sports journalist, Red Smith, for instance, once said, 'There's nothing to writing. All you do is sit down at a typewriter and open a vein.' To which another American, Gore Vidal, probably gave the definitive reply when he wrote, 'When I hear about writer's block, this one and that one! Fuck off! Stop writing, for Christ's sake. Plenty more where you came from.'

Sure it is sometimes a real sweat. Of course, there are stories which seem a confusing and worthless jumble until you have spent many hours wrestling them into shape, and there are times of sheer panic as the deadline approaches with the thing only half done and ill thought out. But the pleasures of capturing something and pinning it down in words, your words, are immense. So too is the thrill of starting a piece with an assortment of disparate information and finding a pattern in it and new ideas about it as you write.

## Newspaper Writing

The articles of a newspaper are invariably printed on one page in several columns. The ending part of an article can appear on a different page; that is done due to space constraints. Pages four five and *six* are normally devoted to articles. In some newspapers, articles and editorials are put on the same page. In many newspapers, articles, regular features, and *three* editorials (in a vertical two-column format) are being printed. Example: We would like to draw the attention of our valued readers to *This India,* a weekly series of articles written by the doyen of Indian journalism,

Rajni Kothari. Our readers can read these articles in *The Hindustan Times* (July-August, 1987). It may be difficult to procure these newspapers.

(A) Remain sensitive towards the broader environment, especially towards those issues that are in tune with your ego sets and interests.

(B) Find the right topic.

(C) Find out the magazine in which, the article is likely to be published. There can be *two* distinct situations:—

(CI) The publisher has a topic and invites you immediate to write it overnight.

(C2) You have a topic. You have to contact the publisher. In such a case, you would take a few days to complete your writing work.

(D) Do the research. Some information may be already present in your files. You have to collect fresh data related to the topic. In fact, you may be having this data when you talk to the newspaper publisher about writing an article. Hence, we can assume that this step and the previous one are intertwined.

(E) Decide the style. You might have defined your style. Newspaper publishers would be well versed with that style. Obviously, only those would place repeat orders on you that like your style.

(F) Do the heading (you can also write or edit it later).

(G) Do the first paragraph. Give the brief news or event that has motivated you to write the article. Give a fascinating fact about it and draw the attention of the reader towards the subsequent paragraphs of the article.

(H) Complete the second paragraph. It would extend what the first one says. However, it can become a backgrounder for the topic.

(I) Continue the third, fourth and fifth paragraphs. These paragraphs are short in terms of extent. A paragraph should not have more than *90-100* words. Within this limit, you can write anything that falls within the purview of the topic. However, the flow of the article must be taken into account. We have scanned many newspapers and found that writers write *88-90* words in a double-width column. If we take the average of various paragraphs scanned by us, the average is *88* words per paragraphs for a double-width column. For a single-width column, the average is *77* words per column. These figures should be followed (at least in India) because typesetting and subsequent make-up of pages of newspapers would be according to a standard format to accommodate these specifications. The newspaper has to look nice because normally, every article is sans colours. Make short paragraphs and let the eyes of the reader take rest after he reads some of them. You can give inset boxes, photographs, sketches, and caricatures to give variety to his mind and relaxation to his eyes.

(J) Decorate it now with tables (give originals to the editorial department of the newspaper publisher as your role ends when you give the article).

(K) Decorate it now with figures and graphs.

(L) Decorate it now with inset boxes.

(M) Decorate it now with photographs.

(S) Send the article to the publisher. You would not be allowed to edit it. A newspaper publisher works according to a time bound schedule. Hence, the editorial department cannot call you for editing the galley; nor he can send the galley to you for editing.

(T) Read the published article and tell experts to pinpoint mistakes in the same.

## Comparative Study

***Radio vs Newspaper Reports :*** By now it should be clear that there is all the difference between the radio and the newspaper insofar as news is concerned. We can summarise the differences as follows:

> The radio has much greater speed and can put hot news into homes even as it occurs—as during live

coverage of sports events like cricket tests. The newspaper is slower if a deadline is near; hours slower, if delivery time is long. The only advantage it has is that it has extra time for checking facts.

The radio presents most news in condensed form and in relatively broad strokes. The newspaper presents most news more fully and certainly with far more specific detail. The only thing it cannot do is to reproduce sound effects.

The radio offers limited selectivity of news—the listener takes what radio presents. The newspaper offers the reader wide choice as to which news he shall read, how much news he shall read and when he shall read it.

The radio delivers its news not necessarily to one person at a time, but often to a small group of audience or a family—usually in the living room. The newspaper delivers its news to one reader at a time.

The radio can dramatise news, thereby adding to its effectiveness both through production devices and use of the human voice, but the newspaper has only the relatively static device of printed words and pictures to achieve dramatic effect. In that sense, the written word has to work overtime to convey what the spoken word can convey instantaneously and sharply.

The radio cannot be readily "checked back". Radio news is evanescent—it vanishes the instant it is broadcast. The newspaper is available for reading, rereading and reference at any time.

The radio can be heard with little effort and can be listened to in almost any circumstance. It does not require the listener's undivided attention. The newspaper requires heavy concentration by the reader who will also make the additional mental effort at selection.

The radio by its very nature, is readily subject to misunderstanding or misinterpretation. The newspaper is less readily subject to misunderstanding. Whatever it says is all there and is probably put together after a good deal of deliberation.

The radio has to be extra selective because of its impact value in dealing with crime, sex, violence and matters of such nature.

The newspaper can write about crime etc. with a greater degree of latitude. Restraint is expected in either case, but in the case of the radio news, the restraint expected is greater.

Far too often, radio news was originally written for newspaper use; the news services do not put out news specially written for the radio. It just puts out news intended for the newspaper. At a radio station, this same news is swiftly edited and in the process subjected to subtle and unintentioned mutations. It is then given to the tender mercies of the news announcer whose voice, inflections, skill and understanding have much to do with the form in which it finally goes on the air.

This is the reason why writing radio news is much harder than writing for a newspaper. The final news script as given to the announcer must not be susceptible to misinterpretation no matter what his skills or biases are. In other words, the news should convey about the same meaning no matter who the announcer is. There is a school of thought, however, that asserts that it is desirable that a given news programme be written especially to suit the personality and "air characteristics" of the person who is to broadcast it. But this suggests that there are several news stations in the same area in competition with each other which would make it necessary to build up announcers as news characters in their own right. This situation does not prevail in India, though it is common in the west, more particularly in the United States.

***One Final Comment:*** Repetition is a priceless tool of the radio newswriter—even when it uses up precious seconds. And emphasis on the source of news, when it concerns a matter of which there may be the slightest doubt is mandatory.

## Writing Editorials

The editorial of a newspaper is its elite ambassador that disseminates latest news, views, and opinions among the masses. The editors of a newspaper are the gems that the newspaper management preserves with utmost care and respect. If the editorial team is disturbed (due to the firing or demise of a senior editor), the newspaper in question may lose its circulation.

## Column for Guests

Normally, a free-lance journalist writes guest columns. He decides his stream of writing and does not move away from that broad stream. Example: Jayaram Ramesh writes for many magazines; his calling in life is politics and not journalistic writing. However, he has been able to draw the attention of the elite masses of India towards burning issues that face India today.

There are exceptions to the aforesaid rule, however. Some journos may be on the rolls of newspapers and magazines. They effectively and creatively contribute to the guest columns of these newspapers and magazines.

Prestige is associated with guest columns. As such, it is imperative to get these columns written from experts, known journos, VVIPs and politicians whose thoughts matter. Examples: The leader of the opposition in the *Lok Sabha,* the PM, the President, a reputed former cricketer, a leading hockey player of the present times, a foreign journo, a VVIP from abroad and many more could with such columns. In fact, many of them get such columns written from other authors or feature writers. These columns are published under the names of these people of repute whereas the real writers remain in the dark corners of anonymity.

The USP of the guest column is the comment of the column writer on the current burning topic that cannot be ignored by the media, elite, politicians, the judiciary or executive. In some cases, NGOs and social action groups are also targeted through these columns. There are no hard and fast rules to write this column. In general, a column writer should:

(a) be thoroughly updated on the topic (good and reliable contents);

(b) show his class through his words (unique style);

(c) remain genuine in terms of overall looks (presentation. should be a paragon).

## Editing of Copy

Every editor edits. That is, the editor decides what shall and what shall not go into his publication on the basis of what he conceives to be the publication mission and philosophy.

Of the various sub-editors who help the editor carry out his job, one is the copy-editor, the man or woman who makes raw copy palatable for the reader.

Although each editor works at different levels, all have to edit Adolph Ochs of the *New York Times* insisted that copy-reading is editing, "A good copy-reader," he said in a talk at the Pulitzer School of Journalism in 1925, "is truly and in the full meaning an editor. The most useful man on the newspaper is one who can edit."

One may describe the duties of the editor, but no one can analyze how an editor works, any more than one can describe how a poet composes a poem. Norman Podhoretz, editor of *Commentary* magazine, came close to defining one obligation of the editor—"to improve an essentially well-written piece or to turn a clumsily written one into, at the very least, a readable and literate article, and, at the very most a beautifully shaped and effective essay which remains true to the author's intention, which realizes that intention more fully than he himself was able to do. He cares about the English language; he cares about the clarity of thought and of grace of expression; he cares about the traditions of discourse and of argument."

Describing a publisher's editor in the *Trade Winds* columns in the *Saturday Review* (February 10, 1968) Herbert R. Mayes gave some attributes that apply equally well to the copy-desk expert: "An editor, like a gardener with a green thumb has a knack. There is no specific training involved. There is no college to offer a doctorate in editing, because editing is an empirical art. There is nothing scientific about it. There are no statistics, except after the fact, that can be relied on. Editing is intuitive. Experience confirms intuition but does nothing to develop it. Intuition is for what is the right writing for a given audience, of course, but no less for what makes the members of any audience laugh and cry, love and hate be decent or vulgar, vengeful or sympathetic, greedy or generous, brave or cowardly.

The copy-editor has been called the midwife to the story, the reporter's best critic. The copy-editor is like the unsung craftsmen in a dramatic production whose skills put the quality into the material that draw the applause for the stars. Rudolph Burke of the *Atlanta Journal,* in a letter to *Editor & Publisher* (July 8, 1967) has said that the byline lures the enthusiastic beginner, but every managing editor knows there is often a great deal of difference between what the reporter writes and what the readers after the story has gone through the hands of anonymous editors.

A few reporters grouse because the copy-editors "butcher all their good stuff," But most writers respect their collaboration on the desk, the ever-alert copy-editor who gives the copy as final look before it goes to the composing room and then to the reader." It was the small author who ever-alert copy-editor who gives the copy a final look before it goes to the composing room and then to the reader. "It was the small author who ever resented the touch of the editorial pencil upon his precious effusions," said Edward Bok in *The Americanization of Edward Bok.*

The term *copy-editor* is more apt than the traditional word *copyreader* because it connotes the essential job of editing copy. It suggests the art of the correcting, refining and polishing a piece of copy. Editing, as crossword-puzzle fans know, means redacting, or bringing back, getting together, collecting, arranging, reducing, composing, framing, translating, selecting or adapting for publication. A redactor, therefore, is an editor. One aspect of redacting is copy-editing, the British equivalent of sub-editing. Editing begins the moment a reporter composes a story. If the writer has been trained in editing as well as in reporting, he or she will double-check the copy for errors of fact and style before submitting the story. The reporters may even have the responsibility of writing a headline for the story.

## Extra-ordinary Performance

An excellent staff without a copy-desk conceivably might produce a fair newspaper. A mediocre staff with a competent copy-desk can produce an acceptable newspaper. But an excellent staff, backed by an excellent desk, guarantees an excellent paper. Such is the testament of a former executive, L.R. Blanchard of the Gannett Newspapers, who added, "No man is qualified to be his own copy editor. No matter what his reputation, his writing will benefit from another's look." And another—this from Stan Amisov of *Neivsday*—"There are many elements that go into the making of a fine newspaper, but one of the least heralded and most important is an outstanding copy-desk. It can make a good newspaper better. It can make a better newspaper the best."

The new technology is making it almost imperative for even the small daily newspaper to place a copy-editor, or some other executive, in-charge of processing and moving copy. Automation is providing more copy from more sources than ever before, thereby demanding a greater degree of selectivity. Also, as will be explained later, the newsroom is becoming increasingly involved with the processes of production so mat much of the responsibility that once belonged to the printer now rests with the editor.

The copy-desk may be viewed as the newspaper's clearing house. Here the flow of copy is sorted, corrected, measured, headlined, scheduled and moved on to compositors. The vision of what the paper will contain and how the pages will look materializes on the copy-desk.

Automation may not radically change content and presentation. As pointed out by Nathaniel M. Gerstenzang of the New *York Times,* new methods may change red ink to black on newspaper balance sheets, put they won't assure publishers of the best and fullest use of the most valuable commodity—-the news column. "The assurance," Gerstenzang said, "can be given, in the last analysis, only by human brains—specifically by competent copy-editors."

The copy-editors has talents that cannot be replaced by *computer.* One of these talents is the ability to edit copy; another is the ability to compose headlines. The first is as important as the second, if not more so, because editing demands many intangibles—judgement, scholarliness, background, memory, aggressiveness, motivation, curiosity, imagination, discretion, cynicism, scepticism and even some genius.

Almost all critics lead lonesome lives, but atleast they have the respect of those they have taught. One of the most demanding of all editors was Harold Ross of the *New Yorker,* of whom Ogden Nash wrote in a letter quoted in James Thurber's *The Years with Ross,* "He was an almost impossible man to work for—rude, ungracious and perpetually dissatisfied with what he read; and I admire him more than anyone I have met in professional life" The copy-editor is a diamond-cutter who refines and polishes, removes the flaws and shapes the stone into a gem. He searches for the ills in copy and meticulously scans the product for flaws and inaccuracy, ever searching for the maximum power of words. He knows when to prune the useless, the redundant, the unnecessary qualifiers. He gets movement in the piece by substituting active verbs for inactive ones, specific for generalities. He obtains colour by changing faraway words to close-up words. He keeps sentences short enough so that readers can grasp one idea at a time and still not suffer primer prose. He strives for pacing. If the sentences clothes several ideas majestically and in the good order, he has the good sense to let the writer have his way. He realizes he is not the story-teller. His talent is in what he can do with another's copy to make it sparkle.

Lest this description suggest that the copy-editor is like a bored teacher correcting English themes, consider that the copy-desk is one of the exciting places in the newsroom. On the desk tumbles all the copy of the day—the major battles, the moon landings, robberies, the cure for cancer, the election of a president, the Kentucky Derby winner, the rescue of a lost child. The desk is the heart that throbs with all the news from near and far, waiting for someone to shape it, size it, display it and send it to the reader. "Because copy-editing is an art," said J. Edward Murray of the *Boulder* (Colo) *Camera,* "the most important ingredient, after training and talent, is strong motivation. The copy-editor must care. Not only should he know his job. He must love it. Every story. Every edition. Every day. No art yields to less than maximum effort. The copy "editor must be motivated by a fierce professional pride in the high quality of editing," No one can tell copy-editors how to edit—they have to experience it for themselves.

A newspaper without a circle of geniuses around the copydesk would have been unthinkable to the sage of American journalism, Carl Lindstrom, formerly of the Hartford *Times.* He regarded the desk as the backbone of the paper, "The copydesk," he once observed, "is the abiding place of curiosity, discretion, cynicism, sympathy—all those human instincts personified in men who give your paper its flavour; news-sounds all, with noses in the air for the scent of human interest and for libel. I salute the copydesk, the sacrificial altar of the sacred cow."

Ask youngster fresh out of a journalism school what they are looking for in their professional lives. The thoughtful ones will reply, "I want a job that offers an opportunity for growth. I want a chance to continue to expand my education. I want a place where I can, by my own incentive, advance to the higher echelons of responsibility." Mention the copydesk and they are likely to repeat the stereotypes of the desk, as the haven for tired, worn out newsmen who spend their days marking paragraphs and hurriedly composing commonplace headline so they can get back to their crossword puzzles. The great and the near great are those of the editors, the reporters, the columnists, the news commentators. Whoever heard of a hero of the copy desk?

Yet, no place on a publication offers a greater opportunity for growth, a chance to continue an education, an incentive to reach the higher places of responsibility. Copy-editors, even if mediocre, must of necessity accumulate a warehouse full of facts compelled to read and edit or from the references they have had to consult to verify information.

Think of him as super-detective, who incessantly search the story for clues that could transform a mediocre piece into an epic. Let them study ocean charts and maps and astronomical formulas, as did Car Van Anda of the *New York Times,* to find the missing links in the routine story. Think of them as lawyers conducting a cross-examination. Let them study Harold Ross, who, as noted previously, made life miserable for writers on the *New Yorker* but who never let a piece escape him unless the meaning was crystal.

The greatness of both Ross and Van Anda was that they were mentally curious, a trait that should characterize all copy-editors.

Few copy-editors today would correct an Einstein formula, as Van Anda did, but—if they are willing—they can probe, question, authenticate and exercise their powers of deduction.

If copy-editors are blessed with a good copydesk chief, they will learn. Day-by-day they will improve. If in college they worked under a wise and experienced professor on the staff, rather than under a graduate assistant who regarded a copydesk lab as a chore, they will probably love editing. The tradition that the copydesk is man's domain is dying. Some of the best copy-editors are women. On some metropolitan papers, women with editing skill have risen to important positions, in charge of copy-editing and layout of sections that run to many pages.

Whether copy-editors, as a class or a craft group, are a vanishing breed is debatable. Some editors think they are. A typical comment might be: A few very good ones exist here and there, but as individuals and not as part of a great fraternity that was with us thirty or forty years ago. Newspapers are poorer because of this, and I suspect that those who survive are lonesome. They were "swift" and could handle large piles of copy with an unerring eye for big and little errors, misspelled words factual faults.

If, in fact, good copy-editors are hard to come by, publishers might start paying more attention to the experts on the desk. A copy-editor with a good education and the opportunity to advance his knowledge will benefit the newspapers more than a reporter will. Let management recommend a copy-editor as a Nieman Fellow, or give him an opportunity to attend the American Press Institute at Columbia University, or give him a leave of absence to ground himself at the London School of Economics, or give him a chance to trade jobs for a year with a copy-editor in another part of the country or invite him to sit in on office conferences where policy and philosophy are discussed.

Editors might keep trainees or interns on the copydesk atleast long enough to find out whether the trainee will make a good copy-editor. By rotating good reporters on the desk, editors might find that both the desk and the reporters will profit.

The emphasis in this book is on copydesk work. It is not intended solely for those who will edit copy for a newspaper, a wire service, a magazine, a broadcast newsroom or even an advertising department or agency. Rather, it is designed to aid the reporter as well as the copy-editor. Editing should start with the reporter's own copy.

# 4

# Origin of News

## Agencies for News

Newspapers, to a large extent, depend on news agencies for general news coverage. Even big newspapers do not have countrywide news network. They have their representatives at the State capitals and at some other important places. In some cases, newspaper representatives are also connected with their own teleprinter lines. Despite this, it is almost impossible to cover all news through their own sources. The newspaper representatives, as a rule, concentrate on important happenings. For other news, newspapers depend on news agency coverage. The medium and small newspapers cannot afford to have their representatives. As such, they are more dependent on news agency reports.

The basic function of a news agency is to survey news and provide news reports of current events to the newspapers and others who subscribe to its service. The UNESCO definition of a News Agency is an undertaking of which the principal objective, whatever its legal form, is to gather news and news material of which the sole purpose is to express or present facts and to distribute it to a group of news enterprises and in exceptional circumstances to private individuals with a view to providing them with as complete and impartial news service as possible against payment and under conditions compatible with business laws and usage. No modern State can survive without an adequate set-up of information-collection and its judicious dissemination.

***The Publicist and News Agencies :*** The publicist feeds the press with a variety of material-news, photographs, features, articles, advertisements, etc., either directly or through agencies. News stories or spot stories, as they are called, are handled by news agencies, photographs by photo agencies, features and articles by feature syndicates or feature agencies, and advertisements by advertising agencies.

The dissemination of information, through a news agency, by the publicist has certain advantages. The news agencies can transmit his message to local newspapers through the teleprinter network in the quickest possible time. As such, the publicist is saved from the botheration of sending his hand-out to local newspapers individually. Also, through news agencies, the publicist reaches the outstation papers in no time which would be otherwise difficult. However, it would not be a wise policy, except in the case of very important news items, to send the news material only to the agencies and not to the newspapers. News agencies may not use the publicist's copy or reduce it drastically before sending it to the subscribers. In that case, newspapers are deprived of a fuller version, and even if they wish to publish the story they would not be in a position to do so.

While the news agency has the biggest merit of getting the widest newspaper coverage in the quickest possible time, it has the disadvantage also of its news not being used by newspapers. By and large, a newspaper does publish a news given by its own correspondent, almost in its full form.

The general principle, therefore, is to send the item to both the agencies and newspapers unless it is decided to 'sell' the story on 'exclusive' basis to a particular news agency or to a single newspaper or category of newspapers based on language, region, or frequency. Where news is given out on 'exclusive' basis to a news agency, the news agency correspondent should be clearly told about it, so that he will do full justice to the material.

## Democratic Structure

The role of news agencies in a democracy with free press is of crucial importance. There are some basic principles which should govern the functioning of news agencies in a democratic set-up. Some of these are:

1. There should not be any monopoly of one news agency. Competitive service freely available to all users is absolutely necessary.
2. The news agencies should not be state-owned or state-controlled. The government should not participate in ownership, nor have any voice in the control of the agency either editorially or administratively.
3. Financial assistance in the form of loans, etc. may be given by the government but without any strings. The payment made for services rendered comes altogether in a different category.
4. The set-up of news agencies should be a public corporation formed on the basis of cooperative efforts of newspapers, other users and interests.
5. In functioning, they should keep in view the overall interests of State and society. They should abide by the laws of the country, as well as by the code of professional conduct.
6. They should develop the system of coverage of foreign news by having their own correspondents at major foreign capitals, and use their despatches to supplement and correct, where necessary, the services of foreign agencies which have the monopoly of world news. Also, they should provide the country's news to newspapers and other media in foreign countries.
7. They should provide adequate coverage of regional news and meet the requirements of regional newspapers.
8. The agencies should provide different types of services-full or comprehensive, brief and summary (for district newspapers) to different categories of subscribers.
9. The tariff should be so devised that the subscribers are charged in equitable manner, or according to the use

made of the service. The subscription rate to be charged from newspapers should be in relation to their number of pages, circulation, income and other factors.

10. In addition to the services provided to newspapers, the news agencies also provide news service, including commercial and special services, to individual subscribers-Central and State government departments, public sector undertakings, business houses, etc. In India, All India Radio, Doordarshan, External Affairs Ministry are important subscribers of the services of news agencies. The payment of subscription from official agencies should be based on sound principles and not on an ad hoc basis.
11. The news coverage should be fast, objective, comprehensive and accurate.
12. Only items which have 'news value' should be selected. While determining 'news value', the appeal to the readers and the significance of the event are to be taken into consideration. The criterion of 'news value' must undergo changes as social, political and economic developments take place in the country.
13. In selection of news, the agencies should have a sense of integrity and impartiality. Selection of news should be made on the basis of importance and priority attached to individual facts. All relevant facts of significance should be reported.
14. The news agencies should not have any specific editorial policy. The agencies should avoid giving views or comments while reporting news. The privilege of comments should lie with the newspapers.
15. The agencies, in giving news, should be fair to different points of view. The views of opposition should be treated fairly and equitably in respect of length and coverage. Since the agencies cater to subscribers of diverse and contradictory views, it will not be proper for the agency to select news to suit the interests of any particular client. The interests or prejudices should not influence the agencies in selection of news. In fact, the conflicting trends

in the country and society should be projected, but in a balanced manner and in proper perspective.

16. News agencies should be free from bias. It should also be immune to pressure from any quarter-governmental, or big business, or proprietorial.
17. As far as possible, news agencies should be viable.

In brief, the news agencies in a democratic society should provide complete, impartial, objective, accurate, countrywide and competitive news services free from slant, pressure, or interference from any source or quarter. It has to guard against the danger of being dominated by any vested interests-economic, social, communal or political.

## Four Agencies

Prior to Emergency, there were two English news agencies, namely, Press Trust of India and United News of India. Two other agencies Hindustan Samachar and Samachar Bharati provided services in Hindi and regional languages.

The history of news agencies in India dates back to just over 30 years. Before Independence, Reuter owned and operated a news agency-Associated Press of India. After Independence, in 1948, Associated Press of India was transferred to Indian ownership and baptised as the Press Trust of India. For years, PTI remained virtually a monopoly. It faced no worthwhile competition from the United Press of India which merely provided an outlet for nationalistic activities. UPI was financially weak and folded up in 1958. For-three years thereafter PTI was all alone in the field. The United News of India came into being in 1961 largely as a result of newspapers' dissatisfaction with the performance of monopolistic PTI. Both PTI and UNI were owned by newspapers as cooperatives.

India's first multilingual news agency, the Hindustan Samachar was set up in 1948. In 1957, it became a society called the Hindustan Samachar Cooperative Society. Prior to its 'merger' into Samachar, it had 14 teleprinter circuits which connected its network of 21 bureaus. The news agency fed news to more than 135 subscribers in 10 Indian languages.

Samachar Bharati, the second language news agency came

into being on 2 October 1966, but became operational only in 1967. The number of teleprinters, prior to its merger into Samachar, stood at 49 connecting a network of 13 bureaus. The news agency supplied news to 50 language papers, particularly the small and medium newspapers, All India Radio and State Information agencies.

### *Samachar*

***Kuldip Nayar Committee Report :*** The four agencies were merged by the government on 1 February 1976 during the Emergency and a single news agency 'Samachar' was formed. Samachar was expected to collect and disseminate news within the country and abroad, and to provide what it called complete, impartial, objective, accurate, and countrywide news service.

After the formation of the new government in March 1977, an Expert Committee was appointed under the chairmanship of Mr. Kuldip Nayar to examine the functioning of Samachar, taking into consideration the freedom of the press, independence of news agencies and possibilities of competitive service freely available to all users.

The Committee recommended that Samachar be dissolved and restructured by creation of two news agencies as 'Varta' and 'Sandesh'. These, in their turn, should jointly set up an organization for international news services which may be called 'News India': The News India will buy foreign agency services and make it available to subscribers of Varta and Sandesh. This whole set-up should be covered by an Act of Parliament.

While Varta was suggested as a news agency to organize and develop news services in Indian languages, along with an English news service, Sandesh was visualized as an exclusively English news agency. News India would not be a separate news agency as such, but would be financed and managed in partnership by the two agencies jointly. News India was to be a monopoly in foreign news. The Committee also recommended that an interim body be set up by the government to bring about the reorganization within a period of three months.

Two of the members, Mr. C.R. Irani and Mr. A.K. Sarkar, differed from the recommendations on the issue of proposed restructuring of news agencies. They suggested that Samachar should be split into two news agencies primarily in English language, since, in their view, the service is demanded in this language. These agencies should also be given back their previous names. As regards news services in Hindi and other Indian languages, these two agencies should be left free to develop them as they may consider best. They should also be free to organize international services separately on their own. They were opposed to granting a monopoly to News India in international news coverage.

For the services given by news agencies to All India Radio and Doordarshan, the Kuldip Nayar Committee recommended a formula of payment based on the number of radio and TV licences (Re. 1 per radio licence and Rs. 5 per TV licence).

The acceptance of Kuldip Nayar Committee report, it was argued by the critics, would create three monopoly news agencies-one each in the field of English language, Indian languages, and international news service. In fact, the critics said that each would be a monopoly in its field-News India in foreign news, Sandesh in English news at home, and Varta in Indian languages. There could hardly be any competition between Sandesh, because it will be only in English and therefore faster, and Varta in a number of languages and, therefore, will have to take to time-consuming translation at each major centre.

The set-up will not have the merit of competition. Also, if the government has to make up the budget deficit of Rs. 1.7 crores every year in respect of the proposed three agencies, the agencies would hardly enjoy any independence. As such, they would also not be self-supporting agencies. Thus, the objective of having news agencies 'completely independent of the government and are not given the right to monopoly' would not be fulfilled.

Some of the other important recommendations of the Committee on news agencies (Kuldip Nayar Committee) on the role and functions of news agencies in India are given below:

— Objectivity, adequacy, and independence are the three main attributes needed for the news agency system of the country.
— The news agency system should adequately cover all aspects of the country's life and not merely political events

and the news from urban areas. The rich milieu of contemporary Indian life should be fully reflected.

— Consequently, the dissemination of news by the agencies has to take place increasingly through the different Indian languages.

— Government must follow a self-denying policy of not interfering in any way with the work of news agencies.

— It is necessary that the news agency system also covers news which is not only outside the orbit of government functioning, but which may imply criticism of authority. It is essential in a democracy that dissent should get adequate coverage.

— The news agency system should not get identified with any vested interests: economic, social, communal or political.

— The news agencies should maintain a high standard of performance, which would itself be a protection against interference from outside sources, including government.

— News agencies, even during such situations as hostilities or international tensions and disputes, should strive to keep the people informed of the realities of the situation and not confine themselves only to the so-called popular view of events.

— Different techniques of internal checks and supervision, as well as evaluation of the news supplied to the subscribers, should be developed by news agencies in order to maintain a high standard of performance.

— Specialization should be developed in reporting system in terms of subject matter and styles of reporting. Expertise should also be promoted to achieve higher ranges of reporting, keeping in view new and modern techniques of writing.

— Programmes for professional training of the staff should be organised on an adequate scale. These should include training in managerial functions also.

— Since news-reporting is a creative activity, selection of

personnel should always be made strictly on merit, and there should be opportunities for promotion of talent.

— News-gathering and distribution is a necessary adjunct of modern society. No modern state can survive without an adequate set-up of information-collection and its judicious dissemination. The democratic society derives strength from wide-ranging debates on various issues before the community. A good news agency set-up should be capable of ensuring a continuous flow of information from and to people.

— An element of social responsibility in the building and functioning of a news agency system has to be recognised as a part of concept of freedom of press.

— A news agency system cannot by itself be the instrument of social change. However, when a community is in throes of social change, a news agency system, adhering to the principle of objectivity, has to cover or reflect the unfolding of such social change; and to that extent, as a medium of mass communication, it induces and supports the process of social change.

***News Agency or Agencies?*** The decision of the Government of India (14 November 1977) to split up Samachar and restore the status quo ante prior to four news agencies' so-called voluntary merger into Samachar on 24 January 1976 was criticised on the following grounds:

1. The decision indicates that the government has no responsibility, whatsoever, in the matter. It is argued that media should be treated as public utility and the government must frame its policy towards media as it has done in the case of science, technology and other subjects. In the name of freedom of press, government should not abdicate its responsibility in such an important matter.
2. In the name of competitive news agencies, there will be lot of duplication in respect of dissemination of news which the country, at this stage of development with meagre financial resources, can hardly afford.
3. For foreign news coverage, the country will have to depend

on foreign international news agencies with all its drawbacks such as poor coverage of Indian news, slanting, etc. Samachar had only five correspondents located in London, New York, Moscow, Kathmandu, and Colombo. It was proposed to appoint 25 more correspondents, particularly in South-East Asia, Latin America and other countries. This scheme would now become non-starter. The decision will also create difficulties in the functioning of non-aligned news agency pool.

4. The government decision is contrary to the Press Commission's recommendation that the news agencies should be converted into a public corporation under Parliamentary enactment.
5. Different news agencies will be more subject to the pressure of big newspapers and other vested interests. This will not be conducive to their proper functioning.
6. None of the news agencies will be viable as they will depend either on subsidy and/or support from the government or big business.
7. It will retard expansion of news agencies' network, both within the country and abroad, which is badly needed in the present stage of country's economic development.
8. The split will badly affect development of Hindi and other Indian language news services.
9. The employees of Samachar will be adversely affected in regard to their emoluments and other service conditions.
10. The country needs a national viable news agency, and Samachar could have been restructured so as to make it independent of government or other control. The leading newspapers could have set up their own competitive news agencies, if they so desired.
11. Competition is a misnomer as newspapers are free to publish or not to publish news items and reports from news agencies. Also, many newspapers have their own correspondents who can act as a check on one-sided news stories emanating from a single news agency.

A contrary view on the subject is held by equally eminent personalities in the newspaper profession. Their reasonings are as under:

1. The government's decision to split up Samachar is intended only to undo 'merger' of the erstwhile news agencies effected under duress during the Emergency. The decision is part of a larger commitment of the government to allow free and unfettered atmosphere for the functioning of all democratic institutions, including the news agencies. The Samachar was a product and a symbol of Emergency. As such, it was necessary to remove this aberration. The decision, however, does not rule out voluntary cooperation or coming together or merger of news agencies, if they so desire.
2. The question of resources is not a valid argument as Samachar, during its one year of existence, was given about Rs. 75 lakhs by the government. The merger of news agencies, therefore, did not result in viability.
3. The argument that Hindi and Indian language services would suffer with the revival of a number of news agencies is also not correct. They can certainly develop as a part of the main news agencies in the country. For instance, PTI and UNI can have effective Hindi and language wings. In any case, news agencies have to be based on actual demand of news from news enterprises, and not on any other considerations. The government has, however, announced that it would extend financial help for the development of news services in Indian languages.
4. It is true that wherever there is more than one news agency, it does result in certain amount of duplication in the dissemination of news. This is avoided in dictatorial and totalitarian countries where there is only one official news agency. Ours is a democratic society and we have to pay this price.
5. In 1954, the Press Commission recommended: "However objective a news agency strives to be, there are certain drawbacks which arise from monopoly, and which could

be obviated only by competitive service available freely to all users." The Government of India, on 22 July 1971, accepted this recommendation as evident from the reply to a question in the Rajya Sabha by the then Minister of Information and Broadcasting.

6. India is in the process of rapid economic development, and there is considerable scope for more than one news agency to develop. It is true that democratic countries such as the U.K. and France have only one news agency. Considering the area, population, geography, language and other factors there is ample scope and future for more than one news agency in India.
7. The basic criteria of news agency services in a democratic set-up are competition and independence. Effective competition is possible only if there is more than one agency. The agency cannot be independent if it is controlled financially or otherwise by the government or other vested interests. The payment for services rendered by the news agencies to TV and AIR is, however, a different matter. This is purely commercial transaction and not financial subsidy.
8. The decision to split Samachar is not going to affect India's participation in news agency pool of non-aligned countries. The agencies can participate individually or jointly through some cooperative arrangement in the pool, and the government has announced its willingness to consider giving financial help for this purpose. The projection of India's image abroad can perhaps be better done by independent news agencies rather than a single officially-sponsored news agency.
9. The Kuldip Nayar Committee had suggested that the government should pay subscription, under an automatic formula, at one rupee per licence of radio set and Rs. 5 per TV set. The collection should be shared between Varta and Sandesh. Since the government is committed to give AIR and Doordarshan an autonomous status, it is extremely doubtful if this formula finds acceptance by the proposed new corporation. The corporation may like to develop its own news-gathering sources.

10. The emoluments of Samachar employees are to be protected by the government through grants-in-aid on a tapering basis for a period of six years. In any case, this cannot be a justifiable argument for retaining one news agency.
11. The via media can be on the lines of French news agency. For the news supplied by the news agencies to official organs such as AIR, TV, government departments, External Affairs Ministry, the government can give matching grants to the agencies equivalent to their income from the non-official sources.

***Press Trust of India :*** The Press Trust of India was set up on 27th August, 1947, as a non-profit sharing cooperative of newspapers, with a mandate to provide economical, efficient and unbiased news service to all subscribers without discrimination. PTI took over the Associated Press of India (a news agency set up in 1908) and the Indian operations of the Reuters news agency and began functioning from 1st February, 1949.

Today PTI's news service in the English language grosses about 1,00,000 words per day. A network of 136 bureaus, a 350-strong journalist cadre, about 300 part-time correspondents, 11 bureaus and about 30 stringers abroad, a support staff of over 1,300 and arrangements with several transnational and national news agencies make up the backbone of this service.

The eighties have been years of modernization and diversification for PTI. As part of its modernization programme PTI's news operations were computerised in 1984. With the objective of delivering news reports faster PTI has now gone for high-speed electronic printers in place of 50-band electro-mechanical teleprinters. With a view to reach its services directly to the subscriber and also to overcome the various snags of the point-to-point transmission, PTI is now increasingly taking recourse to the satellite mode of dissemination through the INSAT satellite. The facility is already available in 14 cities across the country and receiver sets are proposed to be located in another 12 cities in 1990. The accent of PTI's modernization is an adaptation of the latest technology to suit the needs of PTI and its subscribers.

To help in the task of this modernization, PTI has created a separate R&D wing. In collaboration with the Madhya Pradesh State Electronics Development Corporation PTI has also set up a production facility in Bhopal. The facility, called the National Information Technologies Ltd., went on-line in 1988 and catering to PTI's needs of high-speed multilingual electronic printers, equipment for the satellite operations, and controllers for its 'News-Scan' and 'Comscan' services.

The process of diversification has seen PTI bringing out *Economic Service, Corporate Trends* and *Science Service* as fortnightly mailers, and weekly features in English and Hindi. A 'News-Scan' for display of news on video monitors was started in 1982. A 'Comscan' service of commercial news on video terminals has been in operation since late 1987. PTI has also integrated the major Indian stock exchanges in a simultaneous display of inter-market share prices on electronic boards. *India Perspectives,* a monthly in English, French and Spanish languages brought out by PTI's publication wing for the Ministry of External Affairs, has been received well among readers the world over.

This process of diversification has also seen the creation of 'Bhasha', a news service in Hindi language started in April 1986, and PTI-Photo, India's first wire photo service, began in October 1987. In early 1986 PTI also set up a television facility. PTI-TV has been producing news clips, documentaries and video films for Doordarshan and other clients.

PTI has plans to launch a news service in Marathi language on the lines of the Bhasha news service in Hindi. Also on the anvil is a 'Newsbank' facility through which PTI hopes to provide newspapers and other ready to use background material and current data on a variety of subjects.

PTI is a leading participant in the Pool of News Agencies of the Non-aligned countries and the Organization of Asia-Pack News Agencies (OANA). From March 1985 till July 1988 PTI was also the President of OANA. PTI is a major redistribution centre in the news exchange arrangements of both the Non-aligned News Pool and OANA.

Besides the news service in English with about 1,000 subscribers other major services provided by PTI are:

| | | |
|---|---|---|
| PTI Bhasha | — | News Service in Hindi and precursor to like services in other languages. |
| PTI News-Scan | — | Video screen display of news at airports, hotels and banks. |
| PTI Comscan | — | Video screen display of commercial news for banks and business houses. |
| PTI Features | — | Weekly mailer services in English, Hindi and on foreign developments. |
| PTI Economic, Corporate and Science Services | — | Fortnightly mailers. |
| PTI-Photo | — | The first wire photo service of the country. |
| PTI-TV | — | The television arm which services Doordarshan and does contract jobs. |
| PTI Stockscan | — | A national stock exchange network for display of share prices. |
| NITEL | — | A joint venture with MPSEDC for manufacture of communication-related equipment. |

The Bombay and Delhi office of Press Trust of India Limited are located at 357, Dadabhai Naoroji Road, Bombay-400001 and 4, Parliament Street, New Delhi-110001.

***United News of India :*** United News of India (UNI) was registered as a company on December 19, 1959. It started news operations on March 21, 1961. The agency was founded by newspapers themselves to promote competition between the country's two news agencies so that subscribers get the best out of both.

The first seven years from 1961 to 1967 were a period of consolidation. From 1968 started the growth phase. It celebrated its Silver Jubilee on March 21, 1986.

Since 1968, the agency's communication network has quadrupled. It now has one of the largest news agency teleprinter networks in the developing world.

The number of subscribers has increased sevenfold. At the end of March 1989, the agency was reaching more than 950 subscribers by teleprinter. These included a dozen in four Gulf countries, linked to UNI through an exclusive satellite channel.

The annual budget is now fourteen times bigger than in 1968. The work force has more than trebled.

The agency now operates from five times as many towns and cities as in 1968. The number now exceeds 300. UNI wires cover 100,000 words of copy daily by teleprinter.

The agency's pioneering Gulf news operations, launched in 1980, now cover UAE, Bahrain, Qatar and Kuwait. These will soon be extended to two more countries-Saudi Arabia and Oman. A UNI Arabic language news service is on the anvil.

In May 1982 UNI went bilingual when it launched its Hindi service-UNIVARTA. Today UNIVARTA dominates the news columns of Hindi newspapers in all the Hindi States, and even in places as far away as Bombay, Pune and Aurangabad. Cities covered were numbering 70.

UNI's foreign news comes mainly from Associated Press of America. AP has been collaborating with UNI from the very first day of start of operations. Another foreign collaborator since the agency's early days is DPA. UNI also has the collaboration arrangements with 15 other news agencies, including most of the Gulf agencies.

UNI's own correspondents ably supplement agency news coverage from abroad. Nepal was the first country where UNI posted a correspondent way back in 1968. Now foreign reports come from 22 UNI correspondents based in 20 countries in all the five continents.

The first UNI news messages went out on cycle to subscribers in New Delhi. This was on March 21, 1961. Today, UNI news reaches out to subscribers over a dedicated teleprinter network stretching over 90,000 kilometres, linking more than 100 towns and cities of India.

UNI was the first news agency in India to go on to satellite communication. The Bombay-New York satellite channel was commissioned on June 6, 1979 for reception of the AP service. An exclusive UNI Bombay-Dubai channel was commissioned on April 1, 1981.

Growth in UNI has been both vertical and horizontal; growth has come through launching of a number of sister services which besides yielding welcome additional revenue have taken the agency into new area in which it can make itself useful. With 430 newspaper subscribers in the languages, UNI commands a readership of 60 million daily.

UNI was the first news agency to launch National Photo Service, Stock Exchange Service and Financial Service. It is now planning to launch Urdu service on teleprinter for the first time in the world.

It was also the first news agency to earn Foreign Exchange for the country by selling news abroad-gulf countries and Singapore by satellite channel.

UNI is going ahead with its modernization plans including computerisation of its new operations. The electro-mechanical, slow speed teleprinters are being replaced by bi-lingual Electronic noiseless teleprinters.

UNI has many "Sister Services"; these have helped widening the circle of clients the agency can serve:

| | |
|---|---|
| UNIDARSHAN | — News clips and Features for Doordarshan. |
| World TV News in Colour | — News Display on Colour TV sets in hotels. |
| UNICON | — UNI Economic Service-mailers, twice a week. |
| LINEN | — UNI Energy News Service-twice a week. |

| | | |
|---|---|---|
| Agriculture Service | — | UNI Agriculture Service in English and Gujarati-Weekly. |
| Backgrounder | — | UNI Backgrounder Service on a topical subject every week in English and Hindi. |
| UNI Features | — | News Features in English-twice a week. |

UNI plans to launch News Feature Service and the Agriculture Service in Hindi in the near future.

The United News of India is located at 9, Rafi Marg, New Delhi.

***Other Indian News and Feature Agencies***

***Cartographic News Service:*** 13, Todermal Lane, New Delhi-1; Ph. 3311010; Estd. 1958. Specializes in news maps, charts and map features.

***Data News Features:*** Burman Bldg. Gunfoundy, Hyderabad-1; Ph. 231520. Two features a week on Andhra Pradesh in English and Telugu, a fortnightly reference periodical *Data Andhra Pradesh* and *Andhra Pradesh Year Book.*

***India News and Feature Alliance (INFA):*** Jeevan Deep, Sansad Marg, New Delhi-1; Ph. 343330; Estd. Nov. 14, 1959 by Durga Das; News-cum-feature agency. Basic feature service of one article a day in English and Hindi. Also offers a Sunday Magazine Service, State and Foreign Newsletter Service, a news service comprising scoops and off-beat items, three features a week in regional languages.

***India Press Agency (IPA):*** F-24, Bhagat Singh Market, New Delhi-1; Estd. Feb. 1957. Specialising in background and interpretative news coverage, *Industrial Relations Letter* (Wky), Agriculture Review (Fortly), daily Hindi Service *Samvad.*

***National News Service:*** PB 1103, Coronation Bldg., Chandni Chowk, Delhi-6, Ph. 2529693. Multilingual News Service, covers commercial, financial topics; agricultural, industrial markets; maps, graphs on current subjects.

***News Features of India:*** Aminabad Park, Lucknow-18; Ph. 47601; Estd. 1953. Run on cooperative basis, specialises in news and photo features.

## News Agencies Abroad

According to the UNESCO Report on World Communications (1975), there are news agencies in 90 sovereign countries but some 40 countries have none; these include 25 countries with a population of more than one million. News agencies are directly controlled by the state in 50 of these 90 countries; in 40 others, the agencies are cooperatively owned and run by the newspapers and the media. In many of these countries, even where the agencies ostensibly are autonomous corporations due to their political set-up, the state casts a long shadow on the news agencies. By virtue of the size of their operations, their financial and technological strength, five world news agencies are breathing down the shoulders of the rest. These are the Associated Press of America, Reuters, Agence France-Presse, Tass and the United Press International.

A few important foreign agencies are accredited to the Government of India:

1. Associated Press of America (U.S.A.)
2. Reuters (U.K.)
3. Tass (U.S.S.R.)
4. Agence France-Presse (France)
5. United Press International (U.S.A.)
6. Kyodo (Japan)
7. Deutsche Presse-Agentur (Federal Republic of Germany)
8. Ansa (Italy)
9. Central News Agency of China
10. Tanjug Yugoslav Press Agency (Yugoslavia)
11. Polish Press Agency (Poland)
12. Iraqi News Agency (Baghdad)
13. Bangladesh Sangbad (Dacca)
14. Novosty Press Agency (U.S.S.R.)
15. Depth News Asia Manila (Philippines) Non-aligned News Agency 'Pool'

While Indian press is fed by a large volume of foreign news, India has not been able to sell any news abroad, not even in the countries of Asia, Africa, West Indies, etc., where there is a great deal of interest in Indian affairs and events.

There is considerable potential for exporting Indian news to foreign countries, but this perhaps could not be done in the past because the news agencies lacked the necessary facilities. PTI had a few correspondents while UNI had none. Samachar had five correspondents abroad. India, therefore, receives world news through English, American, French or Russian news agencies. There is also no separate international news service which can procure world news for the country's press and disseminate Indian news to the world press.

The non-aligned countries, numbering about 100 and comprising almost entirely the less developed regions of the world, felt concerned with the media situation. 70% of the world population lives in Asia, Africa and Latin America but only 26% of world's daily newspapers are bought in these regions. Again, 70% of the news, served by transnational news agencies, is about the industrialized west. The conference of Foreign Ministers of non-aligned countries, held in Lima in August 1975, decided that a constitution for the news agency pool of non-aligned countries should be framed. A special conference for this purpose was held at New Delhi in July 1976 in which Information Ministers and representatives of news agencies from 62 countries participated. The decisions were ratified at the Summit Conference of non-aligned countries at Colombo in August 1976.

The conference, held at New Delhi, prepared a broad constitution for the News Agency Pool. The underlying principles were:

1. The aim is not to restrict but to supplement and expand the existing flow of news.
2. The pool is not to acquire hard contours and become a supranational news agency; the pool would imply a set of arrangements.
3. Following from the above, there would be no need for the pool to have either a secretariat or fixed headquarters.
4. The utilization of the wordage, received by an agency, would be fully within its discretion.

Before the initiation of the non-aligned pool idea, Samachar relied, for the bulk of its international news, on Reuter (U K), AP (USA) and AFP (France). In addition, it had bilateral agreements with 12 news agencies. Out of these, five were from non-aligned countries.

## The Pool

After the conference, held at New Delhi in July 1976, and subsequent acceptance of the news agency pool scheme, Samachar finalized 'arrangements', for the exchange of news, with 16 news agencies of the non-aligned world. As such, arrangements existed with a total of 28 news agencies including 21 from non-aligned countries. The other seven agencies are from the USSR, Poland, Czechoslovakia, Japan, Romania and Italy.

The arrangements visualized a two-way flow of news, on a selective basis, between Samachar and these agencies. The exchange of news between Samachar and a number of national news agencies in the non-aligned world began on 3 August 1976. Samachar provided 300 to 400 words a day to each of its pool partners, comprising therein four or five news items drawn from its domestic files, as also despatches from its own staff overseas. To most of these agencies, Samachar provided news by international telex. Samachar and Bangladesh, however, exchanged news on their jointly-leased teleprinter link between Calcutta and Dacca, while Sri Lanka Broadcasting Corporation received news from Samachar over Samachar's Madras-Colombo teleprinter link. Samachar exchanged news with RSS of Nepal by telegram to and from Kathmandu. Consequent on the winding up of Samachar, PTI has taken over this work. The other three agencies are also likely to participate in the pool.

The non-aligned news pool is a self-paying project in the sense that the sender of the news pays the cost of the transmission. There is no special investment involved on staff or central headquarters. The recipient is also free not to use the news material received, if he decides that it is unsuitable for circulation among his constituent newspapers.

The present scale of expenditure over news pool arrangement is about Rs.30 lakhs a year. The expenditure to be incurred by India is about one lakh per month-Rs. 85,000 on news on telex and Rs. 15,000 on other items.

The non-aligned countries met for the first time at the level of Information Ministers in July 1976 at New Delhi, and in a declaration took note of "the persistent and serious imbalance in the current global information situation" and its adverse effects on the non-aligned countries, stressed the need "to liberate their information and mass media" from the colonial legacy, and expressed their collective determination to rectify this situation. The declaration called for "the decolonisation of information" and "the establishment of a new international order for information", which was felt, to be "as necessary as the new economic order". To give practical shape to this, the Non-Aligned News Agency Pool was set up on 13 July 1976. The News Agency Pool of the Non-Aligned countries is a system of news exchange based on professional cooperation, equality and coordination among the pool partners.

India, which played a leading role in the formation of the Pool, was elected the first Chairman of the Coordinating Committee from July 1976 to November 1979. India was elected a member of the Pool's Coordinating Committee at its Third General Conference, held in Tunis in November 1982, and re-elected at the Fourth General Conference, held in Havana in March 1986. India participated in the last Coordination Committee Meeting held at Lima (Peru) in August 1987.

The Press Trust of India operates India News Pool Desk of the Non-aligned News Agency Pool. India is currently having direct communication link with Belgrade, Djakarta, Bahrain, Havana, Colombo, Hanoi, Kuala Lumpur, Tunis, London, Harare and, Baghdad through satellite; with Kathmandu, Dhaka and Islamabad through terrestrial link; and with Kabul through radiobeam service.

***Arguments against the 'Pool' :*** Non-aligned news pool has potential to develop into a good instrument of inter-governmental cooperation, particularly in the economic and social fields, but it is argued that it is no substitute for a foreign news agency. According to critics, it is a pool of official publicity material or exchange of government handouts as most of the pool partners and the agencies disseminating the news are not free from official control. They suppress dissent as a matter of course. The non-aligned pool countries are mostly non-democracies (dictatorships, governments of monolithic parties or oligarchies), and as such the agencies have no free hand in the selection of news items. The pool arrangement is at best an investment in international cooperation and-not in any foreign news service. In fact, critics point out that the Press Attaches of the concerned Embassies/ High Commissions çan also undertake this type of work-exchange of official news. Other constraints in the rapid growth of the news pool are non-existence of even a daily newspaper in some of the non-aligned countries, and lack of technological resources and skilled manpower to man the pool. Mr. S.M. Mulgaokar, Editor-in-Chief, *Indian Express,* is of the view that in non-aligned news agency pool "no thought has been given to ensuring objectivity and credibility. Indeed, these are qualities which the non-aligned news agency pool has specifically rejected as irrelevant. Each country in the pool is responsible for gathering news within its borders, and contributing to the pool what it considers fit for dissemination to the outside world. This amounts to acceptance of the totalitarian conception of information as an instrument of state policy, since in most countries in the non-aligned block such national news agencies as do exist are controlled by the government.

Another veteran journalist, Mr. A.S. Abraham is apprehensive of the utility of non-aligned news pool. According to him, the theoretical justification for the pool is sound. Western media, to a large extent, determine not only how non-western countries see the world but often even how they see themselves. Western media do monopolise the flow of information and that monopoly must end.

Mr. Abraham is of the view that this can and must be achieved only by the media in non-western states functioning no less efficiently than what the western media do now. In precise terms, they must aim to be as independent, as fearless, as investigative and as committed to the truth as the western media, by and large, are. If this requires more and better equipment, greater professionalism, more effective training schemes, more liberal publishing laws, cheaper newsprint and transmission rates, then that is what UNESCO should, by promoting worldwide cooperative endeavour in these areas, seek to make these available.

Commenting on the role of media in a democratic set-up, Mr. Abraham says that there can be no compromise on, no dishonesty about, the basic assumption that the media in any truly open society cannot be an appendage of the state. No news pool, non-aligned or otherwise, will achieve parity with western media by propagating state-manipulated information. It is sometimes said that while for western media news means events, for those in the poor world concerned with development, news is a process. Consequently, the argument runs, they cannot assume the adversary relationship with their governments that western media have with theirs. This position is not correct. As for news being an event or a process, reporting or commenting on it in any form can be truthful (and so possibly inconvenient to authority) or expedient (and so always acceptable to authority). It is not as if reporting a process, as against an event, automatically eliminates the choice between truth and the suppression of truth.

***In Defence of the 'Pool' :*** The supporters of the pool argue that in any case it is a good start towards the exchange of direct information among the non-aligned countries. The objective is to supplement and not to supplant the existing transnational news agencies. The idea is to create better direct awareness among the members. There is no intention to have any confrontation with multi-national or global news agencies which have vast resources and superior technology enabling them to land their news in any part of the world at top speed and at a throwaway cost. The pool is not an inward-looking closed circuit system of information. It is only an attempt at greater flow of information among the non-aligned countries. The receiving countries are free to discard any item. The experience has been that while political items are not used much, economic and social news is disseminated more or less freely.

According to Mr. D.R. Mankekar, Chairman, Coordinating Committee of the Non-Aligned News Agency Pool, the four western news agencies, namely, Associated Press and United Press International of USA, Reuter of Britain and Agence France-Presse of France hold the monopoly of world news. The news sent out about the developing countries by these transnational agencies gives a prejudicial image of the developing countries. The developing countries hardly get any regional news, and the world news received by them is qualitatively as well as quantitatively western in content and character. This is understandable as these agencies primarily gather, compose and edit news for their home markets. The newspaper readers in developing countries often find such news out of tune and irrelevant or unsympathetic and woefully inadequate or prejudicial and mischievous.

Mr. Mankekar is of the view that the non-aligned news pool is an attempt to remedy this evil with their own efforts, through system of pooling their news resources and exchanging regional news of interest to non-aligned and developing countries. The non-aligned news pool is an important step to correct certain imbalances, deficiencies or communication gaps in the field of information in the developing world. The 'imbalances', according to Mr. Mankekar, are of three kinds namely: (i) 'Inward file', that is in respect of content, quality and to some extent volume of news received by the developing countries from the outside world through western news agencies. The quality and content of news received at times is destructive and irrelevant, if not harmful; (ii) 'Lack of flow of news' within a region, between neighbouring developing countries. Even when western news agencies cover regional news from developing countries, the story is of western angle and out of tune with the requirements' of the region; (iii). `Outward file', that is news transmitted to the outside world from developing countries by the western news agencies. It is often distorted, prejudicial or frivolous. News is seen through unsympathetic western eyes, and written, edited and selected to cater primarily for the needs of their home markets.

Mr. Mankekar is of the view that while it is true that non-aligned nations are distributed over four continents, in varying stages of development, all of them do not command competence and skills in equal degree, but collectively they certainly have the professional competence and organisational skills to operate the news pool. Also, the argument that several of the non-aligned countries have authoritarian rule and have no independent news agencies and, therefore, the news put out by the non-aligned news pool is packed with official propaganda should not stand in the way of the developing countries to set up national news agencies. The agencies can be converted, in course of time, as independent entities. In any case, some beginning has to be made and this is what news pool seeks to achieve. "Let there be a national news agency first. Credibility will come later. It is of slow growth. Rome was not built in a day, nor Reuter or A.P."

It is particularly in the sphere of regional exchange of news that the non-aligned news pool can play a vital part. The western agencies do not consider it worthwhile or viable to gather and distribute the regional type of news because their home markets are not interested in it. The pool can also deal effectively with developmental news, socio-economic reform, agricultural and industrial progress, cultural activities and news of human interest. The content and angle of news received from western agencies by the non-aligned world can also be rectified, if non-aligned news agencies can expand their corps of foreign correspondents.

Since the news pool service is of a supplementary character, and it is not intended to compete with transnational media in technical efficiency and speed of transmission, the news pool has generally to step off spot news. It should, on the other hand, look for exclusive stories and concentrate on news on economic, commerce, developmental, cultural and human interest relating to agriculture and land reforms, trade and commerce, industrial progress, etc. These should take the form of news features, special articles, situationers, and backgrounders.

The news stories received from the pool, disseminated by national news agencies, can be given credit line of the pool and the country from which it has originated, so as to make it clear about the origin of the news story. Most of such material is bound to be somewhat lengthy in wordage and would not be affected by the time element, and, therefore, could with advantage depend on air mail for their transmission, reserving the expensive electronic transmission channels for important spot political stories of special interest to the developing countries.

The actual experience of handling of non-aligned news pool by India is that basically it is a news service of economic, developmental, cultural and human interest. The high cost of transmission is a serious bottleneck. An effort is being made, by the coordination committee of the non-aligned news pool, to get appreciable concession in cable transmission rates on the analogy of pre-Second World War 'penny a word' British Commonwealth cable rate. Also, the financial burden of international effort of this kind, aimed at bringing closer the non-aligned nations scattered over four continents in goodwill and understanding, through exchange of news and information cannot be borne by the news agencies themselves. As such, the participating governments have to foot the bill.

The non-aligned news pool which has already become operational and the proposed Asian News Exchange network, backed and sponsored by UNESCO, and other similar ventures are expected to remove the imbalances, deficiencies now prevailing in the news system in the developing countries. In the words of Mr. Mankekar, the developing nations need a free and balanced flow of news, and not 'free flow one way' of news by the western media.

## India's Status

While it is necessary to project country's balanced picture across the world, it is extremely doubtful that this can be achieved by any official or officially-sponsored international news agency. It is well-known that responsible newspapers think several times before accepting any material emanating from government-sponsored agencies. It is automatically considered propaganda stuff. In India also, no newspaper worth the name accepts material at face value sent out by USIS or TASS agencies.

Newspapers everywhere give priority to national news and for the limited space left, after national news has been accommodated, over 100 foreign countries compete. Each can, at best, hope to get attention only for news of the widest readers' interest. It is therefore, clear that government-sponsored agencies, by whatever name they may be called, are not at all suitable for giving out Indian news to the foreign newspapers.

News material has a slightly better chance of acceptance if it is given out by independent news agencies like the Press Trust of India or the United News of India. It will be more effective if these agencies are encouraged and given facilities to expand their operation overseas. The setting up of an official international news agency is of little help. Even for PTI and UNI, it will take quite some time before they are able to make any impact on foreign newspapers.

The best way, however, to get into foreign information media is through their representatives functioning in our country. Newspapers, radio and television media, all prefer to get their impressions of foreign countries through their own representatives and their own nationals. The foreign correspondents, therefore, constitute the best channel through which a balanced picture of India can be projected. It is they who write in depth about the country and not the news agencies which generally confine themselves to spot news. The evaluations of foreign correspondents are readily accepted by their principals. The foreign correspondents should be, therefore, provided all facilities to observe, understand, and write anything they like and in the way they wish to write. We are an open society, and if some foreign observer takes a slanted view we need not get upset or lose our balance.

## Other Important Sources

News agencies-Indian and foreign-are no doubt major sources of news for newspapers and other media. Some of the other sources are: news media's own reporters, correspondents and special representatives; monitored broadcasts of different radio stations; publicity material from government departments, business houses, embassies, political parties, trade unions; reports of committees and commissions; and other material emanating from educational, scientific and learned institutions, including research papers and evaluation studies.

During the war the Associated Press lent itself as freely to the uses of the government for propaganda purposes as did the corresponding services in England, France, Germany, and Italy to their governments. Even before we entered the war it carried the wholesale falsifications of the late John R. Rathom of the Providence journal, whose romancing finally became even too vivid for the United States government to brook. It was responsible for a wickedly cruel and false report of a speech made by Senator La Follette in which he was made to say that we had no quarrel with the

Germans over the sinking of the Lusitania, when he said precisely the opposite. No other alleged quotation from his lips did so much harm to this brave and patriotic American citizen, whose statue now stands with those of the greatest men of our public life in Statuary Hall in the Capitol at Washington. Not until years later was this wrong corrected on the initiative of the writer of this article. During the years prior to our entrance into the war the A.P. quite failed to obey the injunction of President Wilson to be neutral in thought and deed—an exception to its rule always to obey authority.

As for Russia, the Associated Press always knows well where its duty to God and our country lies. In the early days of the Bolshevik government the Associated Press was as eager as the *New York Times* to grab any absurd rumor and spread it abroad. It still believes in the high news standards of its service, but can it look back with anything but shame on some of its Russian reports? Thus, in April, 1918, it overthrew the Bolsheviks and reestablished the old regime under the Grand Duke Alexis. In August it had Lenin and Trotzky running hand in hand to Kronstadt for safety. On the eighteenth of that month it kindly allowed the Germans to seize Kronstadt. On September 1 it reported Lenin as back and in charge, for it announced that he had been shot by a girl.

The next day he died, only to be resurrected by the Associated Press, for three days later he had a relapse—to see Petrograd revolting and peasants "storming the city" a few days later. On October 17 poor Lenin was shot again. In December he was about to flee to Sweden; before he could make his getaway, doubtless at the instigation of the Associated Press, he was arrested on January 9 by Trotzky himself and imprisoned in the Kremlin. Fortunately the Associated Press was soon triumphantly able to report that he had escaped to Barcelona; a couple of days later he had buried the hatchet and was making speeches with Trotzky in Moscow. All of which is delightful romancing, but hardly worthy of a service which believes that its reports are the most accurate and reliable and unbiased in the world. If its news from Moscow has now steadied down, it is in no wise as valuable as that sent by Walter Duranty to the *New York Times*.

Now such things happen during the hysteria of war time, or

of events leading up to war. But the continuance of the policy of playing the game of the men who are temporarily delegated to run our government at Washington, and of letting them give out their propaganda anonymously, is just a little bit too much for journalists to stand who believe in fair play and professional ethics. Yet the practice goes on, and not only in the purlieus of our Capital, as witness the fact that during a large part of the American occupation of Haiti the Associated Press has been represented in that island by an officer of the Marine Corps, just as if this officer were in a position to report freely and frankly the Haitian criticisms of the Occupation, of which the Associated Press correspondent was an official and uniformed member, or the acts of his superiors. If the revelations of the justified Haitian criticisms of our occupation, which led President Hoover's commission to that island to reverse our policy there, came as a surprise to the American people it must be in large part due to the fact that the Associated Press has had a marine officer as its correspondent.

It is only just to add that when trouble broke out there the Associated Press immediately rushed to the island a civilian correspondent, and that it did its utmost to bring out the truth about the Aux Cayes massacre. But no amount of good intentions or actual honorable achievement in a crisis can atone for the fact that during periods of quiet the only news source of the Associated Press in Haiti was an officer of marines. For it was in the quiet periods that those policies were formulated which so aroused the population of Haiti against us that there would have been worse bloodshed than ever had not the commission fortunately intervened just when it did. Nor is the excuse that the Associated Press could not afford to maintain a special correspondent in Haiti a valid one. It maintains correspondents at places far less important than Haiti, especially if one considers that what we did in Haiti aroused the bitterest indignation against us in every Central and South American country, to our financial as well as moral cost as a nation. As I write, it is about to begin a service of "comic strips" to its members. This it can finance; but it was unable to raise the money needed to insure a fair and accurate report of a situation which to all South Americans was a touchstone of our national good faith and of our honourable intentions toward all of Latin America. Unfortunately, in Nicaragua, in Mexico, and in our other extra-territorial ventures the Associated Press invariably regards every situation through the spectacles offered to it by our officialdom.

Here, as has been said, is the greatest weakness and the greatest danger of the Associated Press. I find myself far less interested in the decay of the character and quality of the news service, which has deeply stirred other critics of the service, notably Mr. Dewey M. Owens in the *American Mercury* for April, 1927. It is true, however, that Melville E. Stone must be turning in his grave if he is aware of the kind of sob stuff that is now appearing in the Associated Press reports—banal and bathetic stuff of the kind to shame a college sophomore despite the fact that the rules of the A.P. urge "a simple narrative style" and deprecate fine writing. Here are two examples quoted by Mr. Owens:

> Death advanced and beckoned for the last time. The tired, worn-out man drew a long breath, there was a slight flutter of the eyelids, an almost imperceptible twitch of the nostrils.

Woodrow Wilson's soul had drifted out on the great dark tide that runs around the world.

Outside a sickly sun broke through a cloudbank. A little native warbler, a pilgrim venturing forth in search of early spring and sun, stopped for a moment and from his twig aloft twittered a happy note. Almost at that moment Mr. Wilson was passing out. Luther Burbank, withered by age, died here early today amid the flowering fruits and blooms he had created for the benefit of mankind.

The noted horticulturist passed on to the great adventure of a hereafter in which he had no faith. Only a few weeks before the end he had declared that he could not believe in a life after death.

And as life ebbed away and he stood on the brink he did not falter in his conviction.

If this is the sort of stuff the 1,250 members of the Associated Press want how can we expect to find anything else, seeing that we are dealing with a cooperative news service? Mr. Kent Cooper, the present able general manager, who rose from the ranks and represents an entirely new school from that of Melville E. Stone, has to face an intense, rapidly growing, and successful competition from the virile and liberal United Press. He has broken with tradition after tradition of the service—the comic strips are his latest venture. So the Associated Press has long since abandoned its original conception of being a service devoted exclusively to the gathering of news; it is now engaged in the merchandising of purely amusement features. Side by side with a vast deal of really admirable and altogether praiseworthy reporting of the vital happenings of the world, a great deal of it well, soberly, and accurately written, it disseminates a line of trivial and often nauseating human-interest stories wholly devoid of any news value. I append two of them which I clipped from the first page of Mr. Noyes's worthy *Evening Star* on January 18, 1930, when I happened to be in the capital:

***By the Associated Press***

Waukegan, Ill., January 18.—Trixie, George Van Valkenberg's police dog, isn't dead after all. She's sick, but the doctor says she'll be all right. Several days ago Trixie's master arranged to put her out of her misery via chloroform. Afterwards he took Trixie to the garage to await suitable burial weather.

Yesterday the grave was dug, and Van Valkenberg went to the garage to get Trixie. From her blanket shroud the dog scrambled up and ran to her master.

***By the Associated Press***

Chicago, January 19.—Animals, real and imaginary, have driven Mrs. Sophie Seidler to seek a divorce from Walter.

She says her husband imagined the existence of pink elephants and wiggly snakes, and that they annoyed him dreadfully. In an effort to get rid of them, his wife asserts, he got real animals and took them to bed with him. One night he would come with a cat, another night a dog, and sometimes with a rabbit, a pigeon, or a chicken.

Mrs. Seidler told of a strange pastime favored by her spouse. When funds for beverage purposes were scant, she charged, he would run around and around the room in circles until he got dizzy.

She wants, besides a divorce, custody of their child.

The purpose of this sort of thing is, of course, to help publishers to sell their "stuff" by "brightening up" their numerous pages. Here let us recall that in his memoirs, "Fifty Years a Journalist," Melville

E. Stone declared that "the Associated Press is writing the real and enduring history of the world, and is not chronicling the trivial episodies, the scandal, and the chit-chat"! Plainly Mr. Cooper has no use for such sentiments. Other times, other morals! The amazing part of it remains that this descent to coarse vulgarity and trivial banality is the work of an organization which has no private-profit motive. It is what one might have expected of Hearst, but never of the men who fell heir to the Associated Press which was founded in its modern form in 1893 with such high hopes, such high standards, and such a sense of responsibility to the American public and to their profession that the founders never could have stooped in any such way to conquer large circulations.

The fact is, however, that the newspaper profession in America has changed in our time from a profession to a business—a purely money-making affair in which the professional aspect has disappeared in all but a few of the dailies of the country. They are being affected by the great economic currents that are hourly producing greater and greater aggregations of capital, larger and larger financial and economic and industrial units. The newspaper owner, as I have so often pointed out, is caught in the vicious circle of steadily rising costs, steadily increasing competition, and the demand for larger and larger circulations and more and more advertising. To the great merchants of the newspaper world the Associated Press is delivering the goods. Why all this tiresome nonsense about ideals and standards in its journalism? The Associated Press is what its members are willing that Mr. Noyes and Mr. Ochs and Mr. Cooper shall make it. They have much to be proud of, can boast of many fine things done, and have many admirable personal achievements to cite in reply to their critics. What does the rest matter as long as Cyrus H. K. Curtis and William Randolph Hearst and our other newspaper barons are content, and Washington officialdom finds their society wholly congenial? Let only those who are chronic fault-finders dwell upon the curious fact that it is the cooperative non-profit-making service which is illiberal and is so rapidly lowering its standards, and that it is the money-making United Press which has wide human sympathies and considerable idealism.

***The United Press :*** In the history of the Associated Press the

Year 1929 will surely rank with 1914 as one of the darkest of all. For it was during this period that a dreadful blow descended. Incredible as it seems, the *New York Herald Tribune* and the Chicago *Daily News* subscribed to the news service of the United Press. If Mr. Hoover were to hoist the red flag on the White House some morning and Secretary Mellon were to denounce the right to hold private property, the Associated Press would surely not be more startled. The *Herald Tribune* blazoned forth its treachery in full-page advertisements. And the Chicago heresy must have been particularly distressing, for the *Daily News* was the organ of the late Victor F. Lawson, one of the men who took the lead in founding the Associated Press, of which he was for years the most powerful director.

What is this United Press that is fluttering the dovecotes of the Associated Press in such an agonizing way? It is a purely mercantile undertaking designed to make money, and it has been doing just that for the past twenty years. By its aggressiveness and enterprise it has built up a clientele of 1,250 papers—as large as that of the Associated Press—with this difference, that only 900 are in the United States while 350 are outside our boundaries. The United Press was founded originally to supply news only to evening papers. Ten years ago it enlarged its service to include morning papers, though the bulk of its clients are still evening newspapers. Within the past twelve months it has added no less than sixty-nine dailies to its list, some of them extremely important, such as the Philadelphia *Record*, the Houston *Post-Dispatch*, the Louisville *Times*, the Wheeling *News*, the Mobile *Press*, and the Springfield, (Mo.) *Press*. With two such dailies as the New York *Herald Tribune* and the Chicago *Daily News* surrendering to the charms of its service, the United Press may well look forward to capturing many other Associated Press strongholds. Indeed, one may even ask whether the competition of the Associated Press and the United Press will not eventually be within the pages of all leading dailies, instead of, as at first, between two groups of dailies each taking one service only.

The United Press lacks every one of the cooperative features which distinguish its great rival, the A.P. It reports news for purposes of sale only. Its members have no more control over it than the subscribers to a circulating library have over its management. In either case, the subscribers can give up the service if it is not up to the standard desired; they have no other direct way of modifying its policies. Whether this is or is not an effective veto every journalist will judge for himself. The members of the United Press are never even called into its councils. Whereas the Associated Press is what its directors and members wish it to be the United Press is today what Robert Paine Scripps, Karl Bickel, Roy Howard, and their immediate associates say it shall be. Mr. Scripps is the controlling owner. In practice the management rests with Mr. Bickel, James H. Furay, Hugh Baillie, Robert J. Bender, James I. Miller, and the other United Press executives, all of them part owners. To them belongs the credit for its good features and to them the blame for its weaknesses. They say for what and how the $6,000,000 disbursed each year for the gathering and distribution of news shall be expended. They do not pretend that theirs is a public-spirited enterprise; on the contrary, they constantly declare that it is just another commercial, profit-seeking institution. They rarely speak of themselves as journalists, but usually as businessmen. With equal frankness they declare that the United Press has no policies of any kind and no desires save "to present to its clients throughout the world a world-wide service of news, objective and impartial, without prejudice of any kind, national, sectional, economic, social, or religious."

Theoretically, then, the organization of the Associated Press is, as I have already pointed out, far superior to that of the privately owned United Press. Yet the latter happens to be the more liberal agency for gathering news, happens to have much more sympathy for the under-dog, happens to be far less sensitive to the great capitalistic press influences which gather around the directors' table of the Associated Press. This is purely accidental, for it was only by chance that the United Press was founded by the late E. W. Scripps, who was opposed to a monopoly in news and faced American problems from the good, old-fashioned liberal point of view. Nor is there any guarantee in the form of its organization that twenty-five or fifty years from now, when the present managers and owners have passed from the scene, the United Press will not be an entirely different affair run with a totally different spirit.

For the steady progress of the United Press there are several explanations. In the first place, no one can question the unusual ability of Roy Howard and Karl Bickel. They have been fortunate in having the complete confidence and the unlimited financial backing of the Scripps family with their liberal point of view, which is also the actuating spirit of the twenty-five Scripps-Howard newspapers. They were untrammeled by conventions. The very fact that they were the dictators of the organization made it possible for them to go ahead rapidly without first having to consult the heads of a number of their member dailies. They could snap their fingers at any dissenter. In order to establish their service they had to avail themselves of every new device and to think up new ways of getting their news cheaply and quickly. Thus, they were first to utilize the facilities of the American Telephone and Telegraph Company for telegraphic news transmission. Mr. Bickel boasts that it was the United Press which first developed the use of the telephone for the transmission of a "pony" (i.e., small) news report; this made it possible to provide a larger service than by telegraph and for less money.

It was the United Press which first extensively used the printer-telegraph machine, operating extensive circuits without any operator attendant on a one-way basis—something that had been said to be impossible. It was quick to welcome the radio, in which it saw not a competitor, but a valuable ally, and it lays the unction to its soul that its use of a national hook-up on the occasion of the general election in 1924 brought about the final acceptance by its rivals of the radio as a necessary adjunct of any news service. Mr. Bickel himself attributes the remarkable expansion of its world service to the fact that it has not belonged to the so-called "official-agency" group, and that it has always been free from nationalistic bias. This may have been accidental; that is, if the Associated Press had not already been linked up with Reuter, Havas, and the other official or semi-official foreign agencies, the United Press might have been happy to make use of their services. But undoubtedly it was a blessing both for the United Press and for the general public that it had to be independent. There are only a couple of exceptions to this rule. It has a connection with the Nippon Dempo Tsushin Sha, the largest agency in Japan, and a slight one with the Australian Press Association. It covers Japan, however, with its own separate correspondents as well. There is a widely held belief that in South and Central America the United Press has done much to improve our relations with our southern neighbours and has gone out of its way to do so.

At home the United Press collects its news not from member newspapers, as does the Associated Press, but by means of correspondents appointed in various localities. Its officers, of course, believe that this is a better system; that it does not place them at the mercy of the news standards and facilities of their members. On the other hand, it places upon the United Press a very heavy responsibility in picking its representatives. Most of them are paid only for what they send in. In the South, for example, their representatives are just as much subject to local prejudices as are the representatives of the Associated Press. The United Press, however, can change its correspondents as rapidly as it pleases, and its officers are bound to realize that the quality and reliability of their service depend upon the care taken in the selection of their local representatives. In Haiti, by the way, the United Press also chose an American officer as its correspondent but mitigated the offense by using a Haitian too.

It would be ridiculous, of course, to assert that the United Press service has been all that it ought to be. It has suffered from growing pains, from the errors made in the building up of a new organization, and there have been big gaps in the territory it has tried to cover. One who was for years a trusted United Press representative abroad is of the opinion that its sense of values has not always been of the best, for the reason that it is an attacking organization, whereas the Associated Press has been entrenched in its position. He adds this in explanation:

> The A. P. can take aim before firing, but the U. P. must be quick on the trigger and must sometimes fire from the hip. I think this explains why the U. P. occasionally fires a whole broadside at a fleeting target and lays down a barrage on subjects not worth a pot shot. It is apt to be more interested in providing entertainment than instruction, in surprising rather than in being profound. I suspect that sometimes it chooses not to

> verify a good story too exactly, lest it [the story] should blow up and disappear.

It is interesting to note his belief that since it is the more commercially minded the U. P. feels more responsibility toward its client newspapers than toward the ultimate public. He adds that if he were a publisher he would prefer the U. P. service, but if he were a careful and thoughtful reader of newspapers he would prefer the Associated Press because its news, though sometimes slower, would probably be more thoughtfully prepared. There, he declares, are not unfriendly observations: "I got a great kick out of working for the U. P. I am enthusiastic about it, its people, and its purposes, and I think it is a most necessary and precious stimulant to the A. P." It seems as if the case could hardly be stated better.

I find, however, other criticisms from worth-while sources. One is that the United Press does not pay its correspondents enough. This charge is emphatically denied by the United Press. The belief is probably due to the policy of the whole Scripps group of organizations of paying low salaries to those at the bottom and rewarding the executives and key men with stock as well as large salaries, which makes them interested in keeping expenses down and profits up. Otherwise they might be more interested in building for the future, for the day when they will be established beyond injury by competition and can set themselves primarily to making their news service as authoritative as that of their chief rival. It is an interesting fact that while the A. P. has been letting down its standards the U.P. is being compelled by the logic of events to move in the opposite direction. Evidence of the way the United Press has been drifting in the direction of the Associated Press is the fact that its executives have been for two years working on the question of broadening its contractual relations with its clientele to give "due recognition of the values that a client confers on the United Press locally as a result of long-time relationship." This means that although founded for the express purpose of preventing a monopoly in news, and as a protest against the Associated Press policy of permitting a member newspaper to prevent others in its immediate territory, under given conditions, from obtaining the Associated Press service, the United Press is now trying to find some way of protecting a client without at the same time violating its policy of "non-exclusivity"—to use its own awkward word.

In Washington the United Press at times seems weak. Sometimes inexperienced men are found in foreign positions of great importance—good men who have to learn their jobs at the cost of the service. Sometimes, as it would be easy to prove, these men "force" their stories because of their desire to get in the human-interest note. In its Washington service, also, there is too much hitting of the high spots, just as there is too much banality throughout its news reporting, though that is more excusable in a new service than in the Associated Press, which under Melville E. Stone denounced that sort of thing and at all times has boasted of its high standards, its superior virtues, and its shining rectitude.

Like the Associated Press the United Press has stooped to conquer. It was the pioneer in adding to its service such features as sports, women's page-matter, cartoons, comic strips, and "human-interest" stories. It gave, in fact, the poor example which the Associated Press followed in this field. It, too, has found it necessary to cater to that recent development in accordance with which the daily newspaper is getting away more and more from the original conception that it was solely a purveyor of news and opinion and is entering the amusement field in competition with the movie and the radio. Cross-word puzzles, children's corners, bedtime stories, advice to the lovelorn, news pictures, and sport pictures—these are all part of the effort to meet the new and threatening competition from outside the business and the never-halting demand for larger and larger circulation.

It was the ill fate of the United Press to perpetrate the greatest hoax in modern press reporting—the fake armistice announcement of November 7, 1918. The world literally went mad with joy when the premature news was flashed that hostilities had ended. In a sense the false report served a useful purpose in that it made officials everywhere realize how deeply the people desired a cessation of bloodshed. Naturally the Associated Press made full use of this bad break of its rival. A careful examination of the evidence in the case plainly proves that the United Press, in the person of Roy Howard himself, was the victim of an error of the naval attache of our Embassy in Paris who telegraphed to Admiral

Henry B. Wilson at Brest as follows: "Armistice signed this morning at eleven. All hostilities ceased at 2 p.m. today." When Roy Howard called upon the Admiral on November 7 the latter casually showed him the telegram. Not unnaturally Howard made immediate use of it. It seemed as if the biggest news scoop in history had fallen into his hands by accident, for he was then at Brest not to obtain news but to take ship to the United States. Had the Paris dispatch been a truthful one, Howard's fame as a journalist would be supreme. As it was, there came down upon his head and upon the United Press an avalanche of abuse and denunciation enough almost to wreck them both. It took a long while for the United Press to work out from under the shadow of this victimization.

Since then Mr. Howard has gone on the active headship of the Scripps-Howard newspaper group, with Karl Bickel taking his place as head of the United Press. Both are still comparatively young men, respectively forty-seven and forty-eight years old. They have already made their mark upon the journalism of this country and of the world and they may continue to do so for years to come. As long as they are at the head of their respective organizations the United Press service will be the one to which reformers and all interested in liberal causes and better human relations will turn first in the belief that they will be received with sympathy and understanding. There are those who think that this liberal attitude is in part inspired by recognition of the fact that it is good business for the United Press to be liberal in contradistinction to the Associated Press. I prefer to believe that the main motive lies in their own convictions and their attitude toward the problems of mankind. Whatever their motives, the fact that the United Press under their leadership is what it is of enormous importance to all who believe that the America of the future should be something different from the self-satisfied and socially and politically reactionary country in which we live today.

***Multiple Ownership :*** To whom the credit belongs for starting the first chain of dailies is a moot question. The pioneer was probably Edward W. Scripps, who in 1875 was associated with his brother in the founding of the Detroit *News.* Three years later he established the Cleveland *Press,* which was in turn followed by the Cincinnati *Post.* These were the leaders in a chain which is now the largest in the country, numbering twenty-four dailies including the New York *Telegram,* with the Ira C. Copely holdings and the Hearst chain following with twenty-two dailies each. Altogether fifty-five chains are listed by the *Editor and Publisher,* but as seventeen of these comprise only two dailies each, they ought really to be deducted. No one, for example, considers Mr. Ochs the owner of a chain because he possesses the *New York Times* and the Chattanooga *Times;* nor can the Pulitzer group, the New York morning and evening *World* and the St. Louis *Post-Dispatch* be rightly included.

All told there are sixteen major groups comprising five or more dailies each. Besides the Hearst, Copley, and Scripps-Howard chains, the more important are the Macfadden, Paul Block, Booth, Brush-Moore, Cox, Fentress-Marsh, Gannett, Howe, Lee Syndicate, Macy-Forbes, Lindsay-Nunn Palmer, Stauffer, Thompson, Ridder Brothers, and Scripps-Canfield. Even here, however, it is to be noticed that some of these are entirely within one State and comprise small-town papers only; thus, all but two of the Macy-Forbes newspapers are in Westchester County, New York. The list naturally takes no account of the weekly newspapers which may also belong to the owner of a chain. As this article is written comes the news of the purchase of a group of thirty-five weeklies, semiweeklies, and small dailies in Ohio by the "Ohio News, Inc," whose real ownership is not yet revealed. In most cases the desire to own a large string is evident. No one can say just how rapidly a chain may grow. Colonel Copley, for instance, is reported to have bought his eighteen California dailies in a day after having withdrawn nearly all his millions from certain public-utility companies through which he had amassed his fortune. His remaining four dailies are in Illinois and of a distinctly different kind from his small-town California properties.

Here we have a characteristic number of chains—a lack of balance. The Scripps-Howard dailies seem better coordinated and more wisely distributed than any other; unlike Mr. Hearst the owners of this chain do not own more than one daily in a town. They are thus represented in twenty-four cities, whereas Mr. Hearst's dark journalistic shadow has happily as yet fallen upon but eighteen. Curiously enough, the Pentress-Marsh chain seems not to go into a city until it acquires all the dailies or the only daily in that town. Other chains are oddly put together. For example, the Ridder brothers, the sons of the late Hermann Ridder, of the *Staatz-Zeitung,* have added to that daily such diverse journals as the New York *Herald* (also German language), the New York *Journal of Commerce,* a business daily, the Jamaica, New York, *Long Island Press,* the historic St. Paul, Minnesota, *Pioneer-Press,* the St. Paul *Dispatch,* the Aberdeen, South Dakota, *American* and News, and the Paterson, New Jersey, *Press-Guardian,* besides holding a minority interest in the Seattle Times.

The most striking rise of a chain is undoubtedly that of the Frank E. Gannett group, now sixteen in number, of which all but two are published in New York State. It includes such important dailies as the Brooklyn *Eagle,* the Hartford, Connecticut, *Times,* one of the two or three most influential newspapers in New England, and the Rochester *Democrat and Chronicle* and *Times-Union.* Mr. Gannett's experiment is the more interesting because he has made use of the new technique of selling bonds and preferred stocks to the public and keeping control through the possession of the common stocks, doubtless with the expectation of making such savings in costs by large-scale purchases and other economies as to be able speedily to buy out the public. That, aside from the question of personal power is the chief lure of the chain.

It is still too early to assert that the newspaper chain has finally demonstrated its financial stability. Several of them are suffering a good deal in the present depression, which has severely affected the advertising of practically all Eastern dailies. It is easy to carry a combination of dailies when conditions are good throughout the country; it may become a dangerous burden when times are bad. Mr. Hearst's chain has a number of very weak links. There is nothing, for instance, about his morning dailies in Washington or New York to indicate prosperity, and there is a general belief that if he could find some means of giving away the New York *American* without too great loss of prestige it would be done. Baltimore is still a bad spot for him, and so are one or two of the up-State New York cities, this despite the fact that his business management has been much improved during the past several years. Mr. Gannett has had difficulty with the Brooklyn *Eagle,* for which he probably paid too much—the price of dailies have been as much inflated since 1920 as were farm lands in the boom war years. It was to finance the purchase of the *Eagle* that Mr. Gannett procured a loan of $2,000,000 from the International Paper and Power Company and its "public-spirited" president. When the fact was brought out and the transaction was severely criticized, Mr. Gannett felt it to be his duty to obtain the money elsewhere in order to repay the paper trust. Other reasons also have combined to make the situation of the *Eagle* a difficult one.

Except in the case of Mr. Hearst, who increased his holdings rapidly in the days when he sought to be Governor of New York and President of the United States, I do not feel that political motives have played any great part in this newspaper development, certainly not at all in Mr. Gannett's case. Mr. Gannett was once asked if had in mind any definite purpose in creating his chain, such as the endeavor to influence public opinion in increasing measure. His reply was in the negative; he merely enjoyed enlarging his personal field of activity. He had no more conscious motive than that which leads a man to buy six more drug-stores if he has made a success of one or two. Undoubtedly the newspaper chain is as much a response to an economic urge or tide as the recent grouping of railroads and the development of the chain cigar or food stores. It is in the air; it is part of the transformation of almost every business which is going on under our eyes, and if it had not been Scripps, Gannett, or Copley, it would have been someone else. The economic drift is what counts—the nation-wide combinations to decrease competition, to restrain trade, and to deal in larger and larger units. There was at bottom no reason to expect that the newspaper business would be spared by the economic forces which are remodeling our industrial life and making the relationship of government to the staggering combinations of capital the paramount issue of the day.

If there is as yet no deliberate planning of newspaper chains to control opinion there is no reason why this could not be undertaken. It is already quite in the power of rich men to buy all the dailies in the smaller States—there are only three in Delaware, six in Wyoming, five in Idaho, twenty-two in Alabama, and thirty-six in Washington. Henry Ford could long ago have purchased the sixty dailies in Michigan with the exception of the very rich Detroit *News,* with but a portion of one year's income. Since there are forty-eight towns and cities in Michigan which possess only one daily journal apiece, despite the theory that this is a government by two political parties, the opportunity must be pretty obvious to those with political ambitions. The purchase of the California chain of Colonel Copley was attributed by some to a desire to control public opinion in southern California in favor of the power interests, but this was denied by his employees. The relative worth of the chain, and whether it is a gain or a menace, will depend upon the personal equation, the character and aims of the owners.

So far it is impossible to say that any one chain has been used for specific anti-social or reactionary propaganda, if we omit the Hearst dailies. The Scripps-Howard newspapers are usually liberal, and most friendly to reform movements. It is a pity that their reporting is sometimes poor, their makeup and typography wretched. They sorely lack high standards in these respects, but their answer is the old one—"We must stoop to get circulations in order to put our ideas over." Even the New York *Telegram* lacks typographical distinction and is messy; yet the *New York Times* has made its great success while adhering to typographical dignity and taste, with the *Herald Tribune* following its example. None of the chains, again excepting Hearst, strive for typographical uniformity. It would be welcome if a format of beauty and distinction were to be adopted by one of them; but those two qualities have largely disappeared from the American press.

By using the new technique of getting the public to advance some of the money while the promoter himself holds control there is no reason whatever why we may not see a chain of one hundred dailies controlled by one man. Theoretically at least; whether this would work out well practically is doubted by many. Yet the steady progress of the Cripps-Howard syndicate, despite certain weak members, would seem to prove that it is no more impossible than the creation by one owner of a group of five hundred grocery or five-and-ten-cent stores.

I can see no valid reasons why we should not have much larger chains and, I believe, we shall see them when those having great stakes in the present economic system are sufficiently enriched or sufficiently frightened by the specter of radicalism to seek more directly to public control opinion. Here is where the danger lies. In this connection the action of the International Paper and Power Company in buying its way into a number of dailies in 1928 and 1929, and lending much money to newspaper owners, including Mr. Gannett, is highly suggestive. The purpose of this new policy, the president of the company said in his own defense, was simply to assure the company steady customers for its paper. But the outcry within the press and the disapproval of the public were so great that he was speedily compelled to change his mind about the advisability of this policy and to get out of the newspaper business. Similarly persistent and at times successful efforts by the power lobbyists to get their hooks into daily newspaper are warnings of a tendency that must be guarded against if the press is not to become merely a creature of the great capitalists. It is, heaven knows, today sufficiently in the clutch of the forces which make for reaction and the support of the *status quo.*

Again, the question of absentee ownership sometimes plays a considerable part in the development of the chain. Some of the smaller communities resent the control of their dailies by men living elsewhere. This is not a universal feeling. There might, however, well be dissatisfaction in Pittsburgh, where all three of the dailies remaining in a city which had seven morning and evening newspapers only a few years ago are now owned by capitalists, residing elsewhere—the Scripps-Howard Syndicate, Hearst, and Paul Block. At bottom the owners of the Hearst and Block Pittsburgh newspapers have no more direct interest in the city than have the owners of chain cigar stores. It is true that there are always editorial writers to deal with local problems; that the staffs are still largely made up of local men. The owners of the Scripps-Howard papers make every effort to tie up their editors with the local interests of the cities in which their papers are situated. Local autonomy is the watchword and it is generally lived up to, except in national affairs. The local Scripps-Howard editor is given help to by an interest in the paper and is expected to spend the rest of his life in its service. He is constantly urged to "know your town" and "feel its pulse". Scripps-Howard editors are, however, freely transferred from one city to another. It still seems impossible that there should be quite the same relationship of the daily to its community that exists when the paper is owned by a local man known to all his fellow-citizens, to be seen at local gatherings, and to be held directly accountable to local opinions and desires. It would seem as though no community of the size of Pittersburgh could rest happy under such conditions. They appear to me intolerable.

On the other hand, defenders of the chain allege that there is a certain advantage in this freedom of a chain editor from local entanglements—social, business, and financial. While it was always Mr. Scripps's idea that his editors might purchase stock in the papers they were serving he rigidly ruled that they should not invest their savings in other enterprises which would interfere with their complete freedom of opinion and action. He wished them to be exclusively newspapermen. Another view is expressed by Eugene A. Howe of the Howe newspapers (chiefly located in Texas, where the chain idea is being developed most rapidly and successfully). "I think," he states, "that it doesn't matter who owns a newspaper as long as it is operated vigorously and honestly. The average reader doesn't bother about the paper's masthead. Give him a judicious selection of news and features, give him a good newspaper, and he is satisfied. And the paper usually will be a profitable investment. . . . We are still experimenting in Texas, but we feel we are going a long way in establishing group dailies."

There remains, however, the question of the editorial opinions of a chain of newspapers. Here we have three distinct policies. The Scripps-Howard dailies, while free to deal with local issues, all conform to the national editorial opinions formulated by chief editorial writers, or, as in the case of their support of Herbert Hoover for the Presidency (which they are presumed to be repenting in sackcloth and ashes), as a result of an editorial convention and a free vote of all the editors. Mr. Hearst's editors reflect his own contradictory and changing views and personal whims. Frank Gannett, however, does not alter the political policies of the papers he purchases. Thus the Hartford, Connecticut, *Times* remains Democratic, and the

Brooklyn *Eagle* independent Democratic, while most of the others are Republican. Mr. Gannett is a convinced and sincere dry; it will be interesting to see if it will be possible for him to allow some of his papers to take the opposite viewpoint if the question of prohibition becomes still more acute. His policy seems to me entirely ethical and quite defensible. It is certainly unusual for an owner to grant to his editors the complete freedom of opinion and expression which Mr. Gannett permits.

In another situation, that in which the same company controls all the dailies in one city, the question is a bit more difficult. Thus, in Springfield, Massachusetts, all four papers are owned by one company. Two are Republican in politics, one Democratic, and one independent. Where the facts are known and where, as in Springfield, there is an honest and above board endeavor to advocate the policies of the two political parties and no effort is made to hide to the real ownership, it would seem that no criticism could lie against this procedure. Different is the case, cited by Senator B.K. Wheeler of Montana, of a town in that State in which both the dailies, one Republican and one Democratic, were none the less owned by the same mining company, their respective opposing editorials being written by the same hireling!

As for the standardization of the dailies which results from ownership of groups, I shall touch upon that later. It is necessary to point out here only that his is the inevitable result—and a specially desired one—of the amalgamations. Herein lies part of the great opportunity to make savings by supplying the same cartoons, illustrations, rotogravure sections, and articles. These savings are not always realized, as for example in the case of a white paper, for which a standard price has now supposedly been fixed for all purchasers, large or small, who do not have their own mills and must buy of the large companies. But in the main it would seem as if enormous economies could be made.

It cannot be maintained that the chain development is a healthy one from the point of view of the general public. Any tendency which makes toward restriction, standardization, or the concentrating of editorial power in one hand is to be watched with concern. For the ideal journalistic state of a republic, especially where the two-party system prevails, is one in which papers may easily be created by single individuals, as Horace Greely established the *Tribune* and Alexander Hamilton's friends the New York *Evening Post*, to rise and disappear if need be. If the coordination of the press with the current urge for larger and larger combinations is inevitable, it is regrettable if only because this makes it additionally harder for the man of small fortune to start a daily and compete successfully for public support.

That this Chain development is an international phenomenon does not alter the situation. It has gone farthest in Great Britain, where three groups, those of Rothermere, Beaverbrook, and the Berry Brothers, now dominate the press, and inform or misinform perhaps 80 per cent of the reading public. It is not impossible that within twenty years or less we shall see there three groups owned by a single company or individual. When that comes to pass the government will have to take cognizance of the existence of a power to control and inform opinion that may prove superior to its own—an impossible situation. No independent daily comes up for sale in England today without the three existing groups bidding for it. The Hugenberg chain in Germany is so large and powerful as to have worried many persons lest it menace the existence of the new republican institutions. Even in South Africa the chain tendency is apparent. Thus, the three leading evening journals, the *Star* of Johannesburg, the *Cape Argus* of Capetown, and the *Natal Advertiser* of Durban, belong to the same company, which also owns the *Diamond Fields Advertiser* of Kimberley and *The Friend* of Bloemfontein, besides controlling the two leading dailies of Rhodesia.

The formation of a British company in 1928 for the purpose of owning British dailies and buying into newspaper properties in other countries foreshadows the international chain. Its mere organization aroused a storm of protest in France, and led to the immediate threat in Paris of a law to prevent the holding of any shares of a French daily by foreigners. The heated and, I believe, totally false charges in this country, during and after the war, that a portion of our press is, or was, under British control is proof of the deep feeling which would be aroused if it should appear that foreigners were seeking to control our American sources of information.

# 5

# News Selection

Newspapers fascinate people from all walks of life, but very few have the time or the patience to study the organisation, production and presentation of news. Most people look upon the newspaper, as a comprehensive presentation of news. Most people look upon the newspaper as a comprehensive presentation of all the important events in the past twenty four hours. Some newspapers have mythologised this concept by claiming that they print 'all the news that's fit to print. Apart from the fact that no newspaper can print everything that is worthy of printing and people's attention, there is another implication in this claim: news judgement. The newspaper organisation decides what is fit and what is unfit to print. Selection is inevitable. According to Walter Lippmann.

Every newspaper when it reaches the reader is the result of a series of selections as to what items shall be printed, in what position they shall be printed, how much space each shall occupy, what emphasis each shall have.

Traditionally, the newspaper has been looked upon as a platform of public opinion, a vehicle for moulding public opinion and an instrument to fight oppression and tyranny of the rulers by bringing to light their misdeeds.

Historically, the press has played an adversary role vis-a-vis the government and championed the cause of the people, particularly the middle and upper classes. The role of the press in freedom movements in all countries has been a very significant one.

But the modern newspaper is a different product from a different organisational structure playing a totally different role. Ever since the business and commercial class began to extend its influence on government, the newspaper's attitude to its own role in society had to change. The new commercial newspaper had to depend on the support of the commercial class since it was the product of that class. Its adversary role against government took - a new turn. The newspaper had to become a vehicle for the criticism of those actions of government which went against the interests of the commercial class. Any action by government which smacked of interference in the free trade philosophy of the merchants, industrialists and financiers was jealously watched by the press and criticised vehemently. Somehow people's interests were taken by the new press as identical to those of the commercial class. This was a phenomenon that occurred in the early part of the 19th century not only in the economically advanced countries but also in their colonies. It is still continuing in both the 'developed' and the 'developing' sectors of the world. In erstwhile colonies, the bulk of the press is still in the hands of the entrepreneurial class that uses the newspaper as an instrument to safeguard its financial interests and to prevent or forestall movements, if any, to change the existing economic order. In the advanced countries, the press is in the hands of powerful media conglomerates which have strong banking and financial ties with multinational corporations.

## Selection Process

No newspaper anywhere in the world can print all the news that comes to it from various sources. Severe selection processes are thus inevitable. This section discusses first, the selection of news in general, and then turns its attention to the selection of foreign news in the light of certain major concepts associated with the making of news.

Economic considerations of total space, size and advertisement content put constraints on the amount and types of news and feature materials that go into the newspaper. The dependence of the modern press on the business world can be seen from the heavy advertising content of the modern newspaper. Even the New York Times which is acclaimed by many as the best newspaper of the United States has a 60 to 75 per cent advertisement content on any given day. All the front-ranking newspapers of the world have similar quantities of advertising in them.' Whether newspapers change their editorial policy or news content according to the dictates of industrial giants who are heavy advertisers is open to, dispute; but it is only logical to assume that advertisers as a group do exert an influence on the large circulation press because the press depends on their support to survive the mounting costs of high technology currently being used by it. Another important factor is the crucial interlocking between the news and information industry and other unrelated industries. This is especially true of the big Indian newspapers such as the Times of India, Statesman, Hindustan Times and the Indian Express. These newspapers are connected with vast industrial and business empires such as the Tatas, Birlas, Goenkas, and others. Directors of huge cement, jute, steel and rubber companies guide the destinies of some of these newspapers. The giants among the American newspapers are also connected with giant industries, a fact well brought out by Dreier and Weinber.

In addition to economic considerations, technological imperatives affect the nature and quantity of news, particularly foreign news, in a modern newspaper. In their bid to bring the latest news in competition with the electronic media which are naturally much faster, the newspapers have spent huge sums of money to install the latest electronic machines and computerised systems of news and picture transmission. They also depend heavily on the satellites and the global wire services. This situation affects the content of newspapers to a great extent, because what is electronically transmitted gets priority. The newspaper editors listen to early morning news bulletins from the broadcast media and then follow up the leading stories-from the wire-services.

The wire services play an important role in the selection process in all news organisations that have installed teleprinters. Whatever comes off the wires is considered more urgent and important than reports coming through other sources. In fact, half a dozen major wire services in the world-Associated Press (AP), United Press International (UPI), Reuters, Agence France-Press (AFP) and TASS-determine the type and quantity of the news content in the newspapers of both rich and poor countries. This is particularly so in the case of foreign news. Since newspapers are in the business of producing under pressure, they find it very convenient to adapt readymade wire service reports and meet the deadline. Moreover, most newspapers cannot afford to station their correspondents in major cities that provide most of the news. Heavy dependence on the global wire services is the characteristic of all newspapers. Diversity in news is likely to suffer from the practice of all newspapers depending on the same wires.

## Presentation Procedure

The very nature of newspaper production imposes certain constraints on the product that reaches the audience. Lack of time and stall imposes restrictions on the selection process and hence on media content. Indepth reports have to wait; what is readily available will form the top story since immediacy is a primary consideration of news organisation and news workers. This will put severe constraints on completeness journalists are sometimes torn between two equally opposing forces: the desire for completeness which may delay the transmission of messages, and the desire for immediate release which may affect completeness. If a large enough staff is not available for research, a story may be 'killed' or delayed indefinitely, or alternatively, the story may be reproduced verbatim from another source more readily available. Most of the time, the wire services determine what stories go into the day's newspapers. Since this is the age of computerisation in newspaper production, standardisation becomes inevitable.

But, are technological reasons the sole determining factors is selection? Are there sociological, organisational and hierarchical factors exerting a decisive influence on the selection process?

In order to understand the sociological, organisational and hierarchical factors exerting a decisive influence on the selection process?

In order to understand the sociological aspects of selection, some theoretical matters connected with the definition of news, function of news organisations in society, structure of news organisations and the decision-making process have to be examined.

First, a look at the process of communication itself. There are four components in the process: the communicator, the message, the channel and the audience. Theorists use four other equivalent terms: the encoder, the symbols, the media and the decoder. The communicators and the audience interpret the message properly only when they have the same frame of reference. Those who produce and present the messages and those who receive them should have the same symbolic frames of reference for proper understanding or communication to take place. Normally those messages which are out of the symbolic context or experience of the audience will be left out by the communicators.'

In his case study of selection and communication in a television production, Eliott identified seven distinct stages:

> Programme ideas and outlines; researching and collect on of programme material; programme material; selection of programme material; detailed outlines and scripts; cuts and adaptation; and programme recording- in that order.

If we transfer this model to a news report production, we can identify the following major steps:

1. Selection of an event to report, or an idea to convey. This may be done by the reporter or a source outside the news organisation. For example, a government or private source may contact the news agency or newspaper organisation, or its representatives with a ,story' for possible inclusion in the next issue of the paper.
2. The report prepared by the reporter or outside person.
3. The report goes to the receiver's desk for selection.

   It is here that the fate of the report is decided. The selector here is usually referred to as 'the gatekeeper'. From here the report may go in toto into the next issue of the paper or it may be totally rejected; sometimes it may be modified a little through further consultation with the reporter and the source, or without any such consultation. Cuts, additions and alterations are made here.

4. If the report goes into the paper in part or as a whole, it reaches the fourth selection stage, namely, that of the audience. The audience may or may not see it. It depends on the positioning of the report, the audience's interest in the subject matter, the size of the headline used, and the relevance of the report to the conditions of the time.

In all the above stage, sociological factors affect the selection process.

A closer look at the four stages is important here.

The communicator is not just the sender of a message. Whether he be a reporter, special correspondent or an outside informant, the communication worker has grown up with certain impressions and value judgements about the socio-economic, cultural and political significance of an occurrence. His impressions are not substantially different from those of his compeers and colleagues the media organisation, and ultimately, they are the sa as those of the top management personnel who control the medium. There are some exceptions to this general rule. Some newsmen have left their organisations precisely because of the incompatibility of their vie with those of their organisations. By and large, however the selectors in all stages have certain common bonds selection philosophy which is unwritten, yet visible actual operation. Communication is part of the to socio-economic and political structure prevailing in country. Culture is again manipulable by those who control the ingredients of its social structure: means production (technology), marketing, finance capital and employment capabilities.

In the first step of selection, therefore, the selector leaves out certain aspects of reality (which is one, holistic, and integrated, although consisting of several aspects). He does this either intentionally or unintentionally, probably because of a set pattern of selection in his mind conditioned by his past education, cultural upbringing, his country's national and foreign policies, his social class, or his corporation's economic objectives. The modern newspaper organisation being a huge, capital-intensive, highly centralised and high technology-oriented corporation, stays in business to make profits. Therefore, those who work for it will have to select a story that will sell. Is there any coercion on the selector at this stage? Perhaps not journalists are by nature free spirits who wish to do their job unhindered by their own bosses or by pressure groups or by government. However, as Gans says, journalists, despite their resentment of bureaucracy and toeing the hierarchical or organisational executive line, are in fact, part of a well-formed bureaucratic set-up that 'suggests' rather than 'orders' -specific tasks.

Senior executives in a news organisation exert a certain amount of pressure on the newsmen because like any other business or social organisation, the press is hierarchical in its structure. But the whole hierarchy is conditioned by the socio-economic and political climate prevailing in the country. It is I relevant to quote Gans again as he studied newsroom decisions by participant observation. He writes:

> Because news organisations are assembly lines on which people must work together to manufacture a product against a deadline, they almost always generate conformity. Few top editors are either sufficiently powerful or Machiavellian to manipulate the pressures for conformity ... [Yet] they resolve uncertainty, decide which selection considerations have priority, set tones and some precedents, which then require conformity. Senior editors do much the same in their sections (1979-98).

Informal methods failing, formal authority is used to bring the 'deviant' reporter back to the organisational policy track. In fact, 'deviations are discouraged or prevented by six factors', according to Warren Breed. They are:

> the use of formal authority and sanction, with the possibility of giving controversial stories to 'safe' men to handle' desire of newsmen to get on in their careers, the lack of any alternative group allegiance to support

deviance; the gratifications of remaining in the in-group and finally handling news according to policy becoming a value in itself.

The policy, according to Breed who studied the role of news selectors or 'gatekeeper' in detail, is usually to protect property and class interest.

## The Prelude

The communicator in the first step is, therefore, news organisation, he is still under the influence of the business or government organisation he works for, whether or not be admits it. This factor of corporate influence over selection is of vital significance in modern media organisations because of the trend towards concentration and centralisation of mass communication technology, production, and ownership; and the interlinkage between organisations and out side organisations including some government agencies. As mentioned earlier, communication industries in both rich and poor countries are under the tight control of either huge conglomerates which, have multinational connections or multinational corporations which have direct or indirect control over several media in many countries. This is the age of monopolistic communication practices.

In the second stage of selection, that is preparation of the report, words or pictures are selected in such a way that those aspects of reality selected in the first step are presented effectively. Again, the reporter's subjective decisions play a role at this stage.

In the third stage, when the message reaches the receiving end, that is, the media organisation, the decision-makers there begin their selection. The message goes through the 'gatekeeper'. Kurt Lewin was the first to introduce the term 'gatekeeper' in 1947 with reference to the people in a news organisation who watched the flow of news. David Manning White and Warren Breed popularised the idea. According to Breed, the policy of a publisher gets translated into action by the 'gatekeepers'. McQuail found that the 'gatekeepers' had the power to decide if an item would have to be changed before it was transmitted. At this stage, major decisions are made regarding the selection of stories for the day's issue the decision-makers go through the stories selected by reporters and judge wire service news stories. The decisions are usually made at the afternoon editorial conference where each section editor brings in what he has chosen for inclusion in the next issue. As Lippmann observed, there are no written rules on decision-making, only conventions.

Some scholars have given more importance to the decision-making process at the first step, namely, the news gathering stage. For example, Bass considers the news gathers' decision more important than the news processors' decision. The news gathers, according to him, consist of the writers, reporters, bureau chiefs, and city editors; the news processors include editors, copy readers and translators. But this does not deal with the organisational and sociological imperatives exerting influence on the climate of the news gathering and selection process. For an understanding of this influence, we have to refer to some other studies based on the content of news media.

In their classic study of a demonstration against the Vietnam War, Halloran and others showed how events were selected for news reporting in terms of their fit or consonance with preexisting images. In other words, the news of the demonstration confirmed earlier ideas. Their conclusion was:

> The more nuclear the news item and the more uncertain or doubtful the newsman is how to report it, the more likely it is to be reported within a general framework that has already been established.

Four other factors were cited by Halloran based on the findings of Galtung and Ruge as vital components of news value: reference to elite persons; references to elite states; personalisation or personification; and negativism. Do media select top people and top nations more frequently than others? Is news reporting person centered? Are negative events preferred to positive ones?

Another important finding of Halloran and associates was that despite he outward differences among various newspapers, all of them showed a fundamental similarity in the presentation of factors which made events news. They found little variation in the approach of the various newspapers to the demonstration against the Vietnam War.

Viewers and readers were not presented with various interpretations focusing on different aspects of the same events, but basically the same interpretation which focused on the same limited aspects-the issue of violence.... Events were not so much deliberately distorted or otherwise falsified by presentation, as selected and interpreted for their relevance to the basic and predetermined news issue.... The simple negative image built up for the demonstration story was the only image made widely available to the public by press the television news.

It is in the function of selection and interpretation that the news producers exercise, their value judgements. This function is performed with reference to a framework of ideas and symbols considered important not only to the communicators but the 'communicatees'.

Stuart Hall's comment on the process of interpretation in broadcast media is relevant to that in the mass circulated press as well:

> Every news event is already, completely, assigned to a context which explains it. The broadcaster, or his reporter and camera-man in the field, must already have such a context in mind in order to know what to film, which to select and send back to the editor, which to include in the broadcast.

If we accept this premise, we have to concede that in the process of news selection. Agenda setting is unavoidable lit-cause the recipients of communication should be provided with certain stories presented in a certain way for contextualisation. For many years, researchers have been trying (and they are still trying) to find relationships between media usage and attitude change. Agenda setting is a trend discernible in the mass media and it is resorted to by the media owners to bring about a symbiotic relationship between their priorities and their audience's supposed priorities. The ultimate aim is to find that perfect fit or consonance between the communicators and the audience which is essential to maximise sales of media products and hence profits. Through agenda setting, the media fare will synchronise, it is hoped, with 'what the public wants'.

## Audience Profile

We are now in the fourth selection stage, namely, the audience of media fare. There have been many studies of the audience of all types of news including foreign news; but most of the studies have concentrated on how to effect behaviour modification through appropriate messages to the audience. Since a study of the effects of messages on the audience is not our aim, it is enough to mention that members of the audience select messages depending on their particular needs and interests. Newspapers are aware of their audience's selection of messages, and they hope to reach messages they consider important for the readers by placing them in special positions or displaying them distinctly. The placement of messages and their display is allied to the concepts of selection and agenda setting. Since agenda setting is linked to the fourth selection stage in the communications model, some details of that concept are worth examining.

The press, as Walter Lippmann said in his classic work, Public Opinion, fills in our unseen environment, and helps us to form our mental picture of the world on a daily basis. People exposed to the mass media do learn from them and form opinions based on that learning. Can the press steer the course of their thinking or influence their thinking process? According to Shaw and McCombs, the two researchers who studied this issue empirically, the press presents to the people should be concerned about. It may be argued that enlightened people will have their own independent judgement on all such issues: but research has shown that the press through the agenda setting process provides issues and event to think about, if not opinions to hold. The concept is defined as 'the ability of the media to influence the salience of events in the public mind. It has been derived from two important pronouncements made half a century apart-one by Walter Lippmann in 1922 and the other by Theodore White in 1972. Lippmann spoke about the power of the press in creating pictures of the world in the minds of the readers. White spoke about the press setting the agenda of public discussion.

Through the process of selection, as already explained, the media transit to the audience those national and international issues which they consider newsworthy and hence worthy of the audience's attention. Shaw and McCombs have shown that people form their individual political cognitions based on what the mass media present as salient. The agenda-setting function of the press is put into practice through the following steps:

1. daily selection of news events and issues by the wire service reporters and editors;
2. daily selection from the wire service news and issues by the newspapers' editors (gatekeepers); and
3. placement of the news and views in the newspaper by the new editor.

Placement in the broadcast media is achieved by the numerical order in which the news and views are presented. Whichever is announced first is the leading news story of the hour. In the newspaper, what the news editor considers to be more important news events will be placed on the front page. These -will not only be placed on the front page, but discussed in the editorial and opposite-editorial pages. Among the important stories on the front page, the most important will be presented in large size types, with bold letter synopsis, 'boxing', etc. Sometimes pictures are incorporated to heighten the importance of the event.

Items placed on the left hand corner catch the readers' attention first since people's eyes move linearly from left to right, except in those countries where they read from right to left. What the media emphasise through selection, placement and display go down in the audience's consciousness as salient. According to Shaw and McCombs.

The agenda setting power of the press may be thought of as a process of consensus building between those who have access to the press or whom the press regularly covers with news, the press itself, and the audience or society at large. Agenda setting represents social learning.

The above discussion shows that reporters and news editors or the maker of news have the power to select events and topics. They exercise this power on a daily basis and what the audience gets is the product of their selection. We move on now, to some more conceptual matters relating to news selection and newsmaking.

Access to the press is supposed to be the corner-stone of democracy since it ensures open debate on public issues. The freedom of the press is ultimately people's freedom to express their views even when those views are against the prevailing authoritarian forces. But, can every citizen be guaranteed access to the media? Is the modern, well-established, high technology press small enough to be accessible to the ordinary citizen?

## Technology's Role

Technological progress has changed the structure of media organisations and the very nature of mass communication. The trend towards centralisation of the technology and ownership of the mass media has been referred to already. Big newspapers force the smaller ones out of business and multimedia conglomerates dominate the communication scene. The concentration of the media in the hands of a powerful elite minority is not conductive to citizens' access and to the freedom of the press. In the United States, newspaper monopoly exists in 95 per cent of the cities. In India, there are thousands of small towns and villages which do not have any newspaper circulation at all. Lack of access leads not only to the loss of vital information but also to the stifling of dissenting views and to a lack of diversity. Despite the argument that it is impossible for any newspaper to publish everything that comes to it, it should be recognised that the only way to ensure access is to multiply media voices through alternative media, if necessary. If the media of communication continue to depend on centralised, capital-intensive, high technology, they will remain inaccessible to the average citizen's points of view.

This is a quality often stressed by newsmen. It is closely linked to completeness, but since newspapers are mainly in the business of bringing the latest news, and not that of completing an already broached story with additional facts and figures for the edification and education of the readers, continuity is not often adhered to as an inviolable news principle. A big story of yesterday will be discontinued or inadequately treated today in order to play up today's big story which in turn will be replaced by another story tomorrow. Do various newspapers follow a pattern of omission or inadequate treatment of an already broken-in story? Are there reasons for this other than the desire to bring the latest 'big story and action news' to the readers? Are there organisational pressures or governmental pressures? By discontinuing stories or reporting incompletely, especially news about other countries and cultures and national minorities, will not distortion occur in news treatment? These are questions that have been answered to some extent by Gans and Tuchman who, like Gans, Audied the newsmaking process as a participant observer.

Tuchman gathered, over a period of ten years, relevant data on the process of newsmaking in two television stations and three newspapers. She also interviewed several news-related organisations and workers. Her main theme is that :

> act of making news is the act of constructing reality itself rather than a picture of reality.... Newswork transforms occurrences into news events. It draws on aspects of everyday life to tell stories, and it presents us to ourselves. By accomplishing this second task, it serves us as a basis for social action. But the process of making news is not accomplished in a void, and so a second theme is that professionalism serves organisational interests by reaffirming the institutional processes in which newswork is embedded.

## Systematic Pattern

According to Tuchman, bureaucratic chains of command are developed in the newspaper organisation to keep p track of daily occurrences out of which particular stories are woven into news and in this process, /news worthiness' is bestowed on selected occurrences. Reporters and editors create a 'web of facticity' for the sake of news credibility, and this web legitimates the status quo. Newsmen identify some sources and institutions as the appropriate location of facts and dismisses others. When legitimate leaders are unavailable, new's organisations bestow authenticity to news into hard news, soft news, spot news and developing news. They also call some news items 'continuing news'.

But in their pursuit of more important news every day, they leave out the concept of continuity, although they may claim that a 'fair amount of coverage' is given to all stories. Perhaps certain news events are covered more frequently than certain others depending upon the importance the news organisation bestows on them.

Connected with selection, continuity and access, is the idea of objectivity. Some newsmen consider their papers to present 'objective news' and take great pride in it. Objectivity is, no doubt, an ideal worth striving for. In it are included other ideals such as impartiality, fairness, truthfulness, reality, and total detachment of the newsmen from their sources and their news. Objectivity is not an ideal that can be achieved easily or frequently. In practice, subjectivity is involved in the selection and presentation of news. Even definitions of news are subjectively derived and not scientifically or objectively tenable. At any given moment, what is newsworthy depends on the decision-makers' socio-economic and cultural background, and the political climate that prevails in his country. As members of a social group, newsmen have certain symbols embedded in their consciousness which they use to interpret reality. Very often these symbols help in the perpetuation of the existing order and systems rather than in replacing them with something different or hitherto untried.

Objectivity is usually considered attainable by reporting opposing points of view. In fact, searching for the opposite side has almost become a ritual with newsmen. But there are a thousand shades of opinion between the two sides. On specific issues, many hundreds of people do not take any rigid view based on party affiliations. Since the newsmen's objectivity is limited in scope, the differences they try to bring out from opposing camps are not real differences but artificial ones couched in terms used by opposing camps. This, can create a semblance of objectivity. The average citizens are sometimes misled by the artificial objectivity in news reports. Even in the first selection stage itself, subjectivity determines what news items and which news sources should be let into the news framework. Once newsmen realise and recognise the process of selection that goes on in their day-to-day work, they will not be as vehement in their protestations of objectivity.

An argument put forward by Tuchman is particularly relevant here. She believes that although it is wrong to accuse news workers of bias, and though it is difficult to define objective truth, it is valuable to identify news as an artificial accomplishment attuned to specific understanding of social reality. Those understandings, constituted in specific work processes and practices, legitimate the status quo.

A newspaper does not hold up a mirror to nature or to events because its reflecting scope is limited. News cannot be comprehensive because of the very nature of newsmaking. The 'reality' constructed by newsmen is not, or need not be, the actual reality or the whole reality. It is only aspects of reality which they produce and present to the public. Berger and Luckmann have discussed the concept of 'construct reality' elaborately in their work. That concept is applicable to the newspaper because, irrespective of the nature of external reality, journalists see it only through their own constructs. As far back as 1953, Kuart and Gladys Lang had shown that events covered were themselves journalistic constructs of related phenomena.

The 'medium is not the message', since the message depends on the men who utilise the medium. Communicators work in a national culture constructed out for several sub-cultures but very much under the powerful influence of the dominant group that holds economic, political and military power. This is why Gans calls news among other things, the exercise of power over the interpretation of reality'.

Similar views are expressed by Tuchman who believes that the work of the media should be evaluated in terms of the sociology of knowledge. Since knowledge is power and communication is part of the knowledge industry, those who run the media are doubly capable of strengthening their network of power over society. They, in fact, start from an already powerful position for reasons of conglomeration with other forms of production. Readers and viewers are not totally helpless if alternative media choices are possible, and if journalists try to maintain news credibility and reliability; but as McQuail has said, the media's views ultimately prevail because they have the final say on what gets into the channels and hence on access and availability.

In the interpretation of reality, the news media use certain techniques for attracting the audience, the most important of which is the technique of dramatisation. This is especially true of television news as confirmed by Epstein who studied the news manufacturing process in the three major networks of the United States. There is no doubt that the newspapers are now compelled to imitate television practices to survive the fierce competition from the electronic industry in technologically advanced countries and also in some developing countries where television is gaining strength. Most news stories open with a dramatic lead. The element of fiction in news stories is also not negligible. These news practices will continue because newsmen in the print media listen to the radio and television news bulletins broadcast early morning for lead stories in their afternoon editions, and the bulletins of the evening broadcast for their morning editions.

***The Reservations :*** Newsmen's preoccupation with personalities and their tendency to personalise news are also allied to the technique of dramatisation. It is easier to dramatise an event if colourful and controversial personalities are involved in the news story. Pictures will heighten the dramatic aspects of a news event. Selection of news is influenced by picture possibility as well as opportunity to dramatise the event through well-known personalities. But who are the personalities who usually appear in the news? After studying a six-month sample of stories appearing in alternate months during 1967, 1971 and 1975, Gans found that most of the news was about affluent people; the main actors in most stories were people in the top 1-5 per cent income bracket, although most were distinguished by their geographical, racial, ethnic and religious background far more often than by their economic background. The magazines were found to universalise upper middle class practices as if they were shared by all Americans. Gans concluded that news story selection was based on availability and suitability of news and that it was the economically and politically powerful people whom journalists sought out for news stories. But drama and colour may not be the only considerations by newsmen since most often, those dramatic events and colourful personalities are chosen, who fit the socio-economic and political environment in which the media operate.

Under the influence of the electronic media, newspapers have changed the format of their pages, increasing the picture content and visual appeal of every page. One of the editors interviewed by this researcher said that he had standing instructions to use at least three pictures on the front page-one big and two small, and one picture on each inside page besides advertisement pictures. News items with picture possibilities and readily available pictures naturally find a place on the front or inside page much more easily than those without a picture. Thus, questions of immediacy, objectivity, completeness, continuity, and other values usually held in high esteem by news workers, are affected by the actual process of newsmaking.

The foregoing discussion should convince us that it is essential to look at the newspaper as a product of the, efforts of a professional group of people who have identical interests and who belong to more or less the same socio-economic, political, and cultural systems. The newspaper is not just a picture of constructed reality, but constructed reality itself to those who produce it. It serves socio-economic, political, surveillance, cultural and entertainment functions news does not simply happen. There are occurrences in everyday life in every part of the world out of which news events are woven with due attention to factual correctness, balanced judgement as far as the selected facts are concerned, relevance to the audience, clarity, contextuality, completeness as far as the chosen facts are concerned, authentic references to news sources specially selected for the purpose, the reliability of the facts selected and presented.

One of the substantive considerations among newsmen and newspaper organisations is that domestic news is more important than foreign news; however, when national interests abroad are threatened, foreign news relating to those interests becomes as important as, if not more important than, domestic news. In the study planned here, foreign news presentation occupies the major position and hence a detailed discussion of foreign news selection is necessary.

Newspapers and all mass media disseminate information not only about events happening in their own countries but in other countries as well. The selection of foreign news is stricter for several reasons, some of which are discussed here.

***The Fulfilment :*** Normally, only about one-third of the total space in a commercially successful and profitable newspaper is devoted to news. The rest of the paper is taken up by advertisement matter of one kind or another. And the bulk of the area devoted to news (called newshole) goes for metropolitan, state capital, large town or newspaper town and suburban news. A sizeable portion is cut out for regional and national news. It is the remaining space that is devoted to events occurring in other countries. Completeness, continuity, objectivity, access, authenticity, and other qualities expected in domestic news presentation will suffer heavily in the case of foreign news because of the pressure on space.

In an investigation of the reasons why newspapers rejected most of the foreign news that flowed into them through the wire services, Casey and Copeland found that 20 per cent of foreign news copies were rejected by American newspapers for 'lack of space', 35 per cent for lack of appeal or interest to readers, lack of news value and significance; 16 per cent because of loss of timeliness and 27 per cent for various technical reasons. They also found that large metropolitan papers allotted proportionately more space to foreign news than did non-metropolitan papers. The International Press Institute study of 93 US newspapers during four separate weeks between October 1952 and January 1953 during the Korean war concluded that the average proportion of foreign news material to text space was little more than 8 per cent.

Sunwoo Nam hypothesised that the flow of news reflected the power configuration of world politics and depended on the political alliance and functional proximity of the reported country, rather than on geographical proximity or any other factor. He also expressed the view that the bulk of foreign news is not meant for the general public, but to help specialised audiences, decision-makers and foreign affairs experts in the functions of surveillance. According to his argument, the press in developing countries reports more foreign news because the press in these countries is elitist. Markham and Hart expressed similar views in their studies of the South American press.

Smith indicated that the growth of a country's interest in international communications is directly proportional to its military, economic and political interests in international areas. Gerbner has indicated that the modern mass media are the cultural arm of modern industry and business. A study by Onyisi under Gerbner's supervision concluded that the southern part of the African continent received the most attention in the United States media because the multinational corporations with headquarters in the country had strong economic interests concentrated in that region of Africa. This relationship had already been studied more elaborately by Schiller in the case of the United States and he concluded that the American mass media were part of an American industrial and military complex. Abu-Lughod found that the degree of international coverage in a country's media depended on that country's dependence on other countries. He also hypothesised that the United States received a disproportionate amount of 'big power' coverage because several countries depended on it.

Lent has pointed out that 'national interests, crisis reporting, foreign censors, and a shrinking corp. of correspondents' constrain international coverage in the US media. Gerbner and Marvanyi have graphically represented the many worlds of the world's press after making a multinational comparative study of foreign news coverage, confirming that coverage depends on the big power configuration that dominates the modern world.

But Elliott and Golding have pointed out that foreign news like domestic news is developed by the media organisers as a marketable commodity throughout the world. According to them, the culture to which news, and other aspects of the international system contribute, is not related to any single society or social structure so much as to that network of economic interests and organisations that is international corporate capitalism. Increasingly the growth of the international media system enables the news media to play broadly the same ideological role at an international level as is already apparent nationally in particular developed countries. The international media system is one mechanism by which developing countries are brought within the common cultural hegemony of western capitalism.

## Working Body

Heavy dependence on the global wire services has been cited by some as a determining factor in the selection and quantity of news from other countries. The IPI study, already referred to, found that the news agencies were the paramount source of international news and that the coverage by the news agencies centered heavily on the major countries of the world. To Hachten, the flow of news concerning less developed countries seemed to be more, closely related to the use of a world news agency than to geographical proximities or language similarities.

Most newspapers of the developing countries do not have the economic capability of stationing their own correspondents in foreign countries. In developing as well as developed countries, it is the big chains and conglomerates that have their own wire services staff and special correspondents in other countries. All the rest depend on the big news agencies of the world. This leads to verbatim reproduction of news agency reports, sometimes including spelling and other errors.

Foreign news in most countries' newspapers is likely to have more or less the same content as far as a particular news story is concerned. There may be differences in the stories selected, but not much variety in the presentation of individual stories.

The history of the development of the news agencies have a great impact on the process of foreign news selection and reporting.

The history of colonialism had an equal impact on the growth of the international news media. Towards the end of the nineteenth century, the newly established European news agencies concluded a series of cartel agreements by means of which they divided the world between the, according to the prevailing imperial spheres of influence. These first links in the international media system set a precedent for much that was to follow as the media in developed and developing societies alike became progressively more involved in corporate capitalist economy.

Colonial news agencies are still strong in erstwhile colonies, and several of their reports could reflect the national interests of the countries in which those agencies originated. They reflect their national ethnocentrism which paves the way toward cultural imperialism. They reporting of an event in a developing country may be influenced by the world's leading wire services, all of which are headquartered in the developed countries. The wire services' reports, thus, could lead to distortion and omission of vital aspects of the events, since they tend to interpret the event from their own national and global economic interests.

This leads us to the fourth factor that influences the selection, presentation and quantity of foreign news.

## News from Outside

As mentioned earlier, domestic news becomes foreign news depending on the foreign policy actions of a country. When millions of refugees from East Pakistan fled to West Bengal, and Bihar their plight was first considered a foreign problem, but the stern action taken by India against Pakistan made it domestic news in India. Similarly, news about a country's nationals in other countries, although strictly news of foreign origin, becomes domestic news because of special domestic links with the nationals residing abroad. With the deep involvement of the United States in Vietnam, the latter country became domestic news in the US media. Afghanistan has now become well-known in the US and the USSR, after the latter's troops marched into that country. The conflict in the Falkland Islands became national news in the British news media. Thus, foreign news is not wholly foreign; it is in a way domestic news extended to a foreign country.

Several researchers have found that three types of countries dominate foreign news in a country's newspapers: its closest or most powerful allies; its chief foes and their allies; and the rest of the world when something extraordinary occurs there. Gans, for example, fund that most foreign news in newspapers in the USA was about England, France, West Germany, Italy, Japan, Israel, Egypt, the Soviet Union and mainland China. He observed that:

> Foreign news deals either with stories thought relevant to Americans or American interests; with the same themes and topics as domestic news; or when the topics are distinctive, with interpretations that apply American values... often limit themselves only to the most dramatic overseas events. In addition, they tend to follow American foreign policy, even if not slavishly.... Foreign news adheres less strictly to objectivity than

> domestic news; but... the values it applies are not very different from those that appear, less explicably, in domestic news.

This observation is not only applicable to the US, but to India and other countries as well. In fact, major newspapers of all countries toe the official foreign policy line most of the time.

Issues of nationalism and patriotism might motivate the media to conform to their national government's foreign policy. It is difficult to find consistently favourable reports about socialist countries in capitalist countries' newspapers (unless there is a very special relationship between them) and vice versa. Similarly, it is difficult to find reports, not to mention favourable reports, about enemy countries in a nation's news media unless the government itself wants certain information to be passed on to the people in order to alert them.

Since foreign policy is a major determinant of foreign news selection, most economic and political developments are seen in terms of the East-West ideological conflict or of the Cold War. Smaller countries are usually ignored unless news about them has some relevance to the newspaper's country. Some major countries are seen as allies or foes. Favourable reports about allies appear in the country's newspapers despite the existence of some very grave threats to human rights in those allied countries. Reports about Latin American countries in newspapers of the US are examples of this. Every foreign news event is likely to be interpreted in relation to either the US or the Soviet Union by most newspapers of the world. 'The daily task of constructing the segment of international reality takes place in a particular kind of setting, both institutional and social', says Cohen. His views about the selection of foreign news are relevant to our discussion:

> Effective decisions are made... at a number of different points, although the general news editor and the telegraph editor, who preside over the bank of news tickers, together with whatever assistants they might have, make the major decisions involving selection and layout. These men do not, of course, start the editorial process de novo each day; they approach the

> task with an experience and a perspective that have both long and short term components. Over the long term, particular classes of stories preempt the leading news spaces-economic reform, war, international political competition... In the short run, the editors carry in their heads the knowledge of what the news has been over recent days and weeks. Hence, they come to their tasks every day with half-formed and unarticulated notions of what the news is apt to be like.

Cohen agrees that no newspaper can 'shovel out to its readers as news the total stock of information and stories that it receives/ but he points out that :

> Priorities and not absolutes determine the amount of... foreign affairs news. Foreign news has to compete with other types of news for getting into the paper. Space allocations are not made every day, but as part of a long term policy, which will be changed only by the top personnel. The selection of all types of news is done by editors on the basis of prior decisions on what the readers will buy.

However, it is not always the sales angle that determines the selection and presentation of foreign news. Political or ideological considerations, global economic interests, military strategies, patriotism, national security interests all these exert a decisive influence on the selection of foreign countries and themes for presentation to the newspaper readers. Journalists often willingly cooperate with government when national security is threatened. As Cohen observes, 'personal friendships between government officials and newsmen are common, extending right up to the Presidential level'.

## Chance for Dispute

There may arise an occasional conflict between senior government officials in charge of foreign policy and some journalists who go wrong in their facts. But by and large, there develops a symbiotic relationship between the foreign news correspondent and his country's local embassy officials and this leads to reporting of events from the official point of view. Sometimes, conditions ripe for revolution in a far-off country, or the true facts of a revolutionary movement may miss the attention of the correspondent who hastily accepts embassy hand-outs for transmission to the newspaper's headquarters. The newspaper organisations are willing to cooperate with the government by resorting to self-censorship on matters of national security or safety of citizens abroad. Several instances can be cited from the reporting of the Vietnam war or the Indo-Pakistan war where , journalists as citizens cooperated with the government. Gans even goes to the extent of saying that journalists occasionally report news from distant countries based on slender evidence.

The intimate cooperation between journalists and government has been discussed by Cohen:

> Stories about foreign aid, Christmas food packages, disaster relief packages, etc., illustrate how the press as a system of communication has become an integral part of the battery of instruments by means of which American foreign policy makers try to influence the expectations and the behaviors of other peoples and governments-friends and allies as well as potential enemies and countries with wandering affections.

The mass media's supply of international news is an important factor in everyone's picture of the world. But foreign policy influence on the press affects the public's attitude towards, and image of, the people in other nations. According to Petersons, there is a correspondence between public opinion and official attitudes with regard to foreign policy.

In the formation of national images of international events and personalities, the transnational news agencies play a dominant role. They also play a role in educating the people of poor countries about rich life-styles. There is a view among researchers that after constant exposure to media fare from rich, technologically advanced countries with multinational economic interests, people of the poor, developing countries learn to identify whatever news they receive over the international news agency channels as relevant to their own circumstances. Himmelstrand and Hedman believe that 'in the long run, people's definition of news will become the same as the supply of news, as they will demand the information they are used to receiving from the news agencies. One might say the news agencies create their own demand'.

It must be stressed that the multinational agencies are under the strong influence of their own national government's foreign policy when they report foreign countries.

How newspapers change their attitudes to countries on the basis of changes in their own countries foreign policy has been documented by Sahin, Kreisberg, and by Lynch and Effendi. These three studies were based on the pattern of reporting in the New York Times over long periods of time. Very little news, for example, appeared about China in the US papers during the two decades following the Chinese revolution. But once President Richard Nixon broke the ice, the newspapers began to turn more frequently to China for news.

There is some merit in the argument that foreign news is meant primarily for the benefit of foreign policy formulators and top echelons of government, and that the average citizen is not deeply interested in foreign affairs. Much of the foreign news published may not be read by ordinary citizens. Some theoretical support to this view has been derived from the oft-quoted 'nature of news' theory of Schramm. Schramm's assumption is that by its very nature, foreign news cannot occupy any significant proportion of the newshole since it may not given immediate reward to the average news consumers. For immediate reward, the average reader turns to soft news: sports, crime, disasters, adventures, comics, movies, other entertainment, society, human interest, scandal, gossip, sex, psychological questions and answers and the like. They also turn to personalities, especially colourful personalities, such as kings, queens, dictators, ruthless tyrants, movie stars, mavericks, controversial figures such as racists, atheists, sex therapists and others, who generate more heat than light for the average reader. Then why does foreign news appear regularly in all newspapers? How much foreign news does appear? What countries and themes are more frequently reported?

Past research has indicated that 'prestige' or 'quality' newspapers devote somewhere between 10 and 30 per cent of their newsholes to foreign affairs. The 'popular' newspapers do not report as much foreign news as do the 'quality' ones. Do newspapers of different press systems have different approaches and attitudes to foreign news reporting? A comparison of two press systems operating in widely different environments may yield answers to the above questions, and clarify some of the conceptual matters discussed in this chapter.

While the lead should arouse the reader's interest, the body should sustain it. The body should flow-smoothly and logically from the lead. It should expand each of the points mentioned in the lead and, as far as possible, in the same order. The body should be as complete and as tight as possible. It should provide all the relevant information within the shortest space possible. The essence of good journalistic writing is brevity and simplicity. Do not use two words where one word would do. And do not use a complex or long word where a short word would do. Eventually, you should reach the point at which, choosing the story structure becomes second nature to you. This will, of course, come with experience and practice. You will then begin concentrating on the more creative and experimental aspects of writing.

A good reporter will spend a great deal of his time not sitting in the office but visiting places and meeting people who are potential sources of news. He should always keep his ears and eyes open. He should know where to go for the facts he needs for the story, recognise news when he encounters it, select the vital points for inclusion in his story and discard the inconsequential details.

## Various Levels

Let us now turn to different types of reporting such as objective, interpretative investigative and crime reporting.

Reporting of news, unlike editorial writing, is often described as a coldly impersonal job. A reporter is essentially a story teller and he should tell the story in an objective and truthful manner, without lacing it with personal opinions or subjective comments. He should be fair and impartial and present both sides of the story.

Complete objectivity is a mere concept. The reporter is a human being, not a robot, and he has certain ideas, feelings, attitudes, opinions and prejudices. However, a good reporter should try to rise above them and tell the facts as he has collected them in his search for truth.

No responsible reporter would behave like the notorious American journalist, Janet Cooke, who won the prestigious Pulitzer prize in 1980 for a story about drugs which was later proved to be fictional and fictitious. The journalist committed a deliberate fraud by dramatising a fake scene in which an eight year-old boy is injected with heroin supplied by the lover of the boy's mother.

Nearer home, the story of "mass rape" at a students function in a Madhya Pradesh town, published in a national newspaper was found to be baseless. When the report appeared on the front page of the newspaper it caused a sensation. The Editor asked a reporter to investigate. On arriving in the town the reporter first questioned the reporter of the news item, who insisted that the mass rape did take place. By , way of corroboration he produced a number of eye-witnesses. However when they were cross-examined and asked specifically to reveal only what they had seen, and not what they had heard, the investigator soon realised that the reporter had written the story on the basis of a bazar gossip and field it without verifying the facts. All that had happened was that during a function to celebrate the annual day of a local college, a portion of the shamiana came down, the electricity got cut off and a few students entered the women's enclosure and molested some of the girls.

There is this apocryphal story of a cub reporter, who, on his, first day at work wrote a piece with a cocksureness which was misplaced. On reading the piece, the editor advised him to be cautious and a little circumspect when writing about sensitive issues. The press, the editor reminded him, must not ordinarily violate the various laws on the statute book concerning libel, national security and parliamentary privileges.

The next day the cub reporter submitted a story which ran as follows:

> "Mrs. Gulab Paniwala alleged wife of Mr. Rakesh Paniwala, who claims to be the mayor of Shangrila, gave a cocktail party at her house in Model Town on Monday to bid farewell to Mrs. Jyoti Jariwala, reported to be the wife of the well-known industrialist, Samar

> Jariwala. Among those present at the party were Mrs. Romi Puriwala, said to be the widow of the late Hansraj Puriwala, a former cabinet minister, along with her alleged offspring, Jani Puriwala..." and so it went on.

The reporter had quite clearly gone to the other extreme in writing this report which was quickly consigned to the waste paper basket.

In reporting news, you must remember that facts are sacred. You must check and cross-check the facts from different sources until you are absolutely sure of them. Only then should you write your story. The golden rule is: tell the truth.

Objective reporting is, of course, not synonymous with dullness. It means fair and impartial reporting that is free from personal bias or prejudice.

***Reporting in Depth :*** It is difficult to define the term "investigative" journalism. Some newspapers scoff at the very idea of an investigative journalist. In one way, of course, "investigative" journalism is a redundant concept, since all stories require some kind of investigation on the part of the reporter. However, the investigative reporter is expected to dig deeply beyond the facts stated in the hard news. Though we may face difficulty in defining the term, we cannot ignore the concept of investigative journalism. Many journalism students have an ambition to become "investigative" reporters. An "investigative" journalist sees himself as the conscience of society, pursuing corruption in high places without fear or favour. In his book Press and Law (Vikas, New Delhi 1990), justice A.N. Grover has quoted from the forward of Investigative reporting by Clark R. Mollevhogg. According to the Foreword, investigative reporting has three elements: It has to be the own work of the reporter. Under no circumstance should it be of others. The subject of the reporting should be such that it is of importance for the readers to know; and There must not be any attempt made to hide the truth from the people.

Investigative reporting has made great leaps in western countries. In India, it is still in its infancy. Most Indian newspapers do not have, or do not allocate, the manpower and funds necessary for a first-rate investigative job.

Attempts at investigative reporting, to quote one eminent Indian editor, are like drilling for oil. A fair amount of wastage of effort has to be taken for granted. But when the oil is discovered and becomes marketable, the sense of achievement is usually more than in any other sector of journalistic enterprise.

The best example of investigative reporting in our times, was the Watergate story which led to the disgrace and downfall of U.S. President Richard Nixon. When the two young reporters of The Washington Post, Bob Woodward and Carl Bernstein, started investigating the arrest of four men for a burglary at Watergate, the Democratic Party's national headquarters on June 17, 1972, they had no idea that their inquiry would culminate in the resignation of the President. The remarkable thing about their investigation was that it kept to the highest standards of professional journalism. The reporters did not start gunning for Nixon from the beginning. They merely pursued the burglary attempt and only later came up with startling facts linking the White House with it. "We did not go after the President, we went after the story", they explained.

Though the Washington Post stories led to the downfall of President Nixon, the same paper, later in 1980, got involved in the most celebrated case of journalist fraud in modern times-the case of Janet Cooke, already described in this unit. Janet Cooke's case gives a clear warning that every story whether "investigative" or not, should be handled by editors with great care and caution, otherwise, it will bring the newspaper to disrepute. N.J. Herbert Altsehul! in his book from Milton to McLuhan (Longman, New York, 1990) states how the Janet Cooke story got into the Washington Post. An internal investigation by the newspaper's Ombudsman, Bill Green, blamed "failure of a system" for not checking up thoroughly on Cook's story. The failure to check was in part, Green said, the result of the fact that Cooke was black and that white editors did not want to be seen as racist. The Cooke's story appeared in the Post on 28 September 1980 and the edition featuring 8 Green's report appeared on 19 April 1981. Cooke was fired from the Post and was forced to return the Pulitzer Prize.

In our country, investigative reporters have brought to high a number of scandals-the Bhagalpur blindings incidents by the police, Kuo oil deal, A.R. Antulay's Private trusts, the securities scam involving Indian and foreign banks and stock brokers, etc. An enterprising reporter once got himself arrested so that he could give a first-hand account of life in Delhi's Tihar jail.

With governments becoming increasingly secretive and corruption spreading its tentacles far and wide, the need for investigative reporting cannot be over emphasized. Yet we must remember that investigative reporting is not everybody's cup of tea. It requires hard and sustained work. The investigative reporter should be combination of a crusader, super detective and blood hound and he should have the necessary time and finance to carry out his work.

In the pursuit of his quarry, the investigative reporter must draw a line between candid reporting and muck-raking, mud-slinging, character assassination or blackmail. He should base his report on incontrovertible facts, not on half-truths and lies. He should be wary of lobbies and lobbyists-political or commercial-trying to misguide him, and he should not behave like a peeping Tom or a prosecutor.

The best king of investigative reporting is that which keeps the public interest in mind. It may highlight an injustice, expose corrupt practices or unmask dishonest politicians and bureaucrats.

Experience has been that unless an investigative reporter or a crusading reporter gets the support of the Judiciary, the executive or the legislative, cannot bring his reports to logical ends. The Bhagalpur blinding report would have ended like any other report if a public interest litigation would not have been filed against the police. In the USA the Watergate stories would not have produced any result if they did not get the support of the legislative which threatened the impeachment of President Richard Nixon.

## Crime Reporting

Crime reporting is not separate from the objective, interpretative an investigative form of reporting. Here it is separately dealt with because it is a separate and important beat in all big and medium level daily newspapers.

There is a tremendous public interest in crime stores and no newspaper can afford to ignore them without damage to its circulation and credibility. Attempts made by some newspapers to keep crime out of their columns, proved to be counterproductive and were soon abandoned.

Crime is a part of life and it is a newspaper's duty to inform the readers of what crimes are going on in their city, state or country. However, crime reporting should not aim at satisfying morbid curiosity or sensation mongering.

Although crime reporting is usually assigned to one of the junior reporters in a newspaper, it is a highly responsible and specialised job. The reporter should not only have the ability to shift the grain from the chaff, and the truth from lies, he should also have good contacts in the police and other departments of the administration as well as a working knowledge of the penal codes and law on libel and other relevant matters.

Besides, he must observe a code of honour. He should be as objective as is humanly possible and avoid resorting to sensationalism or cheap gimmicks to catch the attention of the readers. He should not suppress news of public interest. Nor should he seek to settle personal scores with police officers or lawyers or judges. And he must be careful that in the course of this work, he does not unnecessarily, invade a citizen's privacy. There has been much criticism of press reporting of crime and not all of it is baseless. Some reporters have been found quality of unethical standards, thus causing much pain and sorrow to their victims or their families and friends. In the case of the brutal murder of two Bombay nuns, some newspapers published totally baseless allegations conveyed to them by irresponsible police officials that the nuns were in the habit of receiving male visitors. The reports offended all decent citizens, particularly the members of the Christian Community.

A leading newspaper once published a fictitious report about a couple having been waylaid by a gang on the national highway. The report said that the husband was beaten up and the women was molested. The story was subsequently found to be incorrect, the product of the imagination of a reporter anxious his by-line in the paper. Reports glorifying the activities of criminals or making heroes of them should be discouraged as much as a resort to sensationalism. The crime reporter must never violate standards of decency and good taste.

***Crime as News :*** There are several types of crime news-murders, fires, accidents, robberies, burglaries, fraud, blackmail, kidnaping, rape, etc.

***Fires :*** The reporter must get his facts correct about the essential elements of a fire story-the number of persons killed or injured, the extent of damage to property, the loss of valuables, etc. He must also find out if the fire brigade responded in time or was guilty of delaying the fire fighting operations through sheer lethargy or incompetence or a lack of water supply. He should question eye-witnesses about any acts of bravery or cowardice. All these are essential ingredients of a fire story.

The lead in a fire story would normally suggest itself. It, for instance, lives have been lost, it needs highlighting in the lead. Where possible, list the names of the dead and the injured.

A major fire caused extensive damage to New Delhi's Vigyan Bhavan, the premier venue of international and national conferences, on Monday night, a chowkidar on duty received minor burns. According to preliminary investigations, the fire broke out in the kitchen and soon spread to other rooms on the ground floor. The chowkidar raised an alarm which alerted the head clerk on duty who informed the fire brigade and the police. Ten fire tenders soon arrived on the scene. However, their fire fighting operations were hampered by lack of water in the hydrants. By the time water tankers rushed to the site, the fire had engulfed a large area and damaged files, furniture, curtains and ceilings.

The police suspect electric short-circuit as the cause of the fire.

***Homicides :*** In cases of a major murder, the reporter should rush to the scene as soon as possible after receiving a tip and gather all the relevant facts. In nine cases out of ten, crime reporters in, say, Delhi, depend on police information about murders and there is a time lapse before they can begin their investigations.

This often hampers their search for the truth. The reporter must, in any case, exercise great care in how he handles the story. Otherwise he runs the risk of causing offense.

In reporting dowry deaths or alleged dowry deaths, for instance, the reporter should refrain from levelling uncorroborated statements by one party or the other. He must therefore get his facts correct-by talking to the investigating police officer, the girl's in-laws and her parents, and, if possible, the neighbours.

A 25 year old housewife, Renu, died in NN Memorial Hospital on Monday morning from burns received in a kitchen fire. The housewife's parents allege that she was murdered by her in-laws who had been dissatisfied with the dowry she brought at the time of her wedding a year ago.

However, the husband, Kishore, a garment merchant in Chandni Chowk, and his father who were in the house at the time of the accident maintain, that Sushmita's sari caught fire when she was lighting a stove in the kitchen. Since the kitchen door was closed, they did not hear her cries for help.

The police are questioning the women's relatives as well as neighbours and are reluctant to offer an opinion until the investigations are complete. At the insistence of Renu's parents, however, they have registered a case against her in-laws.

***Accidents :*** Most accidents are reported on the basis of police bulletins or information supplied by police spokesmen. However wherever possible the crime reporter must rush to the scene of a major accident to give authenticity to his story.

Three members of a family-husband, wife and daughter-were killed on the spot when a speeding truck rammed into their car on the road to Indira Gandhi International Airport on Sunday morning. A fourth member of the family had a providential escape. According to the police, the truck driver lost control of the vehicle and swerved sharply to the right and hit the car coming from the opposite direction.

Those killed are Ram, a businessman of Agra, his wife, Janki and their daughter, Aasha. The second daughter, Geeta, had a miraculous escape and suffered only minor bruises on her arms and legs. She was treated at the Safdarjung Hospital and allowed to go home.

The truck has been seized by the police but the truck driver, Sasi Singh is absconding.

## Formation of News

All copy reaching a newspaper office from different sources is processed at the news desk. The desk is manned by sub-editors and usually a chief sub-editor leads the team and works as copy taster and also as revise editor or slotman. He sits in the very useful slot of the horse shot shaped copy desk facing other sub-editors on the rim. After distributing copy to other subs he also checks their work for any mistakes and passes to on to the composing room.

The sub-editor does some or all these to every story:

- Reads the story for clarity of language and meaning and rewrites where necessary.
- Shortens the story while retaining the essentials and maintaining coherence.
- Combines one story with another, or perhaps combines running reports from several news agencies, correspondents and reporters to produce a single intelligible report from different and sometimes contradictory messages.
- Saves space when verbosity creeps in.
- Corrects the grammar and checks for house style.
- Checks for apparent errors of fact.
- Checks for taste.
- Adds important background facts and provides answers for any implied questions.
- Writes headlines which attract the attention of the reader and also writes sub-headings if necessary.

The chief-sub of revise editor checks the work of sub-editors ensuring accuracy of details. He also becomes the fist reader of the story and sees whether the headline and copy make sense.

Another senior sub-editor or chief sub looks after the work at 'the stone'. He is called 'stone editor' also. Though with change in technology the stone has vanished but the term persists. The job of the composing room where the pages are made up with metal types and picture blocks or with strips of film or bromide. The stone sub can also be called production editor or make up editor. He deals with minor disharmonies. If the text is too long, he cuts it. If the page plan does not work, he changes it. If there is late news, he makes room for it. He checks the galley proofs and page proofs and finally sends them to the press.

Thus a sub-editor has to know all about news writing and how a reporter should write news copy. He is supposed to improve upon the work of the reporter. He should not change something for the sake of change but he must make sure that every correction or change the makes improves the copy.

## News Supply

The bulk of copy which comes to the news desk is from wire agencies. The teleprinter keeps on creeding information almost all the time during peak news hours of the afternoon and evening. This copy comes in takes the unit of news agency transmission or unit of newswriting.

Foreign news items have their own serial numbers, FG, FS, FES, FTF, PAS and POOL. Whereas FG, FS and FES files carry news items received from Reuter, AFP and UPI and are credited to those agencies, the PTF file is made up of reports received from PTI's own correspondents and stringers abroad. Items taken from the services of agencies like TASS. Xinhua, Antra Bernama, Tangug and other agencies with which PTI has exchange arrangements go under the PAS series. The POOL file is devoted to agencies participating with PTI in the Press Agencies Pool of Non-aligned countries.

Sobhraj-style is slug-an identification tag. Every story even a story consisting of only one take, must carry at the top a suitable slug. Generally the slug is one word which is often the key work in the story. Thus a story about rain would which is often the key work in the story. Thus a story about rain would be slugged "rain" and one about the police firing, "firing". Slugs are nouns and not adjectives pour in from various points, a master slug should be used with sub-slugs for individual story. In the above example Sobhraj is master slug while style is sub-slug.

Play boy of prisons once more outwitted is the headline. This is a new development. Agencies normally are not supported to give headlines but now to lighten the burden of newspaper sub-editors they have also started putting headlines. If the sub-editor. At the newspaper desk likes it he can indicate the type size for the headline.

New Delhi Apr. 7 is dateline and PTI is credit line. It appears just after date line in the fist take of the story and again at the end of each take. All the takes of the story except the last end with More-PTI as in the above example. The last take of the story is closed with PTI. For Spl of Espl services or sometimes for all stories the story can be reopened. In re-opening an item, reference is given to the previous take by its number for instant, "Sobhraj five-New Delhi-re-open Del 33".

RR RT BDS are initials of the reporter, the deskman or deskman processing it and the teleprinter operator punching it on the tape. Each take also carries at the end ,that time at which it is transmitted in the services.

***The Lead :*** In news agency lead is used in the case of developing stories for updating the top, as necessary, in the light of fresh facts as they become available. Examples of such stories could be train or air mishap, a conference or meeting, an election, a state visit by a VIP. Such stories may require one or more leads as the story advances with the day. A lead can also be used to tie up loose ends of dispersed story, or to provide combined top for two or three different items about a single subject or related development.

There can be one or more leads to a story. For example, the leads on an air crash story, slugged "Crash" could be "Lead Crash", "Second Lead Crash", and so on. The final wrap-up story would be "Lead all Crash".

A lead often overhauls a substantial part of a story or even the entire story. Such lead is also called a "round up". Close to deadlines of newspapers roundups are not useful and therefore the lead is in the form of a brief one or two para top, that is, just the new intro. This intro introduces the new element that has emerged in situation. In such cases an appropriate pick-up line is given linking with the part of earlier story specifying the item by number, slug and dateline and giving the location of the point of pick-up.

If an agency wants to withdraw or kill a story which has come on the ticker, it puts out a kill note. The kill note has priority marking 'Kill' and is without a dateline. It gives the number, slug, dateline and subject of the story which it kills and also indicates whether a substitute follows.

Similarly, corrections are also issued specifying the take line and words of the earlier story and then the whole take is re-issued with corrections. Sometimes service messages which are meant for internal use also reach newspapers. Such messages have the word "service" at the top. Ordinarily a service is addressed to the editor at a particular place. These messages should not be confused with messages and stories sent for use in newspapers.

In order to prevent mistakes the words not, now and nor are repeated in news agency copy. While editing the copy a sub-editor should delete one of these words.

News agencies keep on creeding takes of different stories one after the other, while reporters and correspondents also continue filing copy so that subjects covered by news agencies are also covered by the members of newspaper staff. If the same story is covered by a member of newspaper staff his copy should get priority over the news agency copy. Additional information given by the news agencies can be added to his copy giving credit to the agency.

News copy coming from different sources is sorted out at the desk and all copy relating to a particular story is kept separate. This helps the sub-editor doing that story to read the whole-copy, analyse it and do justice with it. This sorting helps also in knowing whether the news agency has completed the story or some more takes are likely to follow.

Judging the importance of the story the chief-sub decides the space to be given to it. This has to be in relation to total news fall. The relative importance of the story also determines the page where the story would go. Except developing or running stories, all other stories are edited as soon as it is decided that they are to be used. For running stories the deskmen wait for more information. When they come close to the deadline of the edition they proceed with what they have. When additional information comes, the story is changed again for the next edition.

A word about copy. Good copy, also called clean copy, has the name of the reporter and the date on the top of the first page. At least a third of this page is left blank to allow room for instructions to sub-editor and the printer. Sufficient margin should be left on both sides of the copy-say one and a half inch on the left hand side and one inch on the right hand side of all pages of the copy. At least a two inch space should be left at the top and the bottom of each page. News copy should be typed double space.

Every page of the copy should start and end with a paragraph. If there is a mistake in typing a word, it should be typed again. Corrections should be made above the line.

A reporter should leave underscoring paragraph, indents and all other typographical markings to the sub-editor. Wrong underscoring and paragraph marks make a mess of copy. At the end of each page before the last 'more follows' or MF is essential and the end of the last page should be marked 'End'.

On the copy the sub-editor crosses out certain things and circles others. Neither will be set in type but the distinction is that what nobody needs to see any more is crossed out, but essential service messages are circled. The page and edition where the story will go are written on the top of the story and encircled. For example, P 1/2 would mean page one of the second edition. Sub-editor's name or initials are also written and encircled, if there is a printer's or proof reader's query it can be referred to the sub-editor who has edited the copy. Type size and columns are also indicated and encircled. For example, 8 x 1 would mean that the copy is to be set in 8 point type of the newspaper text print across one column. There is no need to specify the face or to say that it is in roman. The rule in newspaper setting is to specify the unusual and otherwise to keep the copy clean. The fewer the marks the better it is.

Catch line or slug is also essential on edited text takes and headline folio, the operator setting the text sets the catch line and it can be married, with the other folios of the same story. Thus a story may have 'Rajiv' as slug or catchline. Its headline folio will carry 'Rajiv I' and its first text take would have 'Rajiv 2', and so on.

Every headline is written on a separate folio. The headline should be written clearly-in capitals if necessary. The letter which need capitalisation should be double ticked. Edition and page mark go on the top left hand corner and the catchline on top right had corner. It also carries instructions regarding type and the columns over which the headline will be spread and the headline style. For example, '14 CBLCX1 set left' would mean that the headline has to be set left over single column in 14 point century bold type in lower case. If the normal headline style is set left in that case it need not be specified in the instructions. However, it is essential that the style breaking headlines should be marked with words and symbols.

The first headlines were single column. Now they can be spread over all the columns in the newspaper. Newspapers today use the opportunities for display by mixing single column and multi-column headlines depending on the importance of the news.

Banner headline should not be in lower case because lower case letters across such a wide measure look straggly. Moreover, headlines should be crisp and lower case headline will be unduly wordy. There is a wide range of possibilities regarding arrangements of headline. A newspaper may standardise on one form, such as the centered head, or it can mix them between headlines. But much depends on the skill of the page planners and the ideas they try to communicate.

The basic typographic arrangements are flush left, centered, stepped, flush right and hanging indention.

Many newspapers have switched to this style. The flush left heading has one or more lines which are set flush to the left. This should not touch the column rule. The flush left headlines look better when each line is indented on the column rule leaving 6 points or half an em space on an 11 cm column.

In this type of arrangement each line of headline type is centered on the white of the column. The well-constructed, centered heading, whether of a multiline or a multi-deck has its own symmetry and it is neatly framed in white.

The patterns created by this need slightly more attention than the patterns the flush left heading creates, but neither needs as much attention as some other patterns.

If one is writing a multi-deck headlines they should be centered where they look best. The common double column headline is a single deck of two lines with centered headings. The second line should always be shorter than the first at least by two units: One should never try to write headlines in tight caps. They need more white around themselves for legibility.

In this arrangement the first line is set flush left and the last flush right and the middle lines centered. Each line has to be about the same length, and they look like steps. To achieve a smooth step requires great care in headline writing. This style is discouraged by modern experts of readability. However, the greatest difficulty is that the stepped style depends too much on a precise count and any failure can lead to ugly results.

Each line is pushed against the right-hand margin to create a stepped effect on the left. It has even more limited application than the stepped headline. It may be occasional variant in a paper but it cannot be recommended as a regular style. It is slow to set and difficult to read. The first line is set full out and the others indented, usually to the left. It cannot be a regular style but can be used as an occasional variant.

Old school considered that quotes and dashes were full letters. New school thinks it is an ugly habit. No headline should need double quotes: Only simple quotes should do. With flush left headings the flush line should be, the initial letter of each line-not the quote. The quote should be left to hang in the white.

Writing headline involves half the skill of a good deskman. The difficulty in writing headlines is in conveying in a few attractive words the essence of a complicated set of facts. In half a dozen words the headline has to inform the reader what the story contains.

The headline gives emphasis to a few words in bold types. Hence every word should be weighed. Accuracy, intelligibility and vigour are the requirements and any newspaper which is careless with its headlines is careless about its own purpose and vitality. Wordy and vague headlines leave a newspaper reader confused and irritate him. Where every headline goes to the print with precision or wit, the whole newspaper comes alive.

Headline writing is art and craft at the same time. The art is in imagination and vocabulary and the craft lies in accuracy of content, attractiveness of appearance and practicality.

A headline must fit in the space available to it. A headline with too many letters to be accommodated in the width and type required is called a "bouncer". It bounces back to the desk from the printer's room and wastes time at various levels. The deskman should always write a headline which should fit. But if there is a superb headline which will not fit in the heading scheme, the scheme can be changed to fit it. A chief-sub may consider this if the merit of the headline so demands.

A sub-editor counts the units in the words he writes for a headline. These units must not exceed the number of units allowed by the size of the type, its style and the number of columns the headline is being allowed to run.

The unit count system begins by giving a unit value to every letter and figure in the alphabet. It is based on a count of one for most letters with adjustments for thinner or fatter letters, and for capitals when they are mixed with lower-case letters. While m and w are counted as 1½ units; i, .1, f and t are counted 1h unit. Other letters are counted as one unit. Where capitals and numerals occur in a headline which is otherwise in lower case, allowance must be made for the extra space the capital letter or numerals will take compared with the lower-case letter. In a headline set u/lc (upper and lower case), count any ordinary capital letter or numeral as an extra 1/2 unit, that is, 1½ units. Exceptions are: M and W which should be counted as two units when in caps and I and J and numeral I should be counted as one unit.

If the headline is in all caps the letters M and W should be counted as 1½ unit while I and numeral 1 should be counted as 1/2 unit. Other letters and numerals will be one unit. The space between the words is counted by some experienced sub-editors as 1/2 unit, while others insist that the space should be counted as full unit. It is better to count it as full unit as if it is in excess it is on the right side and it also simplifies the count.

How does one know the number of units available? In newspapers there is always a list of headline types composed and pasted somewhere for ready reference. It may be available in the style sheet or style book.

If it is not available then the sub-editor should prepare a unit count card which gives the various counts at a glance. Unit count card can be prepared from the type schedule or by counting headlines as published in the newspaper for each style, size and spread. Count a dozen representatives of each headline and average the unit count obtained. Working in this way from published examples the deskman can write headings that fit without the need to count them. Experienced sub-editors resort to a unit count only in case of doubt. But the real art in headline writing is in using the language to sum up the news item and attract the attention of the reader. Before writing the headline the sub-editor must read the copy carefully and decide on the basic news point. The sub-editor must think hard about the single element in the story which makes it worth its space in the paper. When he finds one or more such points he should write them on a piece of paper.

Some sub-editors prepare to write a headline first and sub the copy later. Their argument is that it concentrates the mind on the subject of they copy and becomes the test for intro. If the basic news point is not in the intro it has to be re-written. So, while the sub-editor tries to look for basic news point for headline he is also evaluating the work of the reporter. However, in many cases headline has to be given later, after a first few takes are composed. But even in such a situation the sub-editor must write down the basic news sentence. Often when edited this basic news sentence yields a good headline.

However, the headline writer should always be cautious about the meaning of the words when they are written in different lines of the same headline. There are a few rules. Never split a hyphenated word, look for another way of saying the same thing without using a hyphen at all; never split compound verbs or compound nouns between lines.

A sub-editor must pretest the headline on himself. He must read it to himself and at the end of each line think if t means what he wants to say. If there is any doubt or awkwardness he must re-write the headline.

When multi-deck headlines are used, there is no point in repeating the same information in several decks. Only the first deck should be completely self-contained. Once the first deck has declared the subject area, other decks can take it for granted and use the space to supplement and elaborate.

The first deck should have the most important news point. The second deck may elaborate this with a significant detail without repeating any word or -it may add a further newsprint. Repetition of a word should be avoided but in no case should it be replaced by a difficult or confusing word. In that case the general rule is to repeat rather than to confuse. Overline, if it is there, should elaborate or supplement the main deck.

Accuracy and impartiality are the basic requirements of a good headline. A news headline expressed the news and not the views of the sub-editor who is writing it. Care should be taken to write headlines of political stories. They should not look as if the paper is supporting some political party's view point while in fact it is just reporting the view point. To avoid such a situation one may use quotes on name the person or, party in the main deck. The headline writer must put his personal views aside. He must remember that his job is to reflect as accurately as possible the content of the story.

Quotes are one of the devices for dealing with strong opinions in headlining speeches or political party resolutions. One may put the name of the speaker or party in the headline. Headlines entirely in quotes are usually weak and should always be avoided. It is better to use single quotes for the part of headline which really needs them. When headline is in decks often the attribution is, given in the second deck, it is a bad practice. A headline with opinion and without quotes cannot be made acceptable by putting an attribution in the second deck. Attributions must be contained in the same deck as assertions, otherwise the statement in the first deck seems to have the authority of the newspaper for it.

But there should be no quotes when the opinion is obviously of the paper or the critic or columnist. It is unnecessary and may mean- that the critic or columnist has relayed gossip. Another word of caution is that the people in the news, particularly in crime stories should not be identified by race, colour, religion or nationality unless such identifications are pertinent in the news context. It is wrong to indulge in puns when the subject is death, injury or religion. Funny headlines should not be given for serious events. The sub-editor should always check whether the meaning of the headline is the same as the content of the story. Normally it is the duty of the chief-sub to check the work of subs as far as copy editing and headlining is concerned. He must also keep all these considerations in the mind, for he is again a person on whom the headline and the copy is pretested for clarity of language and meaning.

There should always be a verb in the headline. News is activity and verbs bring activity and life to headline. In a normal headline there should be no room for adjectives. Its colour and spice must come from a rich verb. One should avoid using parts of weak verb 'to be' or 'to have' as the main verb in headline. The verbs 'to be' or 'to have' are not needed even as auxiliaries. For example "Sobhraj arrested" is better than "sobhraj is arrested". There are occasions when the very 'to be' should be omitted even though this seems to leave the headline without a very. This verb is better when implied. Its physical presence in the headline makes it weak.

Passive voice has been major culprit in headline writing. A verb should be used in active voice as far as possible. At least before using the passive voice the sub-editor should himself try the active voice and should explain to himself the reason for not using active voice Passive voice normally breeds extra words and burdens a headline. Usually, rejecting a passive voice construction can lead to a more vivid headline. However, care should be taken to see that the main news point is as close to the beginning of headline as possible.

The headlines have been using the present tense to describe events that have already happened. The arguments in support of this phenomenon is that the present tense is active, it puts the reader in the middle of the action and gives him a feeling of participation. The event described in present tense in the headline may be past, but it is recent past and the reader is learning about it now. He also understands the convention and will imply that in the present tense his morning newspaper's headline is giving the news of yesterday. 'Yesterday' is almost never justified in a morning newspaper headline because in that case almost all items could have yesterday in the headline. The reader takes for granted that it was yesterday unless it is otherwise specified.

There is an added advantage in using present tense. It is invariable shorter. It gives the feel of recency to the news below the headline.

Subject is an essential part of a sentence like verb and headline is really a truncated but still meaningful sentence that the reader understands. It should be in the headline either as such or as understood. It may be possible to write a headline without a subject in many circumstances but one should remember a headline with a subject tells more about the story than one without it.

The rule regarding the use of subject in a headline is to give the name if it is well known or the title if he is not well known. One must headline a name in case of obituary even if a person is not so well known.

The weakest form of subject in a headline is 'he' or 'she.'. It is not an identification. But it will be at times good to use 'he' or 'she' headline on a human interest story with a picture of the subject.

'Man' or 'woman' are weak identifications of subject but at times they are unevitable. 'Wife, husband, father, mother's are better because they narrow the field. But they should not be taken as another name for man or woman. 'Husband banned at club' will suggest that he cannot go while wife is allowed. Thus it is better to be more specific about the subject but it should be ensured that there is no distortion. Don't say "child" in headline if the child is not yet two. Better use 'baby' or say boy or girl and give age.

Headlines should be as specific as possible not only in identification of the subject but also in other matters as well. One should be specific about the main newsprint and a headline should

# 6

# NEWS REPORTING

In a real sense, the world's ability to learn the news about itself depends on what gets into the news-flow in the fifteen or twenty open societies with highly developed media systems. Once an important story appears, for example, in New York, London, Paris, Rome, or Tokyo, it is immediately starts flowing through the arteries of the world's news system and will be widely reported elsewhere—but not everywhere and certainly not every story. For the majority of non-Western governments act as gatekeepers, screening news in and out of their nations. These political controls, as well as poverty and illiteracy, deprive the great majority of the world's peoples from learning even the barest outline of major current events. But any major story that breaks in the West has the possibility of being reported throughout the world. Within hours after the explosion of the space shuttle *Challenger,* many millions worldwide heard the news and saw the dramatic pictures on their television screens.

To the few thousand foreign correspondents, the world's nations are strung out on a continuum from "free" or open at one end to "not free" or closed at the other. To illustrate, the Associated Press "has little difficulty in gathering news in open Sweden, since several newspapers there take AP services and share their own news and photos with the agency. In addition, AP correspondents can use other Swedish media as sources and can develop their own stories or easily gain access to public officials.

Sudan, as an example of a partly free country, offers a different kind of challenge. AP has no clients there, largely because the Sudan News Agency lacks the hard currency to buy the satellite-beamed AP world service. The local media are often subject to official controls, and the AP cannot economically justify maintaining a full-time correspondent in Khartoum. Therefore, AP covers Sudan by using a local stringer (a part-timer who is paid for what is used). Periodically, the AP may send in a staff correspondent to Sudan to do background or round-up stories.

At the "not-free" end of the continuum are a few countries that for years have barred all foreign journalists and news agencies. When something important happens in Tirana Albania for instance, AP and the world usually find out about it belatedly from a government-controlled Albanian radio broadcast monitored abroad or from travellers or diplomats coming out of the country. A foreign correspondent often defines a country as free or not free, according to how much difficulty he or she has in reporting events from this country. This may sound narrow and self-serving, but it has validity; the freedom of access that a foreign reporter enjoys is usually directly related to the amount of independence and access enjoyed by local journalists themselves, if local journalists are harassed and/or controlled by a particular government, so very likely will be the foreign journalists.

Throughout the unstable Third World, some nations swing back and forth between freedom and controls. For example, under Indira Gandhi, India, the world's largest democracy, went through a not-free period when the local press was controlled and foreign correspondents were forced to leave or were subjected to censorship. Later, news access opened again and the country regained the free press for which India had been noted.

Despite the widespread availability of impressive gadgets and hardware—communication satellites, telex, video display terminals, computers—collecting news throughout the world is still an erratic and imperfect process. Some significant events are either not reported or reported long after the fact. Certain areas of the world, such as central Africa, rarely get into the world news flow. Datelines from such capitals as Niamey, Bamako, Khartoum, Ouagadougou, Lome, Freetown, Conakry, Bangui, Yaounde, Nouakchott, or Brazzaville seldom appear in Western newspapers unless the stories concern natural disasters, violent conflict, or a coup d'etat. Reasons to this situation are disagreements between professional journalists and government officials over the nature of news.

To the journalist, news is the first fragmentary and incomplete report of a significant event or happening that editors think will be of interest or importance to their readers or listeners. To many government officials, news is "positive" information that reflects well on their nation (and hence themselves) and serves their country's' general interests and goals. Yet those same leaders want to know all that is happening elsewhere that affects their interests and country. Keith Fuller, former head of AP, put it well: "News is what a government official wants to read about somewhere else, propaganda is what the official wants the world to read about him and his country."

## Political Intervention

Politicians and government leaders in every nation from north to south attempt to manage or manipulate the news so that it favours their causes, their programmes, their image.

"What is commonly referred to as the world flow of information," AP foreign correspondent Mort Rosenblum wrote, "is more a series of trickles and spurts. News is moved across borders by a surprisingly thin network of correspondents.... The smaller countries are squeezed into rapid trips during lulls between major stories in larger countries." Rosenblum quoted a comment from a Latin American academic that "news breaks in South America along the direct line of the Braniff route."

Considering the demand for foreign news and the difficulties of reporting it, there are probably far too few correspondents stationed overseas. Rising costs and inflation have made maintenance of a staffer overseas quite expensive. Estimates range from $125,000 to $ 200,000 for maintaining a bureau overseas for one year. The New York Times spends an average of $200,000 a year on each of its bureaus, or about $ 8,000,000 annually. Another $1,000,000 is spent on the Times foreign desk in New York. The Baltimore Sun (with only 170,000 circulation) maintains eight correspondents overseas at a cost of $ 1,000,000 annually. It is not surprising then, that so many news media rely on the news agencies for their foreign news.

The number of American foreign correspondents seems to have stabilized in recent years. AP's foreign news corps grew from sixty-five full time U.S. journalists in 1975 to hundred in 1985, but relies on some 300 plus foreign nationals to cover foreign news in its overseas bureaus.

In 1982, the New York Times had thirty-two full-time foreign correspondents, twenty-five part-timers, and twenty-three bureaus overseas. However, in 1968, the Times maintained forty-eight full-time correspondents overseas. The Los, Angeles Times has been expanding its foreign coverage in recent years and in January 1986 opened a new bureau in Manila, bringing to twenty-four its number of foreign bureaus manned by staff correspondents. The Washington Post has also increased its staff of foreign reporters, which stood at seventeen in 1952.

Other print media with significant foreign staffs were the *Wall Street Journal* with a dozen reporters. *Time* magazine with thirty-five in twenty-two locations, *Newsweek* with twenty-one, *Christian Science Monitor* with eight, and the *Chicago Tribune* with five.

The three major U.S. television networks have decided to leave vast areas of the world uncovered, in part, because of financial considerations. It has been estimated that it costs $ 1,000,000 a year to maintain even one "shoestring" bureau overseas. *ABC* has twenty-two reporters in thirteen locations abroad, *CBS* has a similar number in thirteen cities, and *NBC* has seventeen correspondents in thirteen cities. Increasingly, the networks seem to be relying on news film supplied by the syndicates *Visnews* and *WTN* and other broadcasters for foreign coverage.

Not only are foreign correspondents comparatively few in number, they are unevenly distributed as well. Ralph Kliesch found that 54 per cent of American reporters and 51 per cent of all correspondents abroad were stationed in nineteen European countries. Of these, only 7 to 8 per cent were in three East European nations, mainly the Soviet Union.

The vast expanse of Africa, with over 500,000,000 people in forty-five countries, is very thinly covered by a declining number of Western journalists. However, when a major international story breaks, almost a herd instinct seems to stampede numerous reporters and cameramen and women to the scene. In 1986, about 170 accredited foreign correspondents were based in Johannesburg, due to the continuing racial unrest because it was a hub for air travel and combat transmission for southern Africa, where news was breaking not only in South Africa itself but in neighbouring Zimbabwe, Namibia, Angola, and Mozambique as well. The 1983 civil war in Chad brought the largest number of journalists ever to gather in that impoverished former French colony. The Ministry of Information at N'Djmena, the capital, accredited 150 reporters, photographers, and television technicians from all over the world at the height of the Libyan intervention. A few weeks later, almost all had departed.

During the height of the Iranian crisis when fifty-three Americans were held hostage, more than 300 Western newsmen and women, some 100 of them Americans, were working in Tehran. Such "parachute journalism" does not always provide informed coverage, because many of these reporters have had no previous experience in the country about which they are reporting.

New York and Washington, D.C., are major world news centres, drawing reporters from over seventy countries but principally from Britain, West Germany, Japan, France, Italy and Canada.

According to the USA Foreign Press Centre, 480 foreign correspondents were working in Washington in 1983.

Such statistics reflects the reality that most world news originates in such major news "hubs" as New York, Washington, D.C., London, Paris, Tokyo, Hong Kong, Bonn, Rome, and Moscow, and foreign correspondents, by and large, tend to congregate in cities where news is either made or flow into.

For American readers, at least, serious questions have been

raised about the quantity and quality of the foreign news they receive. The discussion tends to be circular. AP and United Press International editors have long maintained that their services gather ample amounts of foreign news but that their newspaper and broadcast clients do not use very much of it. The clients, in turn, say that their readers and viewers are not that interested in foreign news. Yet critics say that Americans are uninformed about the world because their news media report so little about it.

In one study of sixty daily newspapers in nine countries, the U.S. press ranked last in the percentage of total space (excluding advertising) devoted to foreign news. The data showed that U.S. Newspapers devoted less than one-half (11.1 per cent) the space to foreign news than did the sample papers of Western Europe (23.6 per cent) and the non-aligned countries (22.8 per cent) and less than one-third the space than the East European papers (37.5 per cent) studied. Yet the news hole is larger in most U.S. papers and more foreign news may be carried.

Certainly there is substance to the generalization that the majority of Americans, with access to the world's most pervasive media, are ill-informed on world affairs. Foreigners travelling in the American heartland are uniformly impressed by the lack of world news in local media and the ignorance shown by most Americans about the outside world. By contrast, the average West German, Dane, Swiss or Israeli knows more global news because his or her media carry more.

Part of the problem is that Americans, like Russians and Chinese, have a continental outlook, living as they do in the midst of a vast land mass that encourages a self-centered, isolationist view of the world. With two friendly neighbours and protected by two oceans, Americans are slow to realize their inter-dependence with others.

Thus Americans' interest in foreign news has its ups and downs, depending on the immediacy of the impact on their lives of events abroad. During the Vietnam War, much concern was focussed on happenings in South-east Asia but not in Latin America or Africa. After Vietnam came a pulling back from foreign concerns as the nation became enthralled by Watergate and its aftermath.

But after the rapid increases and then decreases in the price of foreign oil, the Soviet incursion into Afghanistan, continuing Arab/Israeli conflict, and the rising level of terrorism directed against Americans, the average American's interest (if not knowledge) in foreign news clearly increased.

Further, there is some evidence that the public is more interested in foreign news than editors believe. A Louis Harris poll on public attitudes towards news found that "those who work in the media (editors, news editors, and reporters) feel that only 5 per cent of the public are greatly interested in international news. A much higher 41 per cent of the public express deep interest in world affairs being covered in the news media." A subsequent poll reinforced the evidence that Americans do care more about international matters. According to a February 1986 Gallup Poll, Americans cited international problems more than any others as the nation's most pressing concerns. Concerns listed included nuclear war, the arms race, and terrorism.

## Perception of News

Some scholars believe that television is profoundly affecting American's news perceptions. Prof. Neil Postman believes television projects "a peek-a-boo" world, "where now this event, now that, pops into view for a moment, then vanishes again. It is a world without much sense or coherence.... Americans know a lot of things but about almost nothing. Someone is considered well informed who simply knows that a plane was hijacked or that there was an earthquake in Mexico City."

After the U.S. hostages in Tehran were freed in 1981, Postman conducted a study to determine the extent of knowledge about Iran. One hundred people were asked simple questions about the Iranian language, religion, and government. "Because Iran was carried almost continuously on the news for a year, we expected people would not only know about Iran but would be overloaded." Postman said. "But we found that most people couldn't answer our questions. Almost always those who actually knew something had gotten it from print sources."

There is a growing recognition that perhaps the term "foreign news" is a misnomer, that in this inter-dependent world we are potentially affected by any event almost anywhere. American workers who lose jobs in manufacturing due to cheap foreign imports or farmers unable to sell wheat abroad due to the overvalued dollar are becoming more knowledgeable about the world economic trends.

Robert Semple of the *New York Times* said, "Ask yourself, would the U.S. auto industry be in such a bad shape if the Detroit papers had men in Japan and Europe a decade ago? Would the U.S. steel industry be laying off workers if the Pittsburgh papers had been covering the European Economic Community and the Japanese steel industry and their export policies 10 years ago? People won't wake up to the importance of foreign news until a few more banks fail because of lousy foreign loans."

"The use of foreign news in the. U.S. media raises two questions: Are news media fulfilling their obligation of providing essential information so that their readers can make sound judgments on foreign and national affairs? Or are media contributing instead to making Americans more provincial at a time when the world is getting smaller?

A study based on a series of surveys of journalists and newspapers found that American newspapers generally are lax in their coverage of international news. Lester Markel and Audrey March concluded that the majority printed little more than the bare essentials, not enough to provide any clear view of what is going on in the rest of the world.

The surveys determined that news space given to reporting of foreign news totalled 17 per cent of the whole news allotment; however, this figure was misleading, the researchers pointed out, since it included trivia, features, and human interest stories, which if deducted would leave about 10 per cent.

"As for quality, there is often lack of expertness, due to the fact that correspondents are often shifted in order to get a fresh point of view and so do not have the feel of the country that a good dispatch reflects. Interpretation of International news in minimal and in some newspapers, non-existent. Instead of interpretation, one is likely to find opinion in the guise of background."

Furthermore, the evidence indicates that the press is not covering the Third World as well as it once did. Xan Smiley, a former correspondent for the Times of London, has suggested that journalists who reported crisis events in countries like Ghana and Tanzania in the early post-independence year, soon found themselves in direct opposition to the governments of these nations, and with the threat of expulsion hanging over their heads, decided that only the major crisis events were worth reporting. Smiley has noted that heavy self-censorship is a standard feature of reporting by Western journalists throughout the Third World and that nowhere is it more rigorously observed than in Africa.

Markel and March also undertook a week-long look at foreign news on the nightly television network news broadcasts. The amount of foreign news was found to be exceedingly low on all three networks; interpretation was virtually absent; objectivity, difficult to measure on brief stories, was rated adequate. The indictment concludes:

## Critical Aspects

Critics of the newspapers and television news broadcasts charge that they fail to supply the essential facts accurately or in perspective; that they barrage the public with a welter of unrelated news stories; that they fail to separate the significant from the trivial; and, much too often, neglect the minority viewpoint. In general, the view was expressed that the media fail to show that international news is relevant to the lives of readers and viewers at a time when actions by the federal government and events in foreign countries may profoundly affect American lives.

Michael J. Arlen, a perceptive television critic, believed that foreign news as a broadcast commodity has been in a steady decline to such an extent that "it now often seems to be thrown into a network's regular news productions as a kind of after thought."

Even though CBS and NBC claim that the foreign news content of their major news shows average from 20 to 25 per cent, this total, Arlen feels, is actually reached by two narrow types of reporting: semi-official accounts of the overseas travels and meetings of our presidents and secretaries of state and largely reflexive, military oriented coverage of combat situations. "Ongoing interpretive coverage of the world as a whole by U.S. broadcast journalism seems right now to be at a minimum and, despite the profitability of the three networks, shows no signs of becoming more ambitious."

Further, television tends to concentrate for days running on the "big story," such as the hijacking of a TWA plane and taking of U.S. hostages in Beirut, while ignoring significant events elsewhere. Perhaps this is inevitable in a "headline service," as Walter Cronkite called television news, but it does not help to provide a public, which relies on television as its major source of news, with a fully rounded picture of the world.

One public opinion survey by ABC news found a marked criticism of foreign coverage. Fifty-five per cent of those polled agreed with the statement that "television news only does stories about foreign countries when there's a war or some other violent crisis going on." Hodding Carter said the networks "concentrate on showing kids throwing rocks at troops or guns going off or planes bombing or rubble falling. These are the repetitive images that block out the complexities." In addition, he cited the "extraordinary lack of continuity and perspective, which is the shadow of all television news."

There is no doubting, however, the tremendous capacity of television news to focus world attention on some foreign events. Starving Ethiopians had been suffering and enduring hardships for many months, but not until the dramatic colour television coverage of their plight appeared on the NBC Evening News night after night were Americans galvanized to support relief efforts. To paraphrase a propaganda maxim, the colour television report of an event may be as important as the event itself. The obverse is true as well: an unreported event will have little impact.

Inevitably, much of what happens in the world will go unnoted. Wherever he or she may be, the average person does not have the time or interest to follow all the news from everywhere. As one editor asked, "Who wants to read about Zaire if there is nothing going on there?" Gerald Long of Reuters explained move fully: "The prevalent school of journalism throughout the world is a 'journalism of exception,' In other words, you don't report that everything is fine in Pakistan. You report that there has been an air crash."

## The Hostility

The journalism of exception—reporting civil unrest, the coup d'etat, the train wreck, the drought—is at the root of increasing hostility and antagonism towards Western reporting.

Journalists who work abroad say there is increasing difficulty in gaining access to many parts of the world, particularly Africa, the Middle East, and Asia. Typically, when a political upheaval takes place, one of the first measures authorities take is to close their borders and stop issuing visas to foreigners, including journalists. Even when journalists do obtain visas to some Third World countries, many say they find themselves faced with tight restrictions on their ability to travel, to witness events, and to speak freely with officials and local citizens.

Journalists have had particular difficulty in reporting the war in Chad, the drawn-out conflict between Iran and Iraq, and the troubles between the Sikhs and the Indian government. In the Soviet Union, no Western journalist was able to travel to Gorky when Andrei Sakharov, the physicist and dissident, was reported to be on a hunger strike.

Henry Kamm of the *New York Times* believes that the foreign correspondent is becoming a casualty of the self-assertion of the Third World toward the West "Demonstrating suspicion towards correspondents and reducing their access to sources of news, much of the Third World is gradually joining the Communist nations in closing itself off from critical inquiry," he wrote.

The field of activity of the western press is being narrowed increasingly by both formal and informal methods. AP correspondent Mort Rosenblum categorized four forms that such methods can take.

The "Blackout" approach, which seems to be gaining popularity, takes the view that no news at all is better than critical or infiltrating reports abroad, so reporters are simply kept out. "Reluctant

Coverage" means that reporters are permitted in, but access to new sources or officials is severely limited. The Soviet Union, China, and Eastern European countries are examples. The "Subtle Squeeze" occurs in countries that appear to permit open coverage but actually apply indirect restraints on particular stories. Sometimes correspondents are consorted by excessive hospitality that keeps them occupied at some distance from a potentially embarrassing story. The fourth method is "Friendly Persuasion," wherein reports are not restricted, but efforts are made to influence them in as a positive way, American officials have been known to use this method, typified by the press junket—taking reporters to the scene of a new story in hopes they will report favourably on it. Much of what is termed "enlightened public relations" falls within this category.

Reluctant Coverage can often be as effective as the Blackout approach in preventing reportage. On a visit to Tanzania, Henry Kamm was told by a government information official that he should have submitted his precise programme in writing long before arrival so that a special government committee could rule on his requests. Because he had not done do, Kamm was told he could see no government official and must not leave the capital at the risk of arrest. The only official help he received for a story on Tanzanian development was a collection of speeches of President Julius Nyerere, the most recent, three years old.

David Lamb of the *Los Angeles Times* agrees that the doors are closing to the Western press. "Across the continent," he wrote of Africa, news management is becoming tighter, restrictions on journalists more severe and access to countries more limited. More than a quarter of Black Africa's forty-four governments ban foreign correspondents or admit them infrequently and under such controlled conditions that news, in effect, is managed or blacked out. Others admit journalists only for self-serving group tours, then send them on their way.

Increasingly, Africa views foreign correspondents as a nuisance. They distort the news, governments argue, by dwelling on the negative and the sensational—or, at least, by raising issues that are best ignored in the interests of a developing nation.

After months of protest and violence in South Africa that claimed over 1,000 lives— an of all fully reported by Western reporters—the South African government on November 2, 1985, imposed sweeping restraints on foreign press coverage. All reporters, print and broadcast, could cover scenes of unrest only under police supervision. But, most tellingly, pictures and sound recordings of unrest in those areas were banned. If the purpose of the ban was to remove images of violence from foreign television screens, most broadcast journalists said, then it worked. "Nobody wants to be in the position of saying that what the South Africans did has worked," said Peter Jennings of ABC news, "but it has." Subsequently, on June 16,1986, the tenth anniversary of the uprising in Soweto, the South African government banned the use of comsa for live television coverage of any news coming out of South Africa. So while violent confrontation between blacks and whites did not abate in South Africa, the vivid images on television screens did.

A major point of contention is that most developing nations believe the press, including foreign reporters, should serve the host country's national aims, while the Western press believes it must decide for itself what news to report.

Covering wars and civil unrest has always presented special problems, but foreign reporters have faced unusual difficulties in reporting from Beirut and other parts of Lebanon. The very real fears of kidnapping or being killed by various terrorist groups prompted many Western reporters into covering the conflict from Cyprus.

Many reporters are forced to cover individual countries by proxy. Uganda, during its chaotic rule by Idi Amin and Milton Obote, was covered by monitoring Radio Uganda in Nairobi and interviewing diplomats and refugees. Ghanna, Guinea, Guinea Bissau, Benin, Equatorial Guinea, and Angola have at various times been covered from afar because they denied access to Western correspondents. When a violent attempted coup took place in Cameroon in 1984, the story was covered by monitoring the Cameroonian radio in Abidjan, Ivory Coast, because no foreign reporters were in the country.

## Danger in Reality

Foreign correspondents often risk their lives while working in hostile countries. In the Central African Empire in the 1970s, AP reporter Michael Goldsmith was brought handcuffed into the presence of Emperor Jean-Bedel Bokassa I. The ruler suddenly clubbed him to ground, stepped on his glasses, and began kicking him mercilessly. The rest of the emperor's party joined in, and Goldsmith quickly lost consciousness. He awoke in a tiny detention cell, where he spent the next month. Through diplomatic intercession, Goldsmith was finally released and later said, "What happened to me could happen to any correspondent in countries where the ruler is unstable and regards objective reporting as hostile. I'm concerned that this is something that will spread."

This was indeed a bizarre incident, but many journalists around the world face danger while doing their jobs. During 1985, according to the World Press Freedom Committee, twenty-three journalists were murdered: three died in the Phillippines, three in Columbia, the others throughout Latin America, the Middle East, and Africa. In addition, eighty-one other journalists were wounded, 205 jailed, and fifty expelled from countries they were working in.

Louis Boccardi, president of AP, said, "On the international scene, the world continues to grow more difficult to cover. The physical dangers abound. Dozens of journalists have been killed in the last few years and many more injured in the pursuit of a story, their story, wherever it was."

Covering civil wars in the Third World is particularly dangerous for Western correspondents. Lebanon, torn by a protracted civil war, lawlessness, and the Israeli invasion, has been an especially fearful place to work (for any Westerner, not just journalists). A number of journalist-targeted incidents particularly underscore this. Jeremy Levin, Cable News Network Beirut bureau chief, was kidnapped and held by Moslem fundamentalists for over a year until managing to escape. Terry Anderson, Beirut bureau chief of AP, was pulled from his car by gunmen after an early morning tennis match; Islamic Holy War, a Moslem fundamentalist group, took responsibility. Later, an Israeli tank shelled a group of journalists in southern Lebanon, killing a cameraman and a soundman working for CBS News and wounding several other people, reflecting, some said, the animosity between Israel and Beirut based correspondents. Subsequently, a French TV crew and a French free-lancer were kidnapped. Caught in the violent and emotional cross-currents between the Israelis, various Lebanese Christian and Moslem groups, and the Syrians and Palestinian factions, the foreign journalists must work with the constant threat of assassination or kidnapping hanging over their heads.

The drawn-out invasion of Uganda by Tanzanian forces was reported mainly from neighboring Kenya because of hostility to foreign journalists from both sides. In the later stages of the conflict that finally drove Idi Amin from power, two West Germans, Hans Bollinger and Wolfgang Stiens, and two Swedes, Arne Lemberg and Earl Bergman, entering Uganda to report on the war were murdered by soldiers loyal to Amin.

Most often, such violence against foreign correspondents is reported sometime after the tragedy. But the murder in Nicaragua of Bill Stewart, a television correspondent for ABC on June 21, 1979, was viewed by millions the same day on the evening television news. While covering the fighting between government troops and Sandinista rebels (both groups had been hostile to American newsmen), Stewart, explaining at a roadblock that he wanted to interview government soldiers, was told to kneel; moments later a soldier walked over and shot him once in the head with a rifle. The whole episode was recorded by an ABC cameraman from a short distance away. This film report, which shocked the nation, also disputed the Nicaraguans' first contention that Stewart was killed while trying to flee.

In El Salvador, names of foreign journalists have appeared on death lists, some have been fired on by government or guerrilla troops, and more than ten have been killed and others wounded. Six U.S. journalists, on their return from a fact-finding trip to Central America, condemned what they described as the suppression of press freedom and the acts of intimidation and physical violence against domestic and foreign reporters in Guatemala, Nicaragua, and El Salvador.

In Argentina alone during the mid-1970s, more than thirty journalists were killed and 119 others were imprisoned, placed under house arrest, or forced into exile, according to AP and the Anti-Defamation League. Foreign journalists there were pressured as well, Reporters from ABC, NBC, Voice of America, AP, UPI, and the *Wall Street Journal* were detained and questioned for writing about relatives of missing persons.

## Uncertainty in the Business

Western news organizations and their governments are uncertain how to respond to this treatment *of* their foreign correspondents. When the Soviet Union expelled AP correspondent George Krimsky from Moscow, the U.S. Government retaliated by expelling Tass's correspondent in Washington, D.C. When the Soviet arrested a *Los Angeles Times* reporter and accused him of collecting political and military secrets, both the White House and the U.S. Senate denounced the Soviet Union's action.

The most celebrated case of Soviet harassments of an American journalist occurred on August 23, 1986, when Nicholas Daniloff, Moscow correspondent for *U.S. News and World Report,* was arrested and charged with being a spy one week after Gennadi Zakharov, a Russian, associated with the United Nations, was arrested in New York on an espionage charge. A loud and continuous protest over Daniloff being "held as a hostage" came from the U.S. Media.

After intensive negotiations, on October 2,1986, Daniloff was released and flew home, and the following day Zakharov was allowed to leave the United States after pleading "no contest" to the espionage charges. Most journalists regarded Daniloff's release as a straight trade of a journalist for a spy, despite Reagan administration statement that the near simultaneous releases did not constitute a trade. Most journalists said they had hoped to avoid the appearance of an equal exchange, which some said could suggest that Daniloff and other foreign correspondents are spies themselves. Moreover, some felt the Daniloff affair set a precedent so that, in the future, American journalists could be taken hostage and then traded whenever a Soviet spy without diplomatic immunity was apprehended.

Yet the U.S. Government does not respond in kind to harassments of American correspondents in the Third World, Stanley Meisler of the *Los Angeles Times* thinks it should. He wrote:

> What is needed is a recognition of the seriousness of the problem, a cry of warning and some tough talk from the U.S. Government and other governments. The Third World is harassing correspondents more and more. In some areas, a virtual news blackout exists. This should be unacceptable to democratic Western governments that deal with these Third World countries. The peoples of these Western societies have the right to be informed about the countries with which their governments are signing trade, aid, and political agreements.

On the other hand, some journalists feel strongly that the Western press's independence from government is compromised when governments intervene on behalf of foreign correspondents. William Sheehen of ABC urged caution, saying that the U.S. Government should not "directly take up the problems that news gathering organization have and intercede with other governments. I feel that the First Amendment precludes such action, that the government's role should neither be in support nor opposition to the press ... .It is best that the government not set any agenda to attempt to find solutions on behalf of the American press."

The difficulties and dangers Western correspondents face from hostile, authoritarian governments, appear to be getting worse, and a widespread boycott of the Western press in many Third World countries is seen by some journalists as a distinct possibility. Those who believe in retaliation point out that Western newspersons working in authoritarian countries create a unique situation.

Marshall D. Shulman, an expert on the Soviet Union, said: The relationship between the government and a newsman working out of Moscow and Beijing on any centralized authoritarian situation cannot be equated with newsmen working in Western capitals. His housing, his ability to travel, even his access to food shipments from abroad and his fundamental protection is inextricably related to his government. We have to work out new cannons to govern the actions of a democratic society when it is dealing with an authoritarian regime.

## The Shortcomings

In summary, it may be useful to list some of the major shortcomings and inadequacies of the Western system of foreign news gathering. Far too few Western journalists and facilities are deployed in the right locations to provide adequate coverage of world news events. Sparsity of local news media in many nations of Africa, Asia, and Latin America compounds the problem because those media are themselves unable to make significant contributions to world news flow.

Serious obstructions to news flow are erected in authoritarian countries by such devices as denial of visas to foreign journalists, censorship, lack of access, and harassment. Ten or fifteen years ago, most reporters covering the Third World would have said that their major problems were logistical—getting to the story and then getting the story out to the world. More recently, better air travel and telex via comsats have improved communications, but the political barriers to news gathering have increased markedly. It is ironic that at a time when travel and communications technology have made even the most distant corners of the world instantly accessible, foreign reporting has become even more difficult and dangerous.

The limitations and subjectivity of news itself mean that many people somewhere are going to be dissatisfied with how the news is reported. For example, a reporter for the *Los Angeles Times* based in Nairobi (Kenya) is writing for readers some 12,000 miles away in California. His or her stories will be chosen and later edited, not according to what East Africans would prefer to read, but what editors in Los Angeles think their local readers will be interested in knowing. That correspondent in East Africa may regard, say, development problems in Tanzania to be an important story, but the resulting dispatch may be discarded because the editor in Los Angeles thinks there is insufficient interest in the subject.

For news, besides being perishable, is relative and subjective as well as frag.nentary and incomplete. Take as an illustration the news of a sudden increase in the price of coffee. In Chicago, it means that consumers will be paying 35 cents a pound more for ground coffee— and resenting it very much. To readers in Brazil or the Ivory Coast, the price increase means that coffee-producing nations are receiving a well-deserved break at a time when prices of raw materials from poor nations are lagging further behind those of manufactured goods from rich nations.

Furthermore, it is true, unfortunately that ethnicity or racism does directly affect news values at times. The death of a car full of white South Africans in a road mine explosion will probably attract larger headlines in Western newspapers than the death of twenty-five-Africans in rioting in black townships.

Also, Western news media, although relatively independent of their own governments, will still tend to report foreign news from the viewpoint of their country's foreign policy concerns. This is not the result of any conspiratorial link between journalists and a state department or a foreign ministry. Rather, the unsurprising fact is that events abroad are of interest to readers in proportion to the ways their own national concerns are involved. Nonetheless, foreign news coverage too often responds U.S. Domestic politics, and this means that often important foreign stories do not get covered because they lack the "local angle" of high reader interest.

From 1948 until 1972, the years when the United States refused to recognize Communist China, U.S. Reporting about mainland China was generally sparse and negative. However, after Nixon and Kissinger went to Beijing and the United States played the so-called China card, "Communist China" became the "Peoples's Republic of China" in the U.S. Media, and stories about China became friendlier and more positive.

News, it has been said, is what an experienced editor puts in the newspaper. And editors—even those on the same newspaper—do not always agree about the importance, value or credibility of any particular story.

The Western practice of journalism of exception, of stressing the disasters, the problems, the upheavals, continues to rankle critics of the press everywhere. In America, many feel the media report far too much negative news. But as Daniel Patrick Moynihan has said, "It is the mark of a democracy that its press is filled with bad news. When one comes to a country where the press is filled with good news, one can be pretty sure that the jails are filled with good men."

But the emphasis on crisis journalism is only one of a long list of complaints and criticism of Western news gathering that has been heard in recent years.

## Print and Electronic Media

Despite the enormous satisfaction it is quite possible to derive from the business of putting together complicated news stories for transmission in a very short time, there is not much doubt that the glamour image of the average newsroom journalist lags far-behind that of those who appear in front of the camera. For while no viewer would be expected to name any member of the back-room team, descriptions of nationally known news performers-the 'talent' as they are quaintly described in the united trip easily off the tongue. So it is hardly surprising that, sooner or later, many a starry-eyed newcomer to television news begins itching to achieve what is believed to be the ideal-to be seen by an audience of millions through a news report made in some exotic, relatively troubled the other side of the world, enjoying what one member of the international reporting set has summed up as 'a front seat on history's.

That is probably a perfect example of the greener grass syndrome, for there are certainly some reporters who would dearly love to exchange their front seats for what they regard as the calmer back rows in the newsroom television reporters privately admit that, after a while, the apparent glamour and excitement-of their lives begin to fall. Some learn sooner than others to detest rushing to catch planes or deadlines, living out of suitcases, eating hurried meals in unhygienic places abroad, witnessing at first hand unspeakable horrors of which the audience may ultimately see very little. All this is in addition to the real personal dangers involved in covering the stuff of modern television news: war, natural disaster, civil unrest. That professional newsmen doing their job are jut as much at risk as the combatants has been proved time and again by events in South East Asia, the Middle East and Central America. In 1984 alone 23 journalists were killed and 81 wounded according to the International Press Institute, which has produced a survival manual for news people operating in dangerous situations.

Many reporters are married with family responsibilities, and live with the uneasy feeling that nay birthday party, wedding anniversary or other normal domestic occasion may be interrupted by a sudden telephone call commanding them to be on the next flight to somewhere or other. The wife of one former television news general reporter used to say that the one thing which unnerved her above all was the sight of the small suitcase containing spare shirts, underwear and shaving kit, which stood permanently in the hall as a daily reminder of the emergency assignment which might come at any time: that, and not knowing whether the news event would last a couple of days, a month, or more. Understandably, not all marriages endure that sort of strain.

Of course no sensible reporter pretends it is all hectic. Most will readily recall hour wasted at airports, in draughty corridors of government or other buildings, waiting for events to take place or people to turn up. Sometimes they did not. At other times, doors slammed, telephones went dead, the answer was 'no comment' or something less polite.

In contrast there are pleasant, well-ordered and interesting assignments, at which the reporter is greeted with enthusiasm hospitality and a genuine invitation to call again. Do not forget the opportunities for keeping up with professional friends: Reporting television news is the only profession in which you can fly 5000 miles, drive 200 miles to a town you've never visited before, walk round the corner and meet 52 people you know.'

The result of a job will done may be two or three minutes of good pictures, a visual by-line and an enhanced reputation, yet the dominating factor of it all is that the reporter cannot work alone if the assignment is to be carried out properly. For while the sole newspaperman and the radio reporter in the field are as close to he office as the nearest telephone, the television news reporter has to work with a camera crew, an outside broadcast unit, or a television studio linked in some way with home base.

Even in these days of compact, mobile equipment, this is bound to put aloof on the fringe of a story in the hope of eventually being granted special dispensation by the other participants. Despite the fact that the obtrusiveness of the camera, microphone and lights makes the entire team a target for attention and occasional abuse, any reporter who is not up with the herd and sometimes in front of it does not last very long in the job.

And then there is the irony that perseverance and initiative at times work to the reporter's own detriment.

How often it seems that the fruits of a good television interview, grabbed against all the odds, are picked up by other newsmen in the crowd and, with minimal embellishment, are turned into highly acceptable accounts for their own branches of the new business. At other times during he serum it is impossible to discover who has asked the questions which are eventually heard on the sound tack, but that has not always stopped the cracks from blaming television reporters or any bullishness or poor grammar.

In the end, though, the reporter for television news is only as effective, as his last report. There is no glory to be won from the production of a brilliant piece of work which arrives too late to be edited in time for transmission. Time, effort and moneys are wasted it, at he conclusion of an extensive foreign mission, the material is confiscated, never to be seen.

## Experimental Aspects

Four television reporters begin their careers as such. Most graduate from newspaper, news agencies or radio, and so back only the knowledge of television techniques to become successful. Some turn out to be competent enough without ever fully understanding how to construct the well-turned phrase which complements rather than competes with the pictures, and it is not surprising that the best exponents of the reporting art are often those who have served apprenticeships as news-writers.

Leaving aside the matter of journalistic ability, a modicum of which must be assumed, the two basic qualities every reporter must have before being let loose in front of an unsuspecting public would seem to be a reasonably personable appearance and clear diction.

In Britain, ideas have undoubtedly changed about what constitutes diction good enough for broadcasting, for the general increase in news outlets, particularly since the arrival of local radio in 1967, has allowed all manner of accents and speech impediments to become suddenly more acceptable. Whether this is interpreted as a lowering of standards or a individual opinion. However the cruel truth about television is that some expert journalists simply lack credibility in front of the camera in the studio or on location, and that the most carefully researched, well-written material is totally lost to the nine-tenths of an audience fascinated instead by a nervous fie, bobbing Adam's apple or inability to keep the head straight.

That is not the only difficulty. What some viewers consider to be incorrect pronunciation is guaranteed to induce near apoplexy on the part of the critics, amateur and professional alike. Bernard Levin, writing in the London Times, devoted hundreds of words to reprimanding certain broadcasters, television news reporters, included, for sometimes pronouncing the word 'thee' instead of 'the'. To the uncaring it may have been so much wasted printers' ink. Yet Mr. Levin was undeniably correct in his assessment of the result, that the 'ugly. Flat, distorted and meaningless noises made by the chief sinners are so boring that they have the inevitable use of important things we need to know.

Still, at least such misdemeanors are capable of being cured, unlike the expressionless monotones and nasal whines which apparently defy the best efforts of the voice-coachers. Little can be done, either, it seems, for those with voices so light and high-pitched as to make virtually no impact for broadcasting.

Women figure largely among the sufferers, which may account in part for what some interpreted as discrimination against female journalists in television news, although the million-dollar wooing of Barbara Walters from one American network to another and the astonishing upsurge in the recruitment of women which followed the inclusion of Angela Rippon in the BBC Nine o'clock News team of newsreaders may help to give the lie to that notion. Another, more cynical, theory about women television journalists is that male viewers spend all their time nursing lewd thoughts about them during their screen appearances while other females among the audience either hate them on principle or wonder who does their hair. (That may cause cries of 'sexist', but there's no denying human nature.) Either way, all is lost.

For these reasons, chocolate-box good looks and speech which is too precise are considered equally off putting, whether found in men or women. Among all except those who mourn the demise of the Hollywood glamour factories, the preference is for people who look and sound as though they lead real lives off screen.

All this merely goes to emphasize how easy it is to be critical. Given the curious chemistry at work in everybody's likes and dislike's, it is interesting to speculate on the fruits of a computer programmed to produce a picture of the reporter must likely to win universal appeal. No doubt that has already been done. But without the benefit of the computer, it must all be down to intelligent guesswork and a single, old-fashioned word-style.

The novice reporter quickly discovers that there is no short cut on the tortuous route that may eventually lead to general acceptance as a competent television reporter. There is likely to be very little in the way of formal 'coaching', as the average news service cannot afford to have any operational staff missing from its line up, and expects its newcomers to pick up everything except the basics as they go along. This is sometimes euphemistically described as 'on the job training', and comes as a complete surprise to novice reporters who may be expected to be able to master the intricacies of 'filming' from their opening assignment, whether it is an interview with the distraught parents of a missing child or with the beaming winner of an angling contest.

Once some initial progress has been made, usually after a few painful lessons on the way, the new reporter may be taken aside by a more senior colleague and told gently about some of the most obvious flaws. Some of these might be avoided in the first place by attention to three factors which add to or detract from any on-screen performance: speech, mannerisms and dress.

## Delivery Style

Everyone who appears regularly in front of the camera develops a natural, personal style of delivery and emphasis, and although this individuality is to be encouraged, the aim in every case must be clarity, with delivery at an even pace. It must be neither slow enough to be irritating, nor fast enough for the word to run into each other: no audience is able to take in much of what is told by an excited reporter speaking at full gallop.

As part of a general tendency to group words and phrases in a manner which sounds odd as well as ungrammatical, one of the most frequent is the addition of non-existent full stops in the middle of sentences.

The cure could not be simpler; sentences which are too long should be broken up into shorter ones.

Bluffed lines and hesitations inevitably mar otherwise fluent performances and perhaps lead to loss of confidence. The answer is for the reporter to become familiar with the contents of the scrip by rehearsing as thoroughly as possible (mumbling to yourself in a corner, though a poor substitute, in better than nothing).

When serious mistakes do occur there is no shame in asking for a second 'take', for even the most experienced performers expect to trip over their words from time to time. Where any faults persist there is no harm in seeking the advice of speech therapists, who are able to devise little training routines for the tongue which can only increase the performer's confidence.

In reporters with easy going, relaxed personalities, tiny mannerisms may become endearing to the viewer. An occasional frown, raising of the eyebrows or head movement to emphasize a point, probably comes across as genuine involvement in the story at hand. For the rest, stiff, awkward movements, facial contortions and continual passing of tongue between dry lips are among the many tell-tale signs of stage-fright. Usually this disappears once confidence comes, although not always. We know of one former reporter who, while completely at case before the microphone in the radio studio, betrayed his nerves during appearances on television by purifying almost every sentence with the word 'well', even though he knew it did not appear once in the script he had written.

Nervousness is not shared equally between recorded and live performances. In many ways the studio camera seems to magnify mannerisms which, to the consternation of studio staff, reveal themselves only under the strain of live transmission. Some reporters slouch back in their chairs, others tilt like the Leaning Tower or hunch their bodies so that one shoulder is thrust forward aggressively across the desk. Possibly worst of all is the fear which has the reporter sitting literally on the seat edge. The result is a close resemblance to a jockey on horseback, except that to the viewer the rider here seems posed to leap out of the set and land in the front room. At least twitching hands are usually hidden by the camera angle.

To all those who suffer from it, this stage-fright (no respecter of persons), can become increasingly confidence-sapping. Practice will make the biggest contribution towards overcoming it, especially if backed up by the close scrutiny of recordings of personal performances. The advice of production staff, given and accepted in the right spirit, will also help the novice to isolate and then dispose of the main problems which, if left to develop, might lead to permanent bad habits.

The medium itself imposes some restrictions on dress: the sensitive mechanism inside electronic colour cameras seems unable to digest certain striped or checked patterns which set off disturbing visual hiccups known as strobing, and some colours (notably shades of blue) create 'holes' through which studio backgrounds appear. Aside from that, some news-type programmes have recognized how dress contributes as much as set design to the identity they wish to create.

Breakfast programmes in particular seem to like the casual look, and one ask anyone who appears, visitors included, to dress accordingly. This fits in with the general requirement for reporters to wear what is in keeping with the programmes they are working for and the stories they are covering. For example, and open checked bush shirt and denims would be entirely appropriate for reporting a desert war, while a pin-striped business suit and Homburg would not, while a formal studio interview calls for jacket collar and tie so long as these remain convention.

The important thing for any reporter of either sex is to avoid clothes and colours which the majority of viewers would consider eccentric or inappropriate. For women therefore enough smart, business-like styles available to preserve femininity without resorting to anything fussy, although almost anything they wear on television seems to be regarded affair game for criticism and comment from fashion writers and others. As for grooming, it would be unfair to expect the viewing audience to accept uncombed hair or a two-day heard where the reporters' families would not, except in those situations where such appearances are relevant to the story.

Beads, jangling bracelets or long earrings are best avoided, as their movements are inclined to create distraction. In the, wrong moment, especially if they fall off. Lapel badges, in particular those which use defy identification are fraught with danger. So is the whole range of 'club' ties. The possibility here is that the viewer might miss all that is being said while concentrating hard to see whether the coloured blob three inches below the knot is of real significance or just a gravy stain.

## Role of Reporter

While local television stations may expect their reporters to find and collect many of their own stories, then supervise the detailed editing of them, in most centrally run news services the reporter's duties are more limited, with daily on-location assignments carried out on the instruction of programme editors or the semi-independent assignments staffs who control newsgathering activities.

A certain amount of briefing is usually given, even if it is limited to the approximate outline any contribution is expected to follow to enable it to take its place within the rest of the programme. Where an assignment is foreseen as representing only one segment of wider coverage of a single topic, briefing is much more detailed. Good preparation is vital at any time. Given reasonable warning of the nature of an assignment, a diligent reporter will make a virtual fetish of reading up any available background material. On foreign assignments, this may run to dossiers built up from previous visits and include a diversity of facts ranging in importance from currency exchange rates down to the names and localities of reliable laundries. To ensure speed off the mark, those news services able to afford it provide individual reporters with office cars, complete with two-way radio telephone links, or at least contribute fuel costs towards the reporter's private transport. For those unwilling or unable to tie-up large amounts of capital in fleets of cars, reporters are expected to travel with the camera crews or simply jump in taxis, either paying as they go and recouping the money later, or as part of official arrangements with taxi companies, signing the driver's log at the end of each journey.

Some news services operate a pool transport system to ferry all operational staff to and from assignments, but this has its drawbacks. There are apocryphal tales of news teams stranded miles out of town at headquarters officially unable to move until an office car became available, while some government building went up in flames at the hands of rioters.'

Once on location, technical matters are clearly the business of the camera crew, but except on those occasions where the unit is accompanied by a field producer, it is the reporter who has to shoulder the 'managerial' mantle with overall responsibility for the shape and content of coverage.

In between lies a fascinating, ill-defined area of ground which in non-news location work would be covered by a director. For reasons chiefly of cost and mobility, it is generally accepted that television news does not need to have separate directors, the role being shared by reporter and cameraman on the spot. So it is probably here that the greatest scope exists for disagreement between members of the crew. The ideal working compromise consists of a reporter with journalistic skills an den eye for pictures sketching an outline to be filled in by a sympathetic, experienced camera crew. Detailed discussion about the best way of achieving the desired-end product is advisable before a single shot is recorded. But, in the final analysis, it must be the cameraman who decides what is technically possible, depending on numerous factors including the available light and distance from the subject.

Once a general storyline has been agreed, the reporter then has to trust the crew to supply what they say they are supplying. Long arguments about the closeness of a close-up or the speed of a pan from left to right only hinder the completion of an assignment, and no professional news cameraman would tolerate a reporter's demand to look through the camera viewfinder before every shot.

Relationships are therefore important, particularly on some dangerous foreign assignments, where the degree of mutual trust between members of the team could make all the difference, literally, between life and death. Sometimes a reporter and crew will build up personal friendships and respect over a series of difficult, successfully completed assignments. Between others, the ,chemistry will be all wrong, and no amount of attempted peace-making will put it right. To team a lazy reporter with a go getting crew or vice-versa and still expect the screen to reflect only successful results is wishful thinking. Far better to ensure that, where possible, incompatible factions are kept well apart.

Even when prospects for cooperation are good, there is no sure recipe for success. The reporter must always remember to be considerate and tactful in the treatment of his professional colleagues, resisting any attempts by misguided outsiders to create separate categories of 'officer' (reporter) and 'other ranks' (crew). The reporter who allows himself to be swept off to the executive dining room while the crew makes do in the factory canteen deserves the inevitable opprobrium.

Equally the camera crew must be patient with a nervous or out-of-sorts reporter. After a long, tiring day with very little to eat or drink, it is often tempting for the cameraman to give the thumbs-up to a reporter's performance he knows deep down to be flawed, just as the timid reporter, suspicious that something may be wrong, is prepared to accept a personal second best rather than risk offending the crew by encroaching on meal times.

Getting the story right must come first. As one experienced cameraman has put it: 'If the reporter fails, we all fail'. In addition to the constant awareness of deadlines, there also has to be recognition of the need to be economical in the use of tape or film, not so much for the sake of cost as for the reason that the greater the volume of material, the longer the time necessary for viewing and editing.

With the assignment completed and the pictures received at base' the reporter's role becomes blurred, for one of the main planks of the intake-output system is that it is the editorial staff back at the office who assume the final responsibility for shaping material for inclusion in the programme. Although the reporter's guidance may be sought, the theory is that those most closely involved in the creation of items are necessarily the best placed to make objective judgements about their value.

This is apart from the possibility that all manner of developments may have taken place which downgrade the original importance of the assignment. Yet many reporters, as specialists in their subjects, quite understandably recent being told which are the 'best' bits of their interviews. Modern video 'packages' especially are so dependent on the reporter's ability to mesh the various pieces together, no producer or news-writer coming old to a project would probably be able to understand much of it anyway.

It is at this stage that the strict dichotomy of intake and output must seem an expensive luxury for the smaller, less wealthy news services. For them the solution lies not in dealing their editorial talent into watertight compartments, but in seeking to create genuine allrounders.

Each would be an amalgam of news editor, researcher, director, script writer and reporter, well-versed in the skills of overseeing picture editing and writing studio introductions for themselves to read on transmission.

## Relevance Today

Although electronic news gathering has almost entirely superseded 16mm. film as the main means of originating news material, most of the reporting techniques being used to present items in a fluent way for the television screen are just as applicable as they were 20 or more years ago, when they were first introduced. Then, as now, no reporter was considered to be competent until he or she had achieved at least partial mastery over a small range of basic skills which go beyond any proven journalistic ability.

These techniques, whether for use on videotape of any format, live on location or in the studio, are used to some extent separately or collectively in every contribution a reporter makes to a programme. Each demands its own careful study and development to a point where it can be applied smoothly and instinctively to add the same veneer of professional gloss to the news report that the experienced actor brings to the play.

Of all the skills needed for television news reporting, the piece to camera is among the most frequently used. Although it is sometimes fashionable to consider it dated (some experienced reporters consider they have failed if they have to resort to it), the piece to camera, which is essentially a vision story told on location in the field, remains a sure means of giving the news lucidly.

It has three advantages. It immediately establishes the reporter's presence on the spot: it is extremely simple to execute, and it is fast enough to be considered a kind of contingency sample, rather like the dust scooped up by the first men on the moon in case they had to return to earth rather hurriedly.

Chiefly because of its speed and the fact that there may be on other pictures to supplement it, the piece to camera can be designed as a complete report by itself, yet it probably has greater worth as one ingredient within a comprehensive news report, being versatile enough to be slotted in at almost any point, not necessarily at the opening or closing stage. The term piece to camera is self-descriptive, being those words which the reporter speaks aloud while looking directly into the camera lens and, through it, to the viewer. The fact that the majority of them are spoken from straightforward positions gives rise to the alternative name of stand-upper.

The technique depends on an ability to write spoken language and to remember it word for word when delivering it to the camera. But in some respects what matters more is the choice of location for the operation. For example there seems little to be gained in travelling thousands of miles and then pointing the camera at reporter standing in front of some anonymous brick wall. Unless the brick wall is germane, or there are legal problems such as exist in filming within court precincts, the aim should always be to show that the reporter is actually where he says he is. To say proudly that our reporter is there is one thing. To prove it to the viewer is something else.

That does not mean going to extraordinary lengths to find a background which is visually exciting but irrelevant to the story. It should be enough to place the reporter in a spot which is appropriate, interesting, but not too distracting. Even if the welcome which greets the news team is not overwhelming, the piece to camera and sound equipment have been tested and known to be working properly, and the reporter is ready with the words.

Most pieces to camera are recorded as the reporter stands full-face to the lens. But the effect of putting the reporter to one side of the frame rather than in the centre is that, any action in the background is not completely blotted out and the figure becomes a part of the picture rather than a superimposition on it. Sensible variations are to be welcomed as long as they do not seem to be too contrived. On occasions these may be forced upon the reporter by the situation sitting in aircraft, cars or trains, crouching under fire or walking along a road. So much depends on the styles programmes establish for their reporters to follow.

Much of the apprehension felt by novices about their first pieces to camera is caused by doubts that they will be able to remember their words. Admittedly this can pose a real problem, for it is a knack achieved more easily by some than others.

Newcomers to television news reporting are haunted by the possibility that even a short, apparently simple piece will require several attempts, resulting in a waste of time, temper and a humiliating starring role on the private tape of mistakes that television technicians love to compile for showing at office Christmas parties. They can take comfort from the admission of some experienced reporters that, even under the least difficult circumstances, they are unable to remember more than a few words at a time. Others get them right at the first attempt or never. The majority have occasional off-days but generally survive the ordeal without too much trouble.

Relatively few have memories which allow them to recall prodigious numbers of words without a moment's hesitation.

For everyone else there is no infallible formula certainly not ad-libbing, which is inclined to come across as uncertainty rather than spontaneity. Perhaps the only answer for the beginner is to keep the length of commentary down to the maximum capable of being remembered without difficult, and not forcing more. Little is worse than watching someone totter to within the final few sentences of a piece clearly too long to memorize.

While there is no way of avoiding the problem posed by the limits of memory, and assuming no portable electronic prompting device is available, three possible escape routes suggest themselves. Two are relatively ugly to look at and are therefore strictly second-best, but, in a tight corner, are preferable to a halting performance which seems likely to grind to a full stop at any moment.

The reporter needs to ensure that the opening paragraph at least is word-perfect. The rest may then be read from a note-book or clip-board which is clearly in shot so that the viewer is not left wondering how the memory is being refreshed. Subsequent raising of the head from written script towards camera fro a sentence or two at a time may add just enough refinement to make the performance tolerable.

Even more than usual cooperation from the camera crew. Here the reporter does not attempt to speak the lines in own continuous take. Instead, the script is learned and recorded in two separate chunks of, say, 15 seconds (45 words). For the sections then to fit neatly different way to avoid an awkward jump cut in the middle. The use of this technique should give the reporter some confidence early on. Later attempts should be made to train the memory to accept longer and longer pieces so that eventually there is no need for the split.

Pre-recording the words on to an audio cassette machine

small enough to conceal in a pocket and listening to the replayed tape through a tiny ear-piece while repeating the commentary to camera at the same time. It is an ingenious technique which seems to many to require more effort than that merely needed to learn the words, but practitioners say the recorders give them a confidence they would not otherwise feel, and if it improves their performance for the camera, then it is thoroughly worthwhile.

The method is not without its hazards, though, for there is enough evidence on film and tape to prove that the all-important ear-piece has a habit of popping out into sight at the wrong moment, and the cassette recorders have been known to malfunction and leave the reporter speechless.

Finally, there is no point in any piece to camera script which fails to refer even obliquely, to what is going on in the rest of the picture behind the reporter. Where the background is general rather than specific, it is essential that script and location, however fragile the real connection between the two, are tied together as firmly as possible, preferably by the opening words.

# 7

# EDITORIAL SETUP

A newspaper office or news agency receives a large assortment of news items. These originate from different sources. The news copy is written by experienced and inexperienced people and hence lack uniformity. In any newspapers, there is always a shortage of space for all news items, which are received in the office. A newspaper's success largely depends on the space and its most efficient, judicious and economic use. Hence, within the space set aside for news, as much news as possible needs to be packed to serve a divergent readership. Considering these factors, editing of the news copy becomes essential.

All incoming news items, collectively called copy, is sifted, before being possessed, to achieve a balance of news between that originating within the organisation and that pouring in from outside. The unwanted matter gets weeded out and only the newsworthy stories are finally selected.

The news room is headed by an editor or a chief editor or an editor-in-chief or a chief news editor. He plans and directs the day's news operations. He is supported by a team consisting of the news editors, chief sub-editors, senior sub-editors. In a news agency, news editors and chief subs looks after the smooth functioning of the news desk. They plan and write 'leads'.

News has a number of characteristic elements:

> The nearer the origin of news, i.e., the closer it is to home, the more is its impact. For example, on a particular day, there may be 45 deaths in a boat tragedy in Bangladesh. But, on the same day, a local bomb blast that kills five people is sure to have more impact on the readers.

News grows old quickly. It decays and perishes fast. The more recent its occurrence, the more worthy it is. On the contrary, an event that happened six months back, but is discovered and reported now could grab the front page. For e.g. the bank securities scam including Ketan Parekh.

Names make news and the newspapers like to use as many local names as possible. For example, if the vice-chancellor of a university gets hurt while playing cricket, few people will take note of the incident. But, if a public figure like a minister is injured in a game, we have a more interesting story.

A reader's interest is aroused in a large measure if an event or occurrence affects him, and more so, if he participates in the event. He is eager to know what will this mean to him in the long run. How will it affect him and his family. A steep hike in the prices of petrol, cooking gas, milk or an increase in water and electricity tariffs will have widespread consequences.

Any interesting story about people and their peculiarities, and their infinite variety, make for wider readership. The human interest stories are pure identification. These are the little things that have happened, or could happen to yourself or to your neighbours or friends. These stories are worth little or nothing as news in any strict sense. Yet these are worth telling.

Ideally read a story, preferably thrice-once for familiarisation, once while you edit and third time to check your work. If the story has no glaring problems and if you fully understand it, you would be ready to edit it.

A news story is divided into two parts-the lead and the body. The lead describes, simply and briefly, what happened and the body documents and elaborates the lead. Adequate attention should be paid to the lead. The intro should be concise and crisp. Details should be dispersed and blended in the subsequent paragraphs.

The most significant information is placed at the top and other details follow in their order of importance. Each succeeding para should add an essential detail without being dependent in content or style on what follows. Next, see if the second para supports the lead. The third para should continue the development implicit in the lead and in the second para.

While editing a story, the subeditor should look for errors in spelling, grammar and correct these. But an instant second look might sometimes compel him to rewrite it. Highlight the news point, taking care to avoid distortion and respect the facts produced by the reporter.

When a reader looks for something interesting in a newspaper, it is the heading which catches, his eyes. A story, howsoever well-edited, would not attract him unless it is given a headline. The headline attracts the reader to go through the story. A headline sells the story. Writing a headline is like applying the finishing polish on a well-crafted piece of furniture.

Kicker is another conventional headline, usually a one-line heading with a second line (kicker) above it in a different style and half the type size. It extends no more than midway above the main line.

Hammer is the reverse of kicker, but, usually, in all capital letters. The big type is the kicker and the smaller type the main headline. One word, or two at the most, will suffice of the hammer. By virtue of their size, hammers impress the readers with their importance. But too many hammers on one page may dilute that significance, and destroy the look of the page.

This lead is different from the one already talked about. Suppose there is a train accident at a place 60 km from Punjab. Just an hour before the first edition of a newspaper goes to the press. But we cannot wait till the reporter telephones from the spot or comes back to file the story. We can give a short news about it and wait for further details. Many news items are bound to flow in on the same event, details will pour in once the reporter reaches the site, there shall also be eyewitness accounts. All these are tied together, highlighting the major facts and the lead is written for the newspaper's city edition.

A lead is a device, used mostly in the case of developing stories, for changing the story's emphasis in the light of new information of facts as these unfold.

## Editor at Desk

A copy editor is a bridge between a reporter and the reader. He has divergent roles to perform and docs one or more of these tasks while editing a copy. He need not execute all these functions simultaneously. A copy editor is a gatekeeper and image builder who protects a newspaper's reputation.

***Duties of a Copy Editor :*** A Copy Editor :

(a) Removes rough edges from the copy and polishes it to make it presentable.

(b) Adjusts the copy to the style of his newspaper.

(c) Should carve out each story in a familiar language so that it runs smoothly through the average reader's mind. Smooth writing ensures smooth reading.

(d) Tailors story length to space requirements.

(e) Detects and corrects errors of fact.

(f) Simplifies, clarifies and verifies meanings.

(g) Adjusts stories to make them objective and fair.

(h) Adjusts stories to make these legally safe.

(i) Rewrites and restructures stories extensively, where necessary.

(j) Follow the policy of the newspaper.

(k) Corrects copy in the interest of good taste.

(l) Avoids sensation.

(m) Removes those points that could be called undue publicity.

(n) Deletes doubtful words and sentences.

The production of a newspaper is a delicate and complex process. There is tension since a deadline is to be met. Amidst this tense atmosphere, the sub-editor has to perform his job meticulously. He should possess certain qualities to discharge his functions efficiently.

***Calmness :*** Be calm and composed. You should not get excited when a big story breaks.

***Decisive :*** Take quick and correct decisions. The editorial department has no place for indecisives.

***Non-partisan :*** Never take sides.

***Memory :*** Have a sharp memory for counter-checking facts.

***Grasp :*** Size up the situation as it unfolds, and estimate its relevance.

Know your reader.

***Self Confidence :*** Have confidence enough to correct a bad copy written by anyone.

***Mature :*** Be mature enough to correct only bad copy, and not just make changes for the sake of changing.

***Sceptical :*** Do not accept anything at face value. You should approach everything as a source of potential error.

***Knowledge :*** Be a jack of all trades. A good editor should store most of the information as it comes across, and search for more.

***Stability :*** Have enough stability to work under pressure.

***Tools :*** The copy editor will require a set to tools, the lack of which may lead to loss of valuable time. These aids are indispensable. Often you may come across problems of spellings and facts. You should focus on the errors, and correct the name.

***Language :*** The basic building blocks of journalism are words. You should respect the words, and follow the way these are arranged and strung together. Any misplacement of words could twist the meaning. Hence, you should pay attention to punctuation marks, grammar and syntax. All these are important in the sentence construction.

***Punctuation Marks :*** Punctuation problems start and almost end with a comma. This little mark causes more trouble than the rest put together.

Punctuation marks brings in clarity and better readability. At the same time, too many of these clutter a story. There should be no comma after a verb unless it is immediately followed by a parenthesis.

## Working Knowledge

A news item or story may run into several paras, and also exceed one page. If running into pages, a news story has to be kept track of from amongst various stories, and chronologically arranged. Hence, these paras, in a page, are divided into two of three parts. Then, these parts are 'slugged' and numbered, i.e., given a label, which identifies that story for that particular day, and helps the editor on duty to bring different parts together. Related stories are slugged to make the relationship clear. Slug is an identification mark or tag. It is often the key word in a story and written on top left or right of a page.

As soon as you start editing a copy, the first symbol you use is for paragraph indentation. Even if your para is indented, you should mark this symbol on every para. This would help the typesetter in knowing that you want paragraph to begin at that spot. Always note that editing marks are large and clear.

Pictures submitted for publication in the newspapers and magazines have to be edited to fit into the layout of the page, and also the unnecessary portions cut off, which the photographer might have added in the actual composition. The competent photo editor's job is to see to it that he does not waste space, and trims a picture keeping the main essence of the subject intact. This reduction process is called 'chopping'.

It is the job of the photo editor to select the best photograph which tells the story on its own. The photo editor edits it to suit the space in the page without destroying or distorting the essence of the picture, and gives it a good display. It is the photo editor's duty to give the photographer ideas about the picture possibilities.

A good photographer must be able to handle every assignment the editor gives him to his own satisfaction. One has to work with a great speed on a location. You should actually shoot a news event from several different angles, and let your photo editor decide which picture to use.

The newspaper photographs are based on factual situation. The photographs illustrates an event, bring depth into it, and probably comment on it. Usually, the photographer is given only an idea to work with, and is expected to create an appropriate photograph to illustrate it. This is where a good memory or a notebook will come in handy. The photographic techniques involved in shooting for magazines are not much different from those in newspapers. The technical skill is again taken for granted, and your primary concern is to illustrate the story clearly and completely.

The intelligent photo editors adopt different creative cropping techniques to bring out the exact point of emphasis a 'pix'. They try to enlarge the main image, which will have a better visual impact. A photo editor studies the picture carefully, and decides about the cropping. First, he crops the picture mentally and then decides on the final edited photograph. A badly cropped pix can not be repaired. A good photo editor is one who can visualise how the picture will look like when it is cropped and printed in different sizes and shapes.

In a professional organization, the photographers leave contact sheets with the photo editors to enable them to choose the right frame, and mark the composition. Sometimes, the photographers send the exposed rolls, and leave the rest of the job to the photo editors. In most countries, where there is competition amongst the leading newspapers, the photo editor looks for pictures from the freelancers as well. He chooses the best picture, and places it in the newspaper. It leaves no bad feelings amongst the staffers, because they also know that their newspapers should have the best coverage. This system makes every photographer work very hard on the assignments, and be alert with the competitive spirit.

Even though the news picture is supposed to tell a story on its own, one should say where and when the incident took place. Caption writing is an art by itself, which conies with experience and aptitude. The picture and its caption are complementary to each other, and it is very essential to mention when and where the picture was taken, and who the persons seen in the picture are.

If the photograph is described in the body of the story, then there is no need for a separate caption and the pix could hang in between the paragraphs. Sometimes to box a powerful picture with just a detailed caption brightens the page.

In most coverages, photographer reaches the spot only after the incident takes place, and is able to take only the result of what had already happened. In such special cases the newspaper or magazine might have to depend upon graphic illustrations to detail the activities that had taken place on a particular spot earlier.

However, with the advancement of technology, photo editing is done by the computer, which eliminates all the unessential elements, and gives out only the section as per the commands. Photos can be stored and recalled on the computer as and when required.

The newspaper composing and printing methods have gone through major changes during the past few decades. However, the basic function remains the same, to convert the printing matter into printable format. The composing methods used by newspaper industry range from hand composing to computer-guided operations. The major composing processes are-

> Hand setting is the original method of setting movable type. In this the compositor works with a composing stick, a type case and the metal type itself: letters, punctuation marks, figures, and spaces. The compositor adjusts the composing stick to the desired pica measure or line length. After taking out proofs and carrying out the necessary corrections, the next step is to make up the page. Since the composed matter consists of hundreds of individual pieces, it is essential that it is locked up, may be directly on the bed of the press.

This method involves casting type from molten metal. There are four popular type casting machines:

> These are mechanical methods of composing and casting type in the piece lines called 'slugs'. The name

> Linotype is derived from casting a line-of-type. In both systems, the operator sits at a keyboard. The machine is adjusted to set type to the desired pica measure and leading. The upper front section of the machine carries a slotted metal container, which holds the matrices and when the operator strikes the keys, the matrices fall into positions to form a line-of-type. After the matter is composed the type is locked up. Any change within a line means that the entire line, or even all the succeeding lines in a paragraph have to be reset.

The basic difference between linotype and intertype is of the intertype of matrices. They can be used for casting headlines as well as body matter.

As the name suggests 'monotype' casts the characters one by one rather than as a complete line. It is a combination of two machines, a keyboard and a typecaster. It is a two-machine method of casting individual type characters, mechanically.

To set type the machine is adjusted to the required pica measure and leading. As the copy is typed, it produces a perforated paper roll, which is used to drive the typecaster. A combination of holes dictates the letters, spaces and punctuation marks to be set.

To set type, the perforated roll is fitted on the typecaster, where it directs the casting mechanism by means of compressed air. The air passing through the perforations brings the matrix holder and the specific matrix ready to be filled with molten metal into proper position. Once the type has been cast, it is ejected onto a galley, one character at a time.

This is a combination of handsetting and machine casting operations. The operator sets the type matrices and leading in a composing stick by hand. The composed matrices are then locked up into a casting machine, where they are filled with molten lead to produce the slug.

It is also known as cold type-setting, as it does not involve metal casting. Its first phase resembles that of monotype setting. Unless the perforator or keyboard is attached to a video display unit, the operation is limited to conversion of copy matter into a coded perforated tape. This perforated tape is then fed into a programmed computerised unit, which projects the desired images of type characters onto photosensitive film. This film is then made up in mechanicals from which printing plates can be produced. Photo-composing provides a fast, flexible and reasonable economical method of setting type.

Newspapers come in different shapes and sizes. There are newspapers that provide general public interest news to the readers, there are other which cater to the needs of the specialists. Every newspaper has its own way of presenting news, views and features.

The front page of a newspaper should be attractive, which will hold the attention of the readers. The front page is the "face" of a newspaper.

Newspapers have a name and each newspaper tries to acquire a unique identity by observing different ways.

On the front page, the masthead of a newspaper is much more than just the name of the newspaper. Some of its characteristics are-

— it is in distinctive bold print,

— it is in a big type size,

— it has a fixed place on the front page,

— it remains in the same form for years.

Headlines are a means to attract the readers towards the news items. It is the responsibility of the page-designer to make each headline as distinctive as possible. Headlines are given generally by the sub-editors/copy editors.

Picture is worth a thousand words. On the same basis, it can be extrapolated that a good cartoon is worth at least two thousand words. From a page designer's point of view, it is important to realise that photographs, cartoons and graphic have a special significance. Placing a picture or cartoon at wrong place may not only reduce its utility, but also reduce the design appeal of the total page. A page designer has to examine whether the picture, cartoon, graphic, chart, has an independent value or it has to be juxtaposed with a particular news story. The size may have to be adjusted due to placement or space considerations.

There is a design in the page, a form and a structure. Each page designer has his own concept of beauty and page structure. To bring it out, he uses different type sizes, white spaces, placement of pictures, graphs, charts, cartoons etc.

Inside pages of a daily newspaper differ from the front page in their format, structure and presentation of contents. By grouping news items on specific pages we are able to give the newspaper a structure. The inside pages under one group often tend to cover as many news items as possible. Hence, often these pages may seem cluttered.

The format of this page looks similar in many newspapers in India and abroad. There is a section, on this page, where the editor(s) write their analysis of the major national and international news items. Along with that, there may be one or two articles written by prominent people on current topics.

The design of the inside pages of a newspaper is relatively much more structured than the front page, which is dependent on the major happenings during the past few hours.

Advertisements have special significance for commercial publications. The very existence of newspapers and magazines depends on the revenue from advertisements. Hence, special care must be taken with regard to placement of advertisements along with the news stories on the pages. Advertisements are placed on these pages according to the product or service to be advertised. Large colour advertisements have special significance in page design.

Newspapers are meant to be read. As far as possible the news item should be contained in a neatly defined area. Each letter, each word and each story has special significance. Readability for a page-designer has a different meaning than that for a reporter, sub-editor or proof-reader. Readability from a page designer's point of view depends on placement of the news stories, typography and the overall page layout.

Today with the help of computers one can develop new type faces by incorporating variations in size, form and shape of each letter. It is the size, form and shape that determine and distinguish the type face of a letter. As page designers, we must select type by analysing its visual appearance as well as readability of its type face. While the choices may be many, editors of daily newspapers for the sake of economy, workability and convenience to its readers, make deliberate attempt to limit the variations of type faces used in their page make-up. Many newspapers adopt just one type face in different sizes throughout the newspaper.

Each letter or alphabet has immense potential to be used as a piece of art.

Because of economic and managerial reasons, newspapers use very limited type faces. Some newspapers may use only one. The only variation being the size. However, with the popularity of phototypesetting and offset printing, newspapers have a wider choice in matching and contrasting of type faces.

In page layout, when we want to emphasize or highlight a word, an expression, a sentence, a paragraph or even a portion of the news item, we have many options before us. Some of them are-

- — Use of different type form of the letters such as italics.
- — Use of bolder type face for the word or portion of the news item to be emphasized.
- — Underlining the word or sentence.

The portion to be emphasized may be displayed with the wider margin, different colour or a combination of above alternatives.

## Developments of Recent Past

Speedy transmission of news is as important as the actual news gathering. It has been made possible by the advanced electronic equipment. News is a perishable commodity. The newspaper staff have to be on their toes to ensure that important news items are processed quickly, to meet the deadlines of publication.

But rapid transmission of news becomes meaningless if information being imparted is inaccurate. In this context, the accuracy of the data and apparently minor details of spellings and language, assume importance. Such correction work is done with the help of the computers and 'fax' machines.

The computer are an ideal system for storing data in their memory and this data could be retained at a later stage. The computers act as the data banks, and are very useful sources of reference for the newspapers.

A computer is an automatic electronic apparatus for making calculations, besides storing and processing information. For this data along with instructions on how to process the same have to be fed into the computer. That is called the 'input'. The result obtained from the computer after processing of the data is called the 'output'.

The hardware components of the computers refer to all the physical parts viz. electronic and mechanical parts.

The software components of a computer refer to the set of instructions given to it to perform a specified task. These are fed to the computer in a language understood by it called a 'program'.

The arrangement of captions, photographs and graphic on a page would have to facilitate easy reading, besides being visually appealing. Certain parameters of format are fixed for any newspaper, such as those of the page size, print area, number of columns, positions of masthead, allotment of articles according to their categories and page titles.

## Using Computers

The Desktop Publishing, the DTP for short, refers to both hardware and software that are involved in preparing high quality prints of pages, once these are composed satisfactorily. The prints are used as artwork, and the actual duplication is done by offset printing, owing to the high costs involved in the DTP operations. The hardware of a DTP includes a large-sized colour monitor of the VDU (Visual Display Unit) and a laser printer apart from the CPU, which is programmed to suit the DTP software. The laser printer involves a high-speed, high-quality printer technology.

The DTP software consist of programmes to compose pages and their layout. These perform the function of the word-processing and automatic margin alignment, providing a variety of type-faces, page-numbering, etc.

Although DTP is considered incomparable when it comes to composing a page according to specifications. It handles the entire process with ease, completing the tasks at a rapid pace. But a few limitations persist in the new DTP packages too, like-

(a) It is not possible to obtain on the VDU an exact copy of the colours, as they would appear in the final print.

(b) The monitor is capable of showing the character in white against a background, whereas the actual product is black & white.

(c) The monitor shows only a restricted areas of each page. Such fragmented views make it difficult for an entire page to be visualised.

(d) A change once made in the typography might not eventually be printed as the package would not be programmed for it.

The appearance of a newspaper contributes to its having greater or lesser readership. There are number of readers who get addicted to their daily papers just because they take a liking to its layout and design. Each publication has a tradition which is flexible enough to accommodate innovative changes in the design layout with the passage of time. However, the readers might welcome such change only to a certain point. Both content and style of presentation matter in attracting readership.

## The Authorities

Every journalist unless he is happy to remain a worker for the rest of his life-carries the dream of being an editor. Who is a newspaper editor?

## Principal Authority

He is not, as is commonly believed the man who writes the editorials. He is the man, who conducts a newspaper. Usually at the bottom of the last page of every paper, is what is known as the Imprint Line. The Imprint Line is mandatory and pins responsibility on what goes into print on the men who bring out a daily. Consider this Imprint Line:

Printed and published for the Proprietors, Bennett, Coleman & Co. Ltd., by *T.P. Pithavala* at *the Times of India Press,* Dr. D.N.

Road, Bombay 400 001. Editor: Girilal Jain. Resident Editor: K.C. Khanna. General Manager: Dr. Ram S. Tarneja.... Everything is clearly stated.

If a newspaper in any way contravenes the law, the men responsible-the editor and the printer and publisher-can easily be identified and located and will have to obey the court's summons. The editor's chair in the circumstances, is not necessarily a comfortable one. The man who occupies it does not have an easy job. He bears a heavy responsibility and often has been called upon to pay a heavy price in the discharge of that responsiblity.

There is no one way applicable to all aspirants. Anyone who has the money to set up shop as an editor can become one. There are no rules and regulations, no memberships to be filled, no examination to pass. A mere declaration suffices.

Editors in the formative stage of the Indian Press were men imbued with a sense of mission. Robert Knight who made *The Times of India* into a great institution early in its career came to his job with experience in civil life and the running of public institutions. *The Pioneer* was started by Sir George Allen, a businessman of Kanpur and his son C.T. Allen. Of the three enterprising brothers Hemanta Kumar Ghosh, Sisir Kumar Ghosh and Motilal Ghosh who started the *Amrita Bazar Patrika,* the first two were working as employees in the Income Tax Department. S. Kasturi Ranga Iyengar who bought *The Hindu* in 1905 was a lawyer.

But there were others, men like Arthur Moore, Kalinath Ray, A.D. Mani, Benjamin Horniman, S. Sadanand and Prank Moraes who came to their jobs the hard way. Devdas Gandhi got his experience assisting his father in the running of *Young India.* Sadanand also had his apprenticeship with the same paper. Prank Moraes first worked as-an assistant editor with *The Times of India* from 1938 to 1946 during which, for a three-year period he also doubled as a war correspondent. He became deputy editor in1949 and a full editor only in 1950. Kotamaraju Rama Rao, who became the crusading editor of *National Herald,* had his apprenticeship as a reporter under T.L. Vaswani of the *New Times* of Hyderabad,

Sind. M. Chalapathi Rao worked as an assistant editor first at the *National Herald* and later at *The Hindustan Times* before he became editor of *Herald.* Pothan Joseph worked for a string of papers like the *Voice of India,* the *Indian Daily Mail* and *The Hindustan Times* interspersing his editorial career with a few executive assignments such as that of the Principal Information Officer of the Government of India. These distinguished men give the lie to the belief that editors are born and not made.

An editorship is not a bed of roses and has never been. Easy as his life may seem he works under all manner of pressuresland not all-necessarily coming from the management. Because his is the final responsibility in bringing out the paper he has to bear the brunt of the wrath whether of advertisers or of existing governments', During the Emergency (1975-77) in India, it was the editor who had to shoulder the burden of official wrath. Editors in India have been under pressure for decades, in fact from the very beginning of the British rule in the country. The Vernacular Press Act was passed in 1878 in order to control the *Amrita Bazar Patrika,* then published in Bengali as well as in English-the *Patrika* being bilingual. To get out of the clutches of the Act, its publishers changed over completely to English beginning 21 March 1878.

The *Patrika* has a long history of editorial daring and competence. At one time, the Government of Bengal recommended the deportation of one of the paper's earliest editors, Motilal Ghosh. On another occasion, the paper had to face prosecution in connection with the famous Barisal Conspiracy Case. Ghosh fought the charges and succeeded in getting the case dismissed. In 1932, the *Patrika* was penalized and a security of Rs 6,000 was demanded from it.

Another paper to fall foul of the government was the *Free Press Journal.* So powerful were the writings of its editor-publisher S. Sadanand that he had to forfeit the then phenomenal figure or Rs 70,000 as security. Indian editors were not the only ones to face the British government's wrath. E.G. Horniman of the *Bombay Chronicle* frequently clashed with officialdom and, at one time, the paper's printer and publisher were asked to deposit Rs 3,000 as security which was later forfeited. The history of Indian journalism is full of such instance of editors, fighting valiantly to protect the honour and integrity of the free press.

Many editors have also fallen foul of the owners of newspapers, though, in one instance, when C.Y. Chintamani differed from his-paper's Board of Directors and offered to resign, it was the offending member of the Board, Pandit Madan Mohan Malaviya who decided to quit instead.

No two editors are alike. The only common denominator that can be ascribed to them is their humanity, their concern for people, their interest in new. A delicate problem for every editor is the extent to which he can, and should, delegate authority. In a large paper an editor would have from two to six, sometimes as many as eight assistant editors. Each would have specialized in a particular field of activity such as foreign affairs, national affairs, law, finance, defence, agriculture or whatever. No editor can possibly be an expert in all fields and even if he happens to be an immensely knowledgeable man, he just would not have the time to keep up with new developments. It is amazing how much a writer has to put in by way of reading. It could be new books on the subject, documents pertaining to it or upcoming literature dealing with the issue. No editor is expected to be a know-all. It is an editor's task to know who, among his colleagues, is best equipped to write on an event and to assign the task to him. By this the editor is not surrendering his responsibility, he is exercising it wisely. A good editor should know how best to tap the available talent in his office.

It is common in most editorial offices for the editor to have a morning conference with his staff. Often it-is done around the coffee table where assistant editors can sit informally and not only discuss the day's newspaper but engage in a post-mortem of the news. Depending on what the day's most important issues are, there will be a discussion of some of them at the end of which the editor would lay down his own views and give guidelines. If the editorial staff is fairly homogenous there would be no difficulty in arriving at a consensus as to what editorial line should be taken on any given subject. Often, if the assistant editors have worked over a long period with the editor, they would know instinctively as to what angle would be projected. In any event it is the editor who lays down the policy and the subject of the editorials. Who will write what is also discussed and decided on at this conference.

An editor of a party paper will have no difficulty in the matter of policy as it would have been laid down for him. It would be his task to argue the party case as well as he can; he has a brief. An ideal paper, of course, would be one where its owners would let the editor make his own decisions and argue on the merits of a subject. In that event he would have to be as honest and objective as he can possibly be, placing, as he should, the public interest before anything else. He will know that life is not a bed orroses. He must expect to be subjected to all forms of persuasion, not all of them scrupulous, including flattery, bribery, even physical threats, not to mention behind-the-scene wire-pulling.

Though an editor is once removed from the actual production of a paper, it is in his power to decide what should be published and what shouldn't. In a sense he has to play God. This is a tremendous responsibility and cannot be ducked. It is an insensitive man and consequently a poor editor who has on occasion tortured himself over taking a decision that could possibly have harmed many people. The editors of *The New York Times* have admitted publicly their regret that they did not publish information about the US government's plans to abet the invasion of Cuba. If the paper had published the news, they have argued, the country may well have been saved the embarrassment of the Bay of Pigs fiasco.

Most editors may not be called upon to take momentous decisions, yet editing a paper is one long struggle against time, during: which decisions, one way or the other have to be taken. This is both the charm and frustration of being an editor Responsibility ends with him.

Editors have different methods of dealing with the problem of leader writing. Some dictate and then make the final corrections. Some do their own typing. Some others write laboriously in long hand. Some finish their writing by the end of the evening and place a phone call before retiring to bed to see that events have not-overtaken the editorial. Some others refuse to put down a word on paper until midnight.

## Attempt towards Social Awakening

The important thing for an editor is always to be keenly aware of the needs of the public and to be able to feel its pulse. It is to him that the reader will look to, interpret yesterday's news. An editor-and certainly a good editor-will offer leadership to the country as only he can. But for that, he will have to offer leadership to his staff, in the first instance. What often makes a news paper great is the right combination of inspiration, emphasis design, control, tone and selectivity. It is the editor who will have to see that through his personal leadership, this combination is,achieved. It is not-and cannot be-an easy task.

An editor will soon learn-if he has not by the time-he has become one-that his time is not always his own. In the office he will have to be in constant, if not continuous, touch with his colleagues. Outside the office he will be in demand as a public speaker,-as a guest at dinners and parties. These are chores that may not always be pleasant for him and more often than not are tiring and time consuming. And yet only by listening to friends and foes in various situations can an editor come to know what the public thinks. Dinners may be hard on the waistline but it is during the after-dinner coffee that an important politician may want to unburden himself to an editor to seek his reaction. An editor must make himself available to those who have something important and worthwhile to say. This may not be very conducive to a settled married life, but it is an occupational hazard that editors have to face. A major problem confronting the "ideal" editor-the editor who 'puts public' interest before everything else is the extent to which he should extend cooperation to the government. It is not the job of the editor to give uncritical support to whatever administration is in power. Neither can it be said that his should be an unrestrained attack. Some journalists pretend that no one but the editor and proof reader read editorials. Such a view is extremely misleading. Whatever the situation be elsewhere in the world, in India there is ample evidence to show that editorials are read with interest. Editors often are more influential than they are prone to tell themselves. It may be that editorial influence is more over policy makers than over the public at large. The fact remains that editorials ("leaders") cannot be dismissed out of hand as mere space fillers.

An interesting comment has been made on the subject by James Reston of the *New York Times.* Speaking about the influence or the American Press on the American foreign policy, Mr. Reston pointed out that in his view this is usually exaggerated. "Its influence" he said, "is exercised primarily through the Congress, which confuses press opinion with public opinon. No doubt the press has great influence on American foreign policy when things are *obviously* going badly. It has very little influence, however, when things are going badly but the impending disaster is not obvious and the government is saying, as it usually does, that all is well or soon will be if everybody only has faith and confidence."

This is largely true. When things are going reasonably well, the tendency for the public is to accept government statements; the public frequently wants to be assured and is willing to believe or, at the very least, to suspend judgement. The crunch comes when things go badly and then it is to the critical editor that the public will turn. This was amply shown when, soon after the Emergency in India was lifted, the sales of newspapers suddenly soared to phenomenal heights. The public was turning to the editors to tell it the whole story unvarnished. The circulation of *The Indian Express,* for instance, showed a remarkable rise in the immediate post-Emergency months.

The important thing for an editor is, to be intellectually honest. He does not always have to be right; in the nature of things he cannot be so. But as long as he is honest and is seen to be honest, his responsibility to his profession ceases there. Nothing more can be expected of an editor and nothing more should.

The problem of honesty is more complicated than one thinks. What, for instance, should an editor's attitude be towards Mrs. Indira Gandhi at a time when the Janata Government is at sixes and sevens? Should the editor refuse to support her as a possible leader of an alternate government on the grounds that her role during the Emergency disqualifies her to receive any support any time or should he take the stand that as a leader of proven stature and stamina, Mrs. Gandhi deserves support at a time of national instability? It is here that an editor whose credibility is beyond challenge can get respectful attention from his reading public. In other words, for an editor, credibility is all.

## The Communication

It is important for an editor to be in constant touch with government officials from ministers downward. Senior editors get easy audience with ministers, since it pays the ministers themselves to nave their policies and views understood in the right perspective by the opinion-makers. The editor who lives in an ivory tower is becoming increasingly rare, if ever such a species existed. He cannot afford to be too far from the madding crowd. The crowd is and should be his business. Almost all editors to a person, complain of the heavy schedule that they have to put up with. Consider this average day put in by one editor who usually is up around 6.30 in the morning and, goes for a half hour early morning walk. Then as he has his tea, he reads the morning papers, especially his competitors. If, as frequently happens, an item of interest has been missed by his paper, he will make a note of it for later discussion with his staff. He is in his office by 10 a.m.

10.00-10.45 a.m.: Staff meeting. This is the time devoted to dissecting the day's performance with assistant editors and assigning writing work to them.

10.45-11.30 a.m.: The editor meets the News Editor, the Chief Reporter and the Chief of his News Bureau. The discussion will relate to why some stories were missed, or why some were not adequately displayed or why some others should not have been displayed. The *post mortem* over, the discussion will deal with upcoming stories and how to cover them.

11.30-12 noon: Individual assistant editors will stray in to discuss specific ideas and to get editorial approval for them.

12 noon-2.00 p.m.: The editor will do whatever writing he plans to do for the next day's paper, taking a 15-minute break for a quick lunch.

2.00-4.00 p.m.: This is the time to look into copy submitted to him by his assistant editors, to select articles and special features to go for the next day's editorial page.

4.00-5.00 p.m.: This is Visitor's Hour when public citizens, usually those who have previously made appointments call on the Editor with complaints, suggestions or plain gossip.

5.00-6.00 p.m.: Time to look quickly into New Delhi and provincial papers and also at foreign papers and dispose off work with-the Bureau.

At 6.00 p.m. the editor leaves for his home where he will wash, change and relax.

8.30 p.m.: Dinner engagement. This is not an everyday affair but is sufficiently frequent to be taken as part of the day's work. Before going out, however, the editor usually calls the office and tell where he may be found in an emergency. Usually he himself calls the news-editor to check on late news breaks.

11.00 p.m.: Back home and one more late night call to the office to check certain details. Mostly arrangements are made to send him the final proofs of the editorial page so that should last minute changes become necessary they can be quickly incorporated.

This does not permit much time to engage in sports or hobbies. A major complaint of editors is that they do not get the time needed to refurbish their minds. "I am living on my capital" is how Mr. Girilal Jain expressed his frustration. According to him, in 15 months he had taken only four days off and had seen only two films, which is probably a good average for most editors.

There are editors and editors. What makes for a truly great editor? According to Mr. M. Chalapathi Rau, C.Y. Chintamani was one. The following article written by Mr. Rau for *Swarajya* gives us a clear picture of why he thought so.

"Chintamani was a journalist, mostly an editor, with a pontiff's air but without pontiff's pomp. An editor of his period, enjoying considerable reputation, a legislator and political leader, possessing a muscular, vigourous style, he had a right to pontificate, and he pontificated giving a further lease of life to the leading article, before journalism made news techniques dominate the newspaper.

My acquaintance with Chintamani was brief but interesting my irreverence about eminence coinciding with the climax of career. It was my ambition not to be a journalist and neither the Spenders, nor the Chintamanis attracted me much. But style did, style as an extension of personality and not merely as an assembly of words, even if it was proper words in proper places or the best words in the best order.

With my interest in politics, I was reading in Madras with great interest the leading articles in a weekly edition of the *Leader* published from Allahabad. By then, I was forgetting Mill on Liberty and Morley on Compromise and was a convert to the Congress. So I could not but read the *Leader* critically. But an admiration for the argumentativeness, the consistency of outlook and the vigourous syntax of the main leading articles developed.

As an admirer of the orators who could rouse emotions one could not admire Chintamani, a speaker of cold logic, though with warm interjections, when I first heard him in Bombay. Then I heard him in Waltair in 1936 or so when he delivered his lectures which later became his book *Politics Since the Indian Mutiny,* abroad survey with many personalities, sketches and amusing anecdotes. Dr. S.Radhakrishnan presided. I rememher Radhakrishnan making caustic references to the Liberals and Chintamani reacting to them vigorously. I was among the few who listened to his Table-Talk as he sat at his brother's place in an easy chair-and pontificated off the record. He had no doubt about anything. Sastri had intellectual honesty but no intellectual courage. Sapru had intellectual courage but no intellectual honesty. Sivaswamy Iyer, who had both intellectual honesty and intellectual courage was India's most accurate thinker, and came only after Gandhi and Malaviya as a great man. Gandhi, of course, was one of the greatest men the world had known but he had done immense mischief in politics....

I had no prejudice against Chintamani but my irreverence extended to him. There was much talk of what people called his phenomenal memory. I held even then that memory was selective. If one remembered certain things, one did not remember other things. Chintamani was reputed to remember all the Congress Presidential addresses, the list of all the Popes, the birthdays of famous Indians, when and where he had met Gokhale or Malaviya first and so on. He also remembered British constitutional debates on India or the debates in Indian legislatures. And many other things. But I was afraid he did not remember many other things because he did not care for them or did not care to remember them. He did not seem to care much for foreign affairs though India had no foreign policy of its own then as an appendage of an empire. He could elaborate some historical parallels and narrrate vividly some historical anecdotes. But in general he showed no sense of history. My point is not that he was not sufficiently educated but that he concentrated on a few things and did not care for much else.

*The Leader* was read mainly for its leading articles and Chintamani was admired, even adored, for most of them. He wrote on all important Indian political subjects, leaving South Africa and other matters to his assistants and whenever he wrote, the world knew that he wrote. There was first his vast knowledge of Indian political subjects, there was then no mistaking the conviction with which he wrote, there was finally the force and vigour with which he wrote. To the Liberals, his was the voice of the Mesosiah.... He had read all the best biographies and auto biographies in the English language and remembered them. He did not forget what this Secretary of State or that had said or what this Viceroy had done. The unflagging energy with which he wrote sustained the readers' interest, even when he wrote two columns. My irreverence disappeared whenever I read leading articles written by him.

Above all there was character in whatever he wrote or did. This enhanced his intellectual and moral stature. He would be no turncoat, no Titus Oates. Chintamani had resigned his ministership on a matter of principle, somewhat rare in our history before Independence, and after Independence. The people in D.P. could not forget it. He enjoyed life. He was kind to young people. He was a fine conversationalist.... I found he did not know enough of economics, did not understand what the Gold Standard was. Chintamani had his personal predilections believed in the other world and spirits and while I was hearing, it, he surprised me by saying that Gokhale's spirit had dictated an editorial to him. He wrote even on the transfer of Superintendents of Police and his obituary editorials ended with 'May his soul rest in peace'. When Chief Justice Thorn died, he wrote that 'the summons had come to his Lordship from above' which roused my amusement.

The more I have known of Indian journalism, however, the more reverent I have become about him. As a leader-writer, he was a rare type. Other leader-writers who have given me equal pleasure were Kalinath Ray of the *Tribune* with his logic chopping and N. Raghunathan of *The Hindu,* who at his best reminded me of the leading articles of the old *Times Literary Supplement.* Chin tam ani was a personality; he had character. He was a great editor".

Consider here the qualities that Chalapathi Rau admired in Chintamani: knowledge, ability, good memory, vast knowledge of Indian politics, adherance to principles at any cost, unflagging energy, courage of convictions; style, character. And an overriding ego.

Editors, to be sure, have egos that seem to go with the job. An ideal editor, of course, will have opinions (or what is an editor for?) but will not be opinionated. Some of the great editors of our times have been men with strong opinions, men like Sadanand, "Stalin" Srinivasan, S. Natarajan, Frank Moraes or C. Narasimhan. They lent to the papers they edited their strength of conviction. An editor without an opinion is like a river without water. He will go nowhere.

Chintamani confessed a lack of expertise in economics. No editor, it is fair to say, can possibly be knowledgeable in all subjects but it is expected of him to have a lively curiosity and an abiding interest in what makes the world go. Today's editor, besides, must be more than a leader-writer; to be an effective editor he will have to know something of making layouts, or cropping a picture or reviewing a film; in other words, it would not hurt to be a jack-of-all-trades while being master of a few.

In the twenties, thirties and well into the forties and fifties, a paper could still sell on the personality of the editor, though it is pertinent to remember that newspaper circulation was in the mid 50,000s for most papers and a circulation figure of 100,000 was considered something of a distant dream. But editors of that era were well-known to their readers and they carried something of an aura about them. Editors today are less well-known; editorials are read but they are disembodied views rather than the live thoughts of a man passionately committed to truth. Newspapers no more sell on the strength of editorials no matter how well they are written or argued or presented. There was a time when writing in the *Indian Express* Frank Moraes placed his views on the front page. That did not perceptibly increase the circulation of the *Express.* If a paper is to sell it must take into account popular tastes whether in politics, economics, sports or films. That this is increasingly being recognized can be noticed from the fact that the *Express,* again, is devoting a page for features, an innovation in Indian journalism.

## Taste of Masses

We may take a brief *detour* to examine a subject that editors are continuously called upon to face, the public mind.

As all editors know, the public is not as well informed as it should be and it often does not even care. Editors are seldom known.

M.V. Kamath who has edited *The Illustrated Weekly of India* has had letters addressed to him in the name of H.V. Kamath, an older man and distinguished Member of Parliament whose name has long registered in the reader's sub-conscience. A Carnegie Endowment survey once established that many Americans believed and this in a country with a powerful communication media-erroneously that the NATO Treaty was negotiated through the United Nations. And the *New York Times* disclosed that nearly one third of the Americans surveyed by its reporters did not know that Berlin was located in communist East Germany. Social scientists can document such findings also in India at all levels of public intelligence.

If this be the case what is the public that the editor is addressing himself to? If public knowledge is limited should he, as one writer has facetiously suggested, put out papers that look like Mother Goose rhyme-books and write for readers with an intelligence,quotient just slightly above that of a moron? The fact of the matter is that in India, at least, there is a substantial section of the public that is highly sophisticated. This is borne out by the letters that editors get every day, some of which are witty, provocative and often throwing new light on old problems.

## Editor's Job

An editor enjoys immense powers such as are not often realized even in editorial sanctum sanctora. He can make or mar reputations. This is difficult to prove statistically. It has been said that even if the average mind could be plumbed for its reaction to any given editorial, no standard could be devised to project its long-term effect. The effect of the written word, by its nature, is incalculable. We know, for example, that newspapers down the years have been suppressed and the only conclusion that we can draw from that fact is that governments have always been conscious of the power of the press. Obviously not every editor is powerful. And the size of a paper's circulation is no guidepost to an editor's influence. The circulation of *Harijan* that Mahatma Gandhi edited was not much to speak about. It never really ever touched even the 50,000 mark. And yet, in terms of moving the governments, it was probably the most powerful paper in its time, certainly as long as Mahatma Gandhi was actively engaged in editing it. But it was the Mahatma who made the *Harijan.* These days, too often, it is the newspapers who make the editors.

Nevertheless, editors have certain responsibilities commensurate with their powers. These are *(a)* to the state, *(b)* to their proprietors, *(c)* to their readers, and *(d)* to their own conscience, and not necessarily in that order. An editor without a conscience needs to be watched. He could be an enemy of the people. Unscrupulous editors may one day get their due, but they can do irritrievable damage to a nation's psyche, while they are in circulation.

The problem of an editor's responsibility to the state has never quite been defined though, when efforts have been made by governments to muzzle the press, it has been loudly articulated. During the Second World War, Arthur Moore of *The Statesman* was sought to be muzzled and the Viceroy even suggested that he be repatriated to England, on security grounds. In times of war, of course, governments will clamp down censorship on the press, but it is the peace-time relationship between the government and the press that call for examination. When senior correspondents asked Mr. V.K. Krishna Menon-after the Goa take-over was complet-ed-why they had not been given prior intimation of the "invasion,"

Mr. Menon blandly replied. "How was I to know that you would not leak the information to foreign embassies?" Mr. Menon is not alone in the kind of thinking that goes into government press relations. On 2 October 1962, toward the end of the Cuban crisis week, Arthur Sylvester, Assistant Secretary of Defence for Public Affairs (and a former Washington correspondent of the *Newyork News)* called a press conference. It was a tense session. Newspapermen charged the US government with withholding the facts regarding the Cuban crisis and giving out misleading and even untruthful information. Sylvester responded:

I can't think of a comparable situation, but in the kind of world we live in, the generation of news by actions taken by the government becomes one weapon in a strained situation. The results, in my opinion, justify the methods we use. News generated by actions of the government as to content and timing are part of the arsenal of weaponry that a President has in application of military force and related forces to the solution of political problems, or to the applications of international political pressures.

Sylvester and his State Department counterpart, Robert Manning (who was later to become editor of the *Atlantic Monthly),* signed orders requiring the military and civilian officers talking to the press report to whom they talked and what was discussed. (The State Department order was rescinded a month later but the Defence Department order was in force for full five years). The memorandum for Defence personnel said:

Procedures for handling media representatives.

The subject of each interview and telephone conversation with a media representative will be reported to the appropriate public information office before the close of business that day. A report need to be made if a representative of the public information office is present at the interview.

In such a situation how should an editor handle his job? Sylvester had suggested, by way of justification of the government's handling of information that there is a need to "speak in one voice to your adversary." Commenting on that-and laying down what an ideal editor should do in the circumstances, the *New York Times* said in an editorial on 31 October 1962: "To attempt to manage the news so that a free press should speak 'in one voice to your adversary' could be for more dangerous to the cause of freedom than the free play of dissent, than the fullest possible publication of the facts."

Another and a yet more fitting answer was given by the chairman of the House subcommittee on Information of the Committee on Government Operations, John E Moss. He said: "Government pronouncements during a conflict of wills obviously have an effect upon the outcome of the conflict, but to imply that the entire government information process is part of the manouvers in international relations is to ignore the working of our democratic system."

That, of course, is not how the US Administration saw it. President Kennedy, for example, thought that by not using the information about the presence of Russian missiles in Cuba which the *New York Times* possessed, the paper had made "far-more effective our later actions and thereby contributed greatly to our national security."

There will always be two opinions as to what the true relationship between the government and the press should be and it will be argued that the circumstances in the end will dictate what such a relation should be. By and large it has been suggested that relationship is best which is adversary in nature. The press which means the editor-is better off to be on guard where the government is concerned than to work in cahoots with any administration.

***Information Network :*** The relationship between an editor and the proprietor is an even thornier one than that between an editor and the government. Where the proprietor is himself the editor-as it used to be in the *Free Press Journal* when Sadanand was alive-the problem obviously does not arise. But there were times when Sadanand employed separate editors and with his kind of temperament, conflicts between him and them were routine. On one occasion Sadanand without so much as consulting his then editor S. Natarajan, changed editorial policy overnight. Natarajan thereupon did what any self-respecting editor should do, resigned on the spot.

Pothan Joseph who, in his time, had served many masters and was willing to argue any case has been reported to have said that, an editor, like a lawyer, should have no compunction to posit the owner's point of view. Joseph himself at different times edited *The Hindustan Times* (a paper that strongly supported the Congress) and the *Dawn* (mouthpiece of the Muslim League). Pothan Joseph found nothing wrong in this.

Some old-fashioned editors have held the view that an editor is responsible solely to his conscience and to his readers and that any proprietorial interference in the discharge of his duties is an assault on the freedom of the press that should be resisted. Theoretically such a position is unassailable. In practice, however, many editors have learned that he who pays the piper calls the tune. An editor is well advised prior to his accepting his appointment to see that he is on the same wave-length as that of his employer. That is the best way to save later embarrassment and agony. Most editors are hired on contract and an editor who claims special privileges for himself on grounds of editorial independence may soon find that editorial independence and job security do not always go hand in hand.

***Job of News Editor :*** The news editor is a very important functionary in the organisation of a newspaper. He is the real backbone of the newspaper. The news editor is responsible for doing the most important work in the publication of a newspaper. In certain ways, he can be called the number two man in a newspaper organisation. He is solely responsible for the news coverage activities of the newspaper. It is his duty to see that the news service of his paper is always up to the mark and ahead of its rivals.

The news editor deputes the reporting staff for news collecting activities. He also directs the work of the sub-editors. He is the final arbiter to whom all questions affecting the news columns are referred, and ultimately he decides the fate of every report and paragraph. However, much of this responsibility in actual working may be delegated to his subordinates. In the western countries, sometimes, the news-editor performs the functions of a general supervisor, because his work is divided among other employees of the newspaper like copy testers, planners etc. Generally, his time is occupied with administrative work.

He merely controls the activities of his assistants and makes the most important decisions. The rest of the work he leaves to his subordinates. But in India the position is quite different. In our country, the news editor has to deal with many aspects of collecting the news and making use of it. He is responsible for all the news stories that appear in a newspaper. In fact, he performs many functions which were previously performed by a district editor, copy tester and a planner of news coverage. The news editor not only acts as a senior journalist guiding other journalists, but he also has to deal with the administration of the staff under his control. He is responsible for alloting duties, giving assignments and making leave arrangements for them. The news editor is generally a very experienced person. He knows all the ins and outs of his job.

In a newspaper the news is received from various sources like reporters, correspondents, national and international news services etc. The news is continuously received on the teleprinter which is installed in the newspaper office. It is the news editor who plans how to use the news which is continuously arriving in the newspaper's office from various sources. He prepares the dummy for the next day's paper in which the space to be occupied by advertisements appearing in the newspaper is indicated. In fact, on the basis of this dummy, the next day's newspaper is planned by the news editor. For special reports he obtains photographs to be published in the paper. He tries to be in touch with all the events and news which are taking place or the reports which are trickling in.

He also discusses the coverage of news and events with the chief reporter as well as the editor of the newspaper. The timings of the city edition and dak edition are also decided by him. He tries to coordinate with the printer and the production side for bringing out the newspaper in time. He gives instructions to the chief sub-editor regarding the use of important reports and news items. Although the chief sub-editor is the ultimate incharge of the actual shape the edition will take, yet the news editor always tries to know as to what is happening.

It is the duty of news editor to build up the news service of the paper on a sound footing. No doubt, in the fast moving world of today this is not an easy task. He has to keep in touch with his paper's local reporters, correspondents, foreign as well as the numerous national and international news agencies for collecting the latest news regarding the important happenings. He may have to meet many callers as well as attend to immense correspondence reaching his office.

The news editor has also to make arrangements to cover the unexpected occurrences hurriedly. To meet the rush of work and unexpected situations, things may have to be done in a hurry, yet in a systematic and proper manner. The unexpected is always happening in a newspaper office. It may be report regarding a big air crash or a railway accident, a mining disaster or a huge fire, a gruesome murder or a cyclone involving loss of many lives. Whichever of these occurences it may be, the same has to be dealt with promptly and appropriately, no matter what hour of the night or day the news arrives in the newspaper office. A good news editor evolves cohesion and order, even out of a chaotic situation due to his cool direction.

The successful news editor possesses a highly trained news sense. He has the knack of anticipating events intelligently. A good news editor is a man of tireless and boundless energy. He should have a lot of driving force to direct his staff, sparing neither them nor himself, when a big story is about to break, or when the reputation of his paper is at stake. Above all, he should be able to make quick and accurate decisions in a crisis and remain cool and calm under all circumstances.

***Job of Sub-editor :*** The sub-editor plays a very important role in the publication of a newspaper. He is a very important member of the newspaper's staff. The quality and style of a newspaper greatly depend on the good work done by the sub-editor. It is the sub-editor who prepares the copy for the printer.

Although the editor of the newspaper exercises the supreme direction and legal responsibility, yet it is the sub-editor who performs most of the functions of the editor, as far as the production of a paper is concerned. In a way, we can say that if the editor is the top stone, then the sub-editor is the key stone of the arch. In ordinary matters the sub-editor has undisputed control over every article and paragraph that reaches the newspaper's office. As far as the difficult and important articles of news publicity are concerned, he may be guided by the editor.

The functions of an editor have become very vague now-a-days. His control is now merged into the managenial side of the paper from which side he may exercise both a journalistic and commercial influence. An editor may hardly write much for the newspaper. In fact, it is the sub-editor who does most of the editing work in a newspaper. If the functions of the editor have now become a little less, as far as the production of a paper is concerned, then the functions of the sub-editor have definitely increased greatly.

The sub-editor is mainly responsible for the manner in which a journal or a newspaper is made-up, sent for printing and offered to the public. There is no doubt that the sub-editor must be a man of high ability and judgement. He must know thoroughly the news value of every matter which comes into his notice. He should have the ability to see the importance of even a small paragraph and the competence to reduce a lengthy paragraph to its deserving size. A sub-editor may not generally do much of original writing like an editor, but he should be an expert in revising the news articles as well as supervising the work of those who do the writing work. Thus, a sub-editor must possess the capability either to reduce or to expand a subject matter as per the needs of his paper.

All sorts of news go on trickling into the sub-editorial department all the time. It is just like a raw material out of which a sub-editor produces a finished product (the news to be published in the newspaper).

The sub-editor has the power of life or death over all the newspaper's material that reaches him. Thus, the responsibility of the sub-editor is really enormous. A newspaper receives its copy from a variety of sources like reporters, correspondents, telephones, news agency reports and verbal communications. All this information is filtered by the sub-editor. The sub-editor is actually responsible, more than any other person for what the paper looks like and stands for, to the readers.

There are many ways in which a sub-editor can leave the impression of his personality on the newspaper. The format of a paper is in reality determined by the sub-editor. The sub-editor has the nose for selecting the right type of news. It is the task of the sub-editor to decide as to what is going in for tomorrows's newspaper and in what form. In fact, the sub-editor with a wide experience in his work, is the most suitable person to become the editor in due course of time.

There is always a big pile of news reports and other communications lying on the table of the sub-editor. He is also pressurised by the printing department for the copy. He has to attend to his functions in a very quick manner, using his best judgement as to the relative urgency, importance and the desirability of printing a particular news or article.

The sub-editor has to separate the grain from the chaff out of the great number of news material lying on his table. He should have an eye for accuracy. He must check the facts of a story and look out for the errors, if any. If there are certain facts which are missing, he must ask these from the reporters. The sub-editor has to read every story and sometimes contrive to make it interesting and news-worthy.

Mainly, we can say that a newspaper receives the news from two sources, one from the paper's own correspondents and the other from the various news agencies. Generally, out of these two sources preference is always given to the news brought by the paper's own correspondents, because a good report under the headline 'from our special correspondent' indicates the initiative and enterprise and adds to the prestige of a newspaper.

Sometimes, a newspaper may receive a number of versions of a particular story from different sources. The paper's correspondent may give a different story where as the news agencies may give their own accounts. The sub-editor has to put all these conflicting accounts into one coherent and wholesome story. If the reports contradict or conflict with each other, then he has to believe the story put in by the newspaper's own correspondent. It is thus the responsibility of the sub-editor to make the story clear. He should see to it that the news story is based upon facts, it is as complete as possible and is clear from every angle for easy understanding.

A sub-editor checks the news stories one by one. He goes through every single piece of the copy. Then he adds a catch-line, if the reporter has not already provided a suitable one. He also writes a suitable headline for the story. This is a very important and difficult duty of the sub-editor. After this, he edits the story, cutting the unnecessary matter and trimming the length to the right size according to the space where it has to be printed. He checks the spellings of names and places so that these are not printed wrongly. A sub-editor also has to correct errors of grammar, capitalization, punctuation and abbreviations. He cannot afford to allow even the most minor error in the newspaper.

If a sub-editor feels that the intention of the writer of a story is not clear or the message of the story is very vague, then he can refer the copy back to the reporter and ask him to rewrite the story. Sometimes, he may have to refer to books like 'who's who', encyclopaedias, telephone and civic directories, almanacs etc., to confirm the facts of a story. He may even have to telephone the source of the news item to seek any clarification regarding which a doubt creeps up in his mind.

The sub-editor has to take into consideration the policy of his paper before allowing a news item to be published. He has to breathe life into some dead matter lying before him so that the story is made lively. Sometimes, he tones down a story which is too lively. He may also trim down a story, if it is too dangerous, to make it safe. He has also to decide the suitability of the news stories and articles on the merits of their news value to the particular paper. He has to reject a superfluous article and prune another to its justified size. He is always on the look out to print a news story which is a scoop, well ahead of his rivals.

After deciding the main contents of his newspaper, he has to use his utmost skill in their make-up and display. This is just like the window dressing of a shop which is fully stocked. And it is a very important function of the sub-editor. He has to be careful that in the final rush no mistake creeps into the print and no paragraph gets mixed up or overlooked. The maximum attention a sub-editor has to pay is to the layout of captions and the main news page. Balance and proportion are the qualities which should be aimed at before anything else.

The principal test of sub-editorial capacity in the art of make up is, of course, the appearance of the main news page. It is the page which the majority of the readers read first of all. Some very busy readers only read this page and no more—they simply turn the other pages. Although the eye may be arrested by the heading of the principal news, yet the total effect of the whole page should not be crudely sensational. In fact, the make-up of the first page should be in such a way that a reader is helped to find at a glance how the world has behaved during the last twenty-four hours.

There is no doubt that the make-up of a newspaper is the reflection of the sub-editor's appreciation of news value. Sometimes, the value and significance of a news feature is largely neutralised by an ineffective handling of make-up.

Side by side with the presentation of the news, a sub-editor should also know something about the gathering of news and arrangement of regular features. He should be fully acquainted with the reporters and correspondents employed by his newspaper as well as with the regular contributors who write special features from time to time, which are published in his newspaper. The sub-editor should also know the principal news-agencies which supply news stories to his paper. In fact, now-a-days more and more news is supplied to the newspapers by one or the other national or international news agencies.

The sub-editor should also be acquainted with the important photographers and photographic agencies which supply photographs of important events and news items to his newspaper. In fact, now-a-days every big newspaper has its own staff photographers, who cover the special functions and events for their newspaper. By knowing these sources of news as photographs, a sub-editor can contact them in case of any contingency without any difficulty.

Of course, many of the troubles of the sub-editor will be lessened, if the correspondents and other contributors take a little more pain to make their copy readable. If the reporters and writers try to follow the style in which their writings are presented finally in the newspaper, then they can greatly save a good deal of unnecessary work and worry on the part of the sub-editorial department. Sometimes, a contributor or a correspondent may even have a complaint against the sub-editor for the way in which his article has been cut down by the sub-editor, who may not be sufficiently acquainted with the importance of the material. Every sub-editor should be careful in the use of scissors and the blue pencils, so as not to give any cause for complaint later on to the conscientious writers.

There is no doubt that ultimately the public is the best judge of the work of a sub-editor. The good work done by him in the selection of the news and views will be much liked by the readers of his newspaper, whereas any fall in its standard may result in a reduction in its circulation. It is, therefore, the duty of every good sub-editor to do his best to put as much exclusive news in his newspaper as possible and as early as possible.

# 8

# CRAFT OF EXPRESSION

Ability for writing is the first condition for a career in journalism. In one's career, at some point probably the first day-one will be expected to take to writing. Let us, begin to with, the question, how to write journalistically. Writing for newspapers is not so hard as many editors and teachers may try to tell you it is, nor is it so easy as it appears on the printed page. But-journalistic writing is different, different really from any other kind of writing. Charles McDowell, longtime columnist for the Richmond Times Dispatch and a frequent lecturer on newspaper writing, contends this is because "newspapers have a thousand ways to make the telling of a simple story complicated." There are; reasons for that, also, buried in habit and special needs. The needs, as well as the habits, are slowly, fading. There was a time when newspapers provided the first news anybody got, and some traditionalist papers hold to the old forms and constraints required of that age fifty to sixty years ago.

Because we don't know whether you will be going to a newspaper that still insists on calling cars "motor cars" or to one that uses "twisted" in the sense of being zincked on drugs, e are going to endeavor to prepare you for either. This particular chapter will address the traditional forms and discuss some of the constants. In the following two chapters, we will take you over the edge into stylistic writing, with some tips, examples, and appropriate warnings.

The one thing we can assure you of is that writing is incredibly important at any newspaper. Gone are the days when big-city newspapers had "leg men" who merely collected facts and fed them to a "rewrite man" who wrote the stories with flair and, sometimes, exaggeration. Some newspapers still use rewrite people to help rework stories that others have written or have dictated by phone. Some newspapers also have a kind of writing-by-committee system for special projects, whereby several reporters collect information, which is then handed over to one or more writers on the team. But once the project is finished, those people who have done the leg work return to being writer-reporters again. At today's newspapers, a reporter must also be a writer. And it has been our experience that the better you write, the better you will do in this business. Increasingly, editors seek talented writers, grudgingly admitting that the public can, indeed, get its basic news from TV but not in the substantive, interpretive way good newspaper writers can present it. Before you dash off to the Pulitzer Committee with your treatise on urban potholes, let us start at the beginning, with the fundamentals.

## Writing in Brief

Journalistic writing is concise writing. Points are made quickly and briefly. William Faulkner, one of our most honoured novelists, would never have made it in the newspaper game. Editors would have yelled at him for his two-page sentences. He would have been frustrated by editors' putting apostrophes and frequent periods into his marvelous visions. Ernest Hemingway, another honoured novelist, was also a journalist wrote like one. His short, snappy paragraphs are in, the most durable tradition of journalistic writing. He also shows how much style can be crammed into, something simple.

The concise form was born of necessity. Newspapers must tell many stories on any given day, and there is only so much space. If you simply cannot restrain your gushes of prose, you might consider writing magazine articles or books. At newspapers, you will have to write succinctly. Editors will insist that you do. Saying a lot in a little space, unfortunately, is one of the hardest skills to learn in journalism. You will do it well only after much practice and some merciless editing. However, a few arbitrary, but generally accepted, rules can help force this habit of tight writing:

> Keep paragraphs short. Any paragraph that runs more than five typewritten lines is too long, usually. Three or four lines are preferred. Editors appropriately refer to newspaper paragraphs are graphs, since normally they are not true grammar-textbook paragraphs but paragraph fragments. Rather than being a collection of sentences expressing a complete thought or theme, newspaper graphs often are one-and two-sentence segments of the thought, which is completed after two or three graphs.

As in all things uniquely journalistic, there is a special reason for short paragraphs. They are primarily a newspaper layout tool designed to prevent the newspaper from looking too gray because of too many words jammed together. Editors also assume, rightly perhaps, that readers like to get their information in a hurry and don't want to wade through something that looks awesomely long.

Get to the point in a hurry. Traditionally, this has been done in the first two or three paragraphs, known collectively as the lead. Even in stylized stories, where you are setting some scene or telling an anecdote, the point should be established early on, at least by the fifth or sixth paragraphs.

Use action words. Active verbs add energy and excitement to a story and get it moving in a hurry. A person who dashed through a crowd appears more interesting than one who was running down the street. In addition, the passive voice trends not only to slow down sentences but often makes them awkward.

Keep in mind that you are a selector of detail, not a recording secretary. From the mass of information available to you, you are expected to select the most significant and interesting details and present them in a way that will immediately grab the reader's attention and hold it. As you become more experienced as a reporter, you will find that there is much more to be discarded than to be saved. Saving the best and putting it into the proper order of significance is a measure of the newspaper writer's skill.

There is a time, certainly, for written windiness. Knowing when to expound and when to truncate comes with experience, practice, and heartless editing. At most larger newspapers, the good reporter is forced to develop two skill levels: one of speed, brevity, and patterned thinking, and another of imagination and perspective. Most frustrating to novices, certainly, is that they will be called on to exercise the former far more than the latter in the beginning.

In the newspaper business, you must learn to run with the breaking story before you can crawl through the analytical feature. As we will see, there is much about journalism that is backwards. So let us start at the finish line.

The news story is what it is all about. You are in the news business, and you will be expected to write news stories. To know what a news story is, of course, it helps to know what news is. To be candid, news is pretty much whatever your editor decides it is. It may be a triple axe-murder-suicide or your publisher's favorite charity. As in most matters of uncertainty, definitions vary. One we like, picked up from a wise old journalism professor, is this: News is that which is timely, truthful, and of public interest. If any of these three elements is missing, chances are you don't have a situation worth presenting to your newspaper's readers. A lot of things are timely and truthful that are not at all interesting. (Your editor, of course, may be aware of some interest that you do not immediately see, such as your publisher's interest in seeing a story in the paper about the favourite charity.) Something that is timely and interesting, of course, might not have a grain of truth to it, and to foist a lie upon the public is the cardinal sin of journalism.

Timeliness is the stock and trade of newspapers, and nowhere is that more pertinent than in the basic news story. The news story deals with the immediate, the facts of the moment, "what's happening." It is the story with adrenaline pumping. It demands the best of reporting (news gathering) skills. It demands that the writer be quick, accurate, and not overly sensitive about his or her art, for news stories can be dreadfully, painfully, insufferably dull in the hurried rendering. Only the very best of a vanishing breed of backward-thinking geniuses are able to make high drama of upside-down story-telling with any consistency under deadline pressure.

With deadline-panicked editors on his or her back, the journalist writing a news story often must fall back on an acquired bag of tricks in pursuit of abbreviations of description. A bank robber pointing a pistol in the face of a terrified teller becomes "the gunman"; a person standing neck-deep in water (whose name you forget to ask) becomes "one flood victim" or "one stricken resident"; a state representative babbling lunacies at a press conference seconds before your deadline becomes "the controversial legislator." A talented writer often can put an original make on a news story, even under those conditions, but with precious seconds ticking away and libel lawyers waiting in the wings, the veteran journalist is most inclined to handle a news story in ways that are tried and safe. For the panicked writer there is probably no better form to use than the inverted pyramid.

## Fashion in Order

The newspaper writer is an assembler of facts in that he or she puts together the parts of the story in an orderly fashion. However, in writing the traditional news story, the proper order actually is a kind of disassembling. We start with the bicycle and wind up with a leftover bolt. Traditional news-story writing might be considered upside-down writing. You give the punch line, then tell the joke. In academic circles, this has become known as the inverted pyramid. Although you may never hear the term used in a news room, editors will assume you know how to use the form. Some purists, in fact, will insist that you use the form regularly because it is something they know how to handle when they don't know how to handle other tricks of writing. What is meant by the inverted pyramid, such as a murder in a mystery story, and ending with the resolution, you tell the resolution in the beginning, then move steadily backwards to where the narrative normally would begin. The traditional inverted pyramid form for the news story has three key parts:

***The Lead :*** The lead is the first few paragraphs of any story. In the traditional form, the lead is supposed to tell everything earth-shattering that there is to know, as well as the most relevant details. A sufficient lead often can stand by itself as a short story, as do the leads from the Associated Press write stories that some newspapers compile into news briefs. (In some newsrooms, editors are prone to spell the world led, a holdover from hot type days when lead was pronounced led and meant metal inserted on the plate in the composing room to stretch out a story that was too short.)

***The Middle :*** This includes paragraphs to support the lead, to add details that are significant but not essential. The lead on a murder story, for instance, may mention the motive as a "domestic quarrel." In the middle, you probably will want to quote police or witnesses about what the quarrel concerned. You may also want to include more details about where the body was found, how many bullet holes there were, who was in the house, etc.

***The Expendable Ending :*** A major reason for writing news stories in the inverted pyramid form is so the bottom can be cut without eliminating some crucial detail. Unless you have your editor's word, written in bold, that it won't be cut, never save your best lick for the end. If you do, readers may never see it, for stories almost always are cut a little-often from the bottom-to fit the space. The expendable end should include background information, the murder story, for instance, might include a summary of how many murders the city has had to date. Unless the increase is alarming, in which case the information should go higher in the story, such peripheral matter can be cut without damaging the story.

Regardless of the form-and we shall discuss some others in the following chapters-there are elements that should be included in every story.

***The Five Ws, Sometimes H, and a Few Cs :*** It is true. All stories should include the five Ws: who, what, when, where, why. And most stories should include the how. The news story, particularly, should have these elements high up in the story. Sometimes overlooked in this traditional equation is that stories also should include some conjunctions, those little words that smooth the transitions and keep the sentences hanging together. One oddity of journalistic writing, frowned upon by some purists, is the habit of beginning sentences with such conjunctions as and but. Purists hold that these little words can be used only to separate independent clauses in compound sentences. We are not here to argue sentence structure. All we can tell you is that in journalism, it is down. And, another set of words that are dispensable when shifting points is such conjunctive adverbs as meanwhile, moreover, nevertheless, and therefore.

In the traditional news story, the five Ws come into play early on. At one time, it was considered important to get them all into the first paragraph, certainly somewhere in the first two. This is no longer a rule at most newspapers, although the veteran journalistic writer almost counts them off in his or her head in writing the first few paragraphs, sticking them into sentences.

***Who :*** This is whom the action is about. Who is talking. Who is dead. Who is stealing. And so forth. Sometimes it is a name, perhaps accompanied by a title: Mayor Maynard Jackson, Sen. Blustrous Fatkitty, Mary Jane McSwane, Dr. Joyce Brothers. Sometimes it is a brief description: A 35-year-old DeKalb County man, a deranged Vietnam war veteran, a psychopathic antiwar leader.

***What :*** What happened. It usually includes a verb. (Who) was slain, attacked welfare, shot her boss. It may also include slight description and detail: Mayor Maynard Jackson announced the dedication ceremony for the new airport; a 35-year-old DeKalb County man died of injuries in a head-on collision; an irate secretary shot her boss.

***Where :*** In Delhi or Bombay? Leaving out where an event occurred confuses readers to no end. In covering city news, you may be expected to include a street address. Often it helps to include a landmark as well. Sometimes the building, house, barn, or whatever is important. An address might not mean so much to the reader as pointing out that the incident occurred across from Manuel's Tavern. A decision made at City Hall may be expected, but one made by the city council at Paschal's Restaurant may be unusual. At most larger dailies, the city where you are writing becomes simply here, as in: former President Jimmy Carter announced here Saturday that he finally has finished his memoirs.

***When :*** Simply the day of the week, usually. Like where, it is a reference point for the reader. Sometimes, more specific time is important to include. A downtown murder that occurred shortly after noon during the lunchtime rush hour takes on more immediacy than one that occurred Tuesday afternoon.

***Why :*** Hard to answer sometimes. It usually involves some discussion in the second or third paragraph of why the news event seems to have occurred or why it is significant: the curbside pickup plan is aimed at helping settle the year-old garbage strike; the accident occurred when Jones lost control of his vehicle.

And sometimes how, which usually takes care of the story's middle. How does the mayor plan to implement his curbside garbage pickup? How did Mary Jane McSwane wind up dead? How will the president's umpteenth economic recovery plan finally end inflation?

The ending in the traditional, upside-down news story, often as not, should be whatever is left over: In other action, the council voted to proclaim Thursday "Say Hello to a Stranger" Day.

The hardest part of writing a story is coming up with a lead. So dreadful is the task to some writers that they write the rest of the story first, then go back to put a top on it. One reason that the lead is so intimidating is that it is quite difficult to summarize a whole story in two or three paragraphs. In the traditional form, that usually is what you are expected to do. The task is made none the easier by the quirks of editors who like to see leads written as they were taught to write them, and each editor seems to have been taught something different. Some editors like the ancient form of cramming everything into the first paragraph. Some editors like brisk five-or six-word leads, with everything else crammed into the second paragraph. And some rare editors will let you do whatever seems to work. In the beginning, it is best to go with tradition. Not only is it easier to write conventional leads, since they fit into standard formulas, but the early habit helps prove to your editors that you are not some crazed journalistic radical. However, once you have made that point, it is generally safe-and wise-to try something daring before you get locked into habits that can impede your eventual progress to a better newspaper.

## Different Leads

Various efforts have been made to label different types of leads. We do not intend to contribute to that confusion. No editor we know is going to accuse you of putting a question lead on a story that should have had a suspended interest lead, but if the editor's interest is immediately suspended, you will be accused of writing a bad lead instead of a good one. The one label that does seem to have some merit is the summary end. The conventional lead should summarize, certainly. This may be done in the first paragraph, or in the first three or four paragraphs. Since the inverted pyramid form requires that you deal with facts in descending order of importance, the best way to establish what is important is to summarize it at the outset. A good practice for writing a summary lead is to pretend that you are talking to a friend who has an attention span of about five seconds. How do you get that friend to notice that some calamity has occurred? Gene Fowler, a legendary reporter of the 1920s who had been accused by his editors of "backing into" leads, proved he could get attention in a hurry with this classic lead: Dead. That's what she was. That lead, of course, does not altogether summarize the event, but it is a fascinating start.

Traditionally, the summary lead is an attempt to get as many of the five Ws as possible into the first and second paragraphs. Here is a good example of how that is done, from a story by the Associated Press, which, like the other wire services, has made summary leads a constant bordering on blandness:

> A 16-year-old girl was critically injured and burned, and her dog was killed when the dog urinated on the wiring of an electrified sign here, the Suffolk County police reported.

Here, we have the who: a 16-year-old girl and her dog. We have the what: The girl was critically injured and burned; the dog was killed. We have the where established as here, magnified by the attribution: Suffolk County police. We even have the why: The dog urinated on the writing of an electrified sign. The when is mentioned in the second paragraph.

That particular lead also offers us an opportunity to discuss the issue of when to attribute. Since attributions seems almost an interruption, first paragraphs are more readable without them. In this instance, the attribution "Suffolk County police reported" could have been used to begin the second paragraph. But some editors consider a first paragraph incomplete without attribution, they especially like to stick in the newspaper's name where a big scoop is involved, as in: "Payoffs to building inspectors is a common practice in the city, the Screaming Eagle has learned." Attribution in the first paragraph is also important if you are dealing with sensitive matters, where you want someone else to be held accountable, as in: "Sen. Fatkitty stole $5 million, FBI investigators have charged." Our rule is: When in doubt, attribute; but don't let your attributions become regular interruptions of the flow of a story.

After a while in the business, you will discover that some conventional leads are so automatic that you practically could plug them into a computer with only a couple of blank spaces to fill in later. One of the most common is the bank robbery story:

> Two masked gunmen robbed the C&S branch bank at 3568 Moeland Avenue Friday afternoon and escaped on foot with an undisclosed amount of cash.

Robbers with any savvy at all usually, wear masks and carry guns, Friday afternoon tends to be their favorite time to strike. They normally hit a branch bank. And neither the bank, the police, nor the FBI will tell you how much the robbers took. Actually, robbers usually escape by car, but the last time anybody seems to see them they are still on foot.

The police story becomes a staple for many young reporters, so you probably will run into another standard-the domestic homicide, wherein someone guns down a best friend or spouse. The stories go something like this:

> A 38-year-old Atlanta man was shot to death during a quarrel outside the High Life Bar & Grill Saturday night.
>
> Atlanta police identified the dead man as Wendell Smudwell of 3236 Renaissance Park Avenue SE. Arrested and charged with the murder was John Francis Doe, 32, of 3237 Renaissance Park Avenue SE.
>
> According to Detective Joseph Friday, the two men had been discussing the Falcons' recent losing streak when Doe pulled out a .22 caliber pistol and fired five shots into Smudwell's abdomen.

For some types of stories, such as obituaries, newspapers do, indeed, have what amounts to fill-in-the-blank forms. At the Atlanta Journal, standard obituaries begin: "Services for..." The second paragraph includes a brief biographical sketch, beginning with the name of the deceased. The third paragraph begins: "Survivors include ..." Here is one example:

> Services for Harry Rosenberg, 65, of Atlanta will be Thursday at 2. P.M. at Ward's Glenwood Chapel, with burial at Forest Lawn Memorial Park.

> Mr. Rosenberg, a retired Deltá maintenance department foreman, died Friday. The New York native was a member of the OX-5 Aviation Engineers.
>
> Survivors include his wife, Mrs. Rachel Adams Rosenberg; a sister, Mrs. Ross Kohuth of Brooklyn, N.Y.; and a brother, Joe Rosenberg of Wellesley, Mass.

The form, of course, varies from paper to paper, and even changes at a particular paper. Journal obituaries used be begin: "Funeral for ..." They used to end "Surviving are..." You shouldn't have much trouble wrong obtares, called obits for short, except in making sure you spell all the names right. Nowhere, in fact, is it more operative to get the names right. Would you want someone to misspell your name if you were getting the last recognition you would ever get on this earth? Standard obituaries, however, are not the same as celebrity obituaries. Celebrity obits usually are turned over to veterans for what amounts to eulogizing. A notable citizen always is put away with kind, and often effusive, words.

Another thing to keep in mind when writing the conventional lead is to get as much pertinent detail as possible into the first few lines. This can require some straining to inject the peculiar adjective clauses that set apart newspaper writing from other kinds of writing.

Here is how Ron Taylor backed into a lead one time, endeavouring to set a tone before he had made clear what he was talking about:

> When Raymond Sagoes called his mother at 4:45 P.M. Friday, "he was crying and said he was sick and didn't have no money and didn't have nothing to eat."

Taylor was struck by the sadness of the quote from the mother of a man on the run. His editor, fortunately, was struck by the fact that the man had allegedly killed two people. The editor felt that was a secret worth sharing with our readers at the outset. Here is how the editor fixed it:

> The last time accused double murderer Raymond Sagoes called his mother here at 457 Western Avenue NW was 4:45 P.M. Friday, and "he was crying and said he was sick and didn't have no money and didn't have nothing to eat."

The reason we think it unwise to label leads for convenience' sake is that they are so often dictated by events rather than rules. Some situations seem to invite a certain amount of playfulness. Nothing works so well sometimes as a twist on an old joke or literary reference. To the reader, the familiar is easier to follow, certainly, than the unfamiliar.

Who hasn't heard Johnny Carlson and Ed McMahon doing their stock television routine on the weather: "How hot was it? It was so hot...? So why not this lead?

How hot was it?

It was so hot Thursday that a young woman took the liberty of taking off her clothes in Central City Park in the heart of downtown Atlanta.

After prancing bare-bosomed before a lunch-hour crowd in the park, the woman was arrested.

Given the right circumstances for Christmas, you can always dust off this one:

The Grinch is not the only one who steals Christmas.

A lot of ordinary Americans walk off with stakes of Yuletide gifts they never bother to pay for, and professional thieves work overtime this time of year.

Be warned, however, that there is nothing worse than a pun or a cliche twist carried off to the nth degree of silliness. Our advice is simple: Be original, even with the unoriginal.

Here is an example of how coincidence invited such a twist:

> One of the first things Sam Lowry was told in a class on delivering babies is that they .... usually aren't born in the back seat of a taxi. Well, how about the front seat of a green 1970 Dodge Monaco, in a motel driveway at 12:30 on a Friday afternoon?

That's how Brooke Alan Lowry came into this world, all 7 pounds, 8 ounces and 19½ inches of him.

In this example, you also can see how an unconventional approach can lead to an unconventional rendering of the summary lead. The first paragraph tells us little, but it sets up the next two paragraphs, which tell us everything we need to know before moving on to some elaboration.

A different type of lead, in purpose but not in form, is the second day lead. Second-day leads are written for stories in which the main event already has occurred but some action relevant to the event is continuing. There you have your full lead. Then, we move to the middle for some clarification:

> Pinay's abandoned truck was found near 1.20 between Flat Shoals and Candler roads Saturday. The truck was locked with Pinyan's hunting equipment still inside.

Authorities speculated that Pinyan may have stopped to help a woman change a tire. Pinyan's truck and the woman's car, a 1959 or 1960 Dodge, were sighted in the same area Friday afternoon.

That, in essence, is how you apply the formula. The more experienced you become, the more ingredients you can toss into the recipe without having the cake blow up in your face. The more ingredients, or details, you have, the better, for there is thus more to work with.

***The Peculiar Language of Newspapers :*** The language many newspapers are written in today has its roots in the 1920s, '30s, and '40s, the period when newspapers began to standardize the presentation of information to a public that still got most of its news from newspapers. Then, newspaper leads functioned much as the TV and radio summaries of today. The leads essentially were the same as the banked headlines with the articles and qualifiers filled in. Some reporters today, in fact, jot down possible headlines for their stories as a way of outlining elements they want to include.

Actually, the traditional newspaper language is much the language of headlines. As Charles McDowell, the Richmond columnist who is a leading critic of newspapers' "artificial" prose, points out, "We jab, hit, lambast.... We have peculiar adjective clauses: 'the red-haired, 25-year-old mother of three." It is an instant language that recently has found a home in the most instant of media-television-giving rise to such parodies as: "Soviets launch nuclear attack. Film at 11." It is a language that only gradually, grudgingly is being replaced by a more personal, stylized language aimed at the literate members of television's pervasive audience.

The traditional news story is a form of abbreviation and contraction of sentences. The word that is one of the most frequent syntactical interruptions relegated to limbo. Instead of:

Nixon said that he was not a crook you would write:

Nixon said he was not a crook.

Who and which suffer similar obscurity in traditional news writing.

The person driving the car... rather than

The person who was driving the car...

Or, taking abbreviation a step further:

The driver,

The word on also tends to disappear. It is

He said Monday... rather than

He said on Monday...

He may not have said "Monday," but that is one of the structural oddities we have been stuck with.

Applying the formula, we can reduce ten words to eight:

She said on Monday that she was going to Taiwan.

Now we could write it as.

She said Monday she was going to Taiwan.

Even in your flushes of literary wizardry, you should keeping mind that newspaper writing is not magazine writing and is therefore always shorter and tighter. It is our way of sparing readers our excesses. A story about a university president probably should not begin with the sun rising gently in the east, as was the struggling attempt of one college writer we recall. Once you begin to apply some of the creative touches keep in mind that you still are functioning in a form that demands that the point be made quickly and that the story be told succinctly. Always there are words that can be eliminated and ideas that can be condensed. Only the abusive writer would impose upon the audience something like this.

Sen. Blustrous Fatkitty was moved to deny he had committed

any of the crimes for which he has been arrested and charged, when it all could be said so simply:

Sen. Blustrous Fatkitty denies the charges.

In second references to people and things, you can tighten your sentences by using general, usually shorter, terms for the specific. Thus, you would have such things as:

> Legislators for members of the House and Senate the organization for the National Association for the Advancement of Coloured People authorities for police, sheriffs deputies, and FBI agents residents for people who live in the Morning side community high court for the U.S. Supreme Court aides for the press secretary, administrative assistant, and bodyguards.

There are numerous other possibilities that we won't bother to list. Keep in mind, however, that on first reference you should be specific to make clear whom and what you are talking about. Furthermore, don't take the preceding list as any sort of absolute. Most nouns have synonyms. Use them generously. Aides can become assistants, advisers, associates, or confidants, or, in less polite situations, cronies, henchmen, enforcers.

Editors and journalism professors' insistence to the contrary, newspapers are not-and never have been-written so that any twelve-year-old can understand them. If that were so, police reporters would not persist in adopting the police habit of calling thugs perpetrators, nor would headline writers dig into their Greek vocabulary to identify legislators as solons. Furthermore, today's twelve-year-olds, thanks to the ubiquitous television, are exposed daily to wars, royal pregnancies, assassinations, unclear proliferation, and cereal commercials. Today, editors are less inclined to quibble over the use of such once intimidating words as microcosm and slog, realizing that even children slog through a microcosm of our troubles every day.

Newspaper stories should, nonetheless, be written simply. But simple writing is not simplistic writing. The best writing, in fact, is simple writing. It is easy to follow, and it communicates; and the business of newspapers is communication. Ernest Hemingway maintained that he wrote for people who moved their lips when they read. He preferred simple declarative sentences. That still is the best way to tell a story.

Now that you know something about the formulas and language of newspaper stories, let's take a brief look at the various forms that come from these techniques.

## News Writing

Sure, we have discussed the news story before, but we told you how to write one, not what it is. What the news story is the foundation upon which all other newspaper writing is based. To solidify its place at the heart of the newspaper scheme of things, editors have given its content macho names, such as hard news, to distinguish it from sissy soft news, or spot news, to give it that we-were-there quality. This is our way of warning you that editors will expect you to be a journalistic aggressor. Only when you prove to be hopelessly talented will they excuse you to pursue flighty objectives.

## Features Writing

For those drawn to journalism not by the sound of alarms and disasters but by the restless urge to write, the outlet is the feature story.

The feature story has its different names, too, given by editors fearful that the common term somehow debases the idea that newspapers are solely about the business of news. Hence, we have such recent terms as news feature and soft news, the latter carrying the connotation that fluff carries import, too. To dare apply electronic terms to the printed word, it might be said that the classic news story is the play-by-play and that the feature is the colour commentary.

Newspapers have had feature stories at least as long as they have had news stories, and the two types are by no means mutually exclusive. In the traditional sense, features are what used to be called human interest stories, those wonderful collections of human agonies and victories about everything from the harvest of giant turnips to the joys of panhandling. But the human interest story certainly has its element of news, helping magnify society's current styles and eccentricities. Editors have finally conceded that opinion. One of the easiest ways to spot a critic who is ignorant of the way newspapers function is to listen for the occasional attack upon the editorial pages as biased, one-sided, subjective, and opinionated. They are; that's what they are supposed to be.

At most large dailies, the editorial pages reflect the reputation and integrity of the publication, as well as the will of the corporation, so publishers do not take lightly the selection of employees to serve the function of writing editorials, thus, usually only the old and wise are so anointed.

There are two basic kinds of editorials in newspapers. There are the unsigned editorials, usually called staff editorial because they represent some consensus among the several members of the editorial board, the folks who work in the editorial department, with one writer assigned to go forth and lecture to the public on that issue. Most newspapers run three to five of these staff editorials each day.

Then, there are the editorial columns. These are the opinions with bylines and mug shots that identify the person writing them, these editorials amount to short, personal essays. Most large newspapers carry at least one column by a satirist or humorist to mix in with the prophecies of doom. Newspapers also employ a mix of local editorial columnists and syndicated columnists. Syndicated columns are distributed by syndication services, which pay the columnists fees based on how many newspapers buy the service. (Syndicates also sell other features to newspapers, such as comics, astrology predictions, how-to-do-it articles, and feature stories.)

## Various Columns

Apart from editorial columns, most large newspapers have general, or feature, columns. The featured columnist, as that writer is sometimes called, is allowed the latitude of opinion within certain limits. Such columnists-and some newspapers have several-deal with human problems rather than cosmic truths. Such columns magnify some subject merely skirted or perhaps ignored by the news pages. Featured columnists also are prone to write about their pets, children, and old sweethearts. Some featured columnists are funny; some are sentimental; some gossip about their friends and where they hang out.

The feature column is the stuff of which legends and acclaim are made. In the business, becoming a featured columnist practically takes an act of Congress, so don't expect to have to write a column unless most of your co-workers are dead and gone or unless your editors share the high regard you have for your talents. On smaller papers, luck sometimes strikes. On larger newspapers, you have to be both experienced and very good.

## Critical Writing

Reviews and criticisms basically are editorials applied to the arts. Reviewers and critics, however, do not so much attack the world as the works of the creative. Practically every newspaper has its reviewers and critics for fine arts, movies, television, and restaurants. Traditionally, a reviews is more merciful than a critic in that a reviewer merely sums up the subject, whether it be a symphony concert or the latest episode of "Dallas." The critic is prone to ridicule and occasionally praise. However, newspapers tend to use the terms interchangeably and often call them editors, such as arts editor, music editor, TV editor, and so on. Increasingly, newspapers employ specialists in these areas rather than grabbing someone in the newsroom who happens to like-or loathe-certain movies, TV, types of music, types of art.

***Sports Writing :*** Sports writing basically is news and feature writing about sports. The intriguing thing about sports writing is that it often brings out the best in newspaper writers. One reason, we suppose, is that sports stories are generally action stories. Knowing how to write action is one of the best skills to have in the newspaper game, and a few of the nation's best serious writers have been extricated from newspaper sports departments. Ralph McGill, James Reston, and Tom Wolfe are among the more famous.

Another significant aspect of sports writing is that it has for generation combined the news and feature approaches, telling us first that Bartknowski busted his ribs again, then that the Falcons lost miserably.

# Bibliography

Almond, Gabriel A. and Coleman, James S. : *The Politics of the Developing Areas,* Princeton University Press, Princeton, 1960.

Andrews, C.F. : *Mahatma Gandhi's Ideas,* MacMillan, London, 1949.

Aronson, James : *The Press and the Cold War,* Beacon Press, Boston, 1970.

Balsara, Rati : *Advanced Dictionary of Journalism,* Dominant Books, New Delhi, 2004.

Barnett, Marvin : *Survey of Broadcast Journalism 1970-71 : A State of Siege,* Grosset and Dunlap, New York, 1971.

Bhutto, S.C. : *The Encyclopaedic District Gazetters of India,* Gyan Books, New Delhi, 1990.

Brown, J.W., Lewis, R.B. & Hercleread, A.V. : *Instruction : Materials and Methods,* Mc Graw Hill Book Co., New York, 1964.

Budd, R., Thorp, K.R., and Donohew L. : *Content Analysis of Communications,* MacMillan, New York, 1967.

Clark, T.N. : *On Communication and Social Influence (Collected Essays of Gabriel Tarde),* Chicago University Press, Chicago, 1969.

Cohen, B.C. : *The Press and Foreign Policy,* Princeton University Press, Princeton, N.J., 1963.

Daitota, I. and Sanjay, B.P. : *The Eighteenth Elephant* : *Udayavani's Experiment in Development Jouralism,* Udayavani Press, Manipal, 1990.

Desai, Amit : *Journalism and Mass Communication,* Vikas Publishing House, New Delhi, 2002.

Emest, C. Hynds : *American Newspaper in* 1980s, Hastings House, New York, 1980.

Fiske, J. : *Introduction to Communication Studies,* Methuen, London, 1982.

Frank, H. Krouse : *Media Technique with Youth,* Charles and Mervil, Ohio, 1990.

Gagne, R.M. : *The Conditions of Learning,* Holt Binsort and Winston, New York, 1965.

Gerbner, G : *Mass Media Policies in Changing Cultures,* Wiley, New York, 1977.

Giner, S. : *Mass Society,* Martin Robertson, London, 1976.

Grey, Elizabeth : *The Story of Journalism,* Longmans Young Books, London, 1968.

Jan, R. Hakemulder : *News Reporting and Editing,* Anmol Publications, New Delhi, 2001.

—— : *Print Media Communication,* Anmol Publications, New Delhi, 1999.

Jayapalan, N. : *Journalism,* Atlantic Publishers, ıvew Delhi, 2001.

Jethwaney, Jai shri, N and N. N. Sarkar : *Public Relation,* Sterling, New Delhi, 1998.

Klapper, J.T : *The Effects of Mass Communication,* Free Press, Glencoe, Illinois, 1960.

Kothari, O.S. : *Report of the Indian Education Commission, 1964-66,* Concept, New Delhi, 1966.

Long, L. and Mehta, P.M. : *First Mental Measurement Handbook for India,* NCERT, New Delhi, 1967.

Mac, Iver, R.M. & Page C.M. : *Society and Media,* MacMillan, London, 1950.

Maclagan, Michael : *Clemency Canning,* MacMillan, London, 1962

Madhavan, P. K. : *Careers in Publishing,* Vikas Publishing House, New Delhi, 1997.

Miller, Care G. : *Modern Journalism,* Holt, Rinehart and Winston, New York, 1962.

Moven, Kiran : *Studies in Educational Broadcasting,* Deep & Deep Publications, New Delhi, 1996.

Mujuni, J.P. : *Studies in Media Education,* Deep & Deep Publications, New Delhi, 1995.

Mumtaz, N. : *Journalism Guidance, Measurement & Statistics,* Takshashila, 1996.

Murthy, Nadig Krishna : *Indian Journalism,* Prasaranga, University of Mysore, 1966.

Myers, G.E. : *Principles and Techniques of Vocational Education,* Government of India, Department of Labour, Manager of Publications, Delhi, 1972.

Panickkar, K.M. *: The Foundation of New India,* George Allen & Unwin, London,1963.

Pant, N. C., Joshi M. K. and Jitendera Kumar : *Hindi Patrakarita ki Roop Rekha,* Kanishka Publishers, New Delhi, 2000.

Parikh, R.D. : *The Press and Society,* Popular Prakashan, Bombay, 1965.

Philip, Ed. James and Others : *International Afro Mass Media : A Reference Guide,* Greenwood, New York, 1996.

Rastogi, T. N. : *Encyclopaedia of Professional Journalism,* Anmol Publications Pvt. Ltd., New Delhi, 2001.

Rau, M.C. : *Social Change and the Unchanging Press,* Government of India Publication, New Delhi, 1982.

Reston, James : *The Artillery of the Press : Its Influence on American Foreign Policy,* Harper & Row, New York, 1967.

Stanley, J. Baran : *Introduction to Mass Communication : Media Literacy and Culture,* Mayfield, New York, 1999.

Tahmankar, D.V. : *Lokmanya Tilak,* John Murray, London, 1956.

Thomas, F. Station : *Dynamics of Adjustment,* MacMillan Co., New York, 1953.

Thorndike, R.L. : *Media Psychology and Education*, Wiley Eastern Pvt. Ltd., New Delhi, 2001.

Verma, Adarsh Kumar : *Management Mantaras of Journalism,* Kanishka Publishers, New Delhi, 2001.

Vigneshwara : *Our New Rulers,* B.G. Paul & Co., Madras, 1961.

Vilanilam, J.V. : *Reporting a Revolution,* Sage, New Delhi, 1989.

Wolseley, Roland E. : *Journalism in Modern India,* Asia Publishing House, Bombay, 1964.

Zachariah, Aruna : *Media Power : People, Politics and Public Interest*, Kanishka Publishers, New Delhi. 2001.